D0087381

Latin America
to the Year 2000

LATIN AMERICA
TO THE YEAR 2000

Reactivating Growth,
Improving Equity,
Sustaining Democracy

Edited by ARCHIBALD R.M. RITTER,
MAXWELL A. CAMERON,
and DAVID H. POLLOCK

PRAEGER

New York
Westport, Connecticut
London

338.98
L 357

Library of Congress Cataloging-in-Publication Data

Latin America to the year 2000 : reactivating growth, improving
   equity, sustaining democracy / edited by Archibald R.M. Ritter,
   Maxwell A. Cameron, and David H. Pollock.
         p.   cm.
      Includes bibliographical references and index.
      ISBN 0–275–93747–X (alk. paper)
      1. Latin America—Economic conditions—1982-   2. Latin America—
   Economic policy.   3. Latin America—Social conditions—1945-
   4. Latin America—Social policy.   5. Latin America—Politics and
   government—1980-   I. Ritter, Archibald R.M.   II. Cameron, Maxwell
   A.   III. Pollock, David H.
   HC125.L34743   1992
   338.98—dc20   91–22939

British Library Cataloguing in Publication Data is available.

Copyright © 1992 by Archibald R.M. Ritter, Maxwell A. Cameron, and David H. Pollock

All rights reserved. No portion of this book may
be reproduced, by any process or technique, without
the express written consent of the publisher.

Library of Congress Catalog Card Number: 91–22939
ISBN: 0–275–93747–X

First published in 1992

Praeger Publishers, One Madison Avenue, New York, NY 10010
An imprint of Greenwood Publishing Group, Inc.

Printed in the United States of America

The paper used in this book complies with the
Permanent Paper Standard issued by the National
Information Standards Organization (Z39.48-1984).

10 9 8 7 6 5 4 3 2 1

Contents

University Libraries
Carnegie Mellon University
Pittsburgh, Pennsylvania 15213

Tables and Figure

TABLES

FIGURE

Introduction

Latin America is entering the decade of the 1990s after a decidedly mixed experience in the 1980s. In that decade, the region endured a persisting economic crisis that amounted to an "ordeal by fire," creating severe strains on the political systems and social fabrics of virtually all the countries of the region. On the other hand, most of the countries that entered the 1980s as authoritarian military regimes underwent important processes of democratization. By 1990 almost all Latin American countries had installed pluralistic democratic regimes, imperfect though they may be.

The countries of the region confront a number of enormous challenges as they proceed toward the year 2000. On the socioeconomic side, the main challenges include

- reestablishing sustainable economic growth;
- improving the real incomes of broad strata of the populations;
- reemphasizing investment in human development;
- reversing the net outflow of financial (and real) resources from the region;
- reducing the burden of debt service;
- halting intractable processes of hyperinflation in a number of countries;
- continuing the structural changes under way in many countries.

With respect to the political systems of the countries of the region, major tasks for the 1990s would include

- sustaining democracy and improving the authenticity of democratic regimes;
- incorporating indigenous peoples, lower income groups, and women more fully into decision-making systems and political institutions;
- improving the responsiveness of political systems and public policy to the voices, interests, and needs of the broader strata of the populations.

There are a number of additional challenges confronting the region. Perhaps the most important in the long term is environmental in character: namely, ensuring that civilization itself in the region, not merely economic "growth," is sustainable into the distant future. The drug economy is another corrosive and difficult problem area that will also require intensifying action in future.

Where, specifically, does the region now stand with respect to these issues? Can the experience of the 1980s be analyzed and evaluated so that some light may be shed on prospects for the region during the 1990s? The objective of this volume is to provide a range of assessments of the development experience of the Latin American countries during the 1980s and to explore some prospective issue areas for the decade of the 1990s. Although socioeconomic and political aspects of development are emphasized in this volume, issues of equity and the environment are also of especial importance.

In Part I some central issues concerning the region's economy are the focus of attention. According to the analyses of Enrique Iglesias, president of the Inter-American Development Bank, and Gert Rosenthal, executive-secretary of the UN Economic Commission for Latin America and the Caribbean, the economic traumas of the "lost decade" of the 1980s have led a number of countries to implement major internal policy reforms that, in time, should facilitate successful adjustment and economic reactivation. These should promote growth, employment, and poverty alleviation in the coming decade. However, both analysts as well as Albert Berry, whose chapter in Part II focuses specifically on income distribution, were not optimistic with respect to future improvements in distributional equity.

A major new issue of the 1980s has been the acceleration of rapid inflation to hyperinflation, a species of economic "meltdown," in too many countries of the region. Gary McMahon analyzes the inexperiences of combating hyperinflation in Brazil, Argentina, Peru, and Bolivia, and concludes that neither the Latin American "heterodox" approach nor the IMF-type "orthodox" approach are likely to be successful in all different circumstances. Instead, it is more likely that a synthesis and appropriate sequence of policies from both approaches would be more successful. It is of interest that in his analysis of trade and industrial policy issues for the 1990s, David Glover also reaches the conclusion that a pragmatic mix of targeted and selective public policy instruments with economic liberalization (rather than generalized protectionism or comprehensive and immediate liberalization) is required in the 1990s if the region is to fulfill its economic potential. In his discussion of the debt crisis—the "privileged problem" of the 1980s—Myron Frankman argues that in place of the current situation of net financial and real resource transfers out of the region, what is required is the implementation of a formal system of international progressive income redistribution—that is, a global application of the "fiscal federalism" already practiced at the national level in developed market economies.

The chapters in Part II, "Society, Economy, and Ecology: Toward Equity and Sustainability," provide fascinating insights into key issue areas for the future. A gratifying though constrained optimism is to be found in the chapter by Rolf Wesche and Michael Small on Brazilian Amazonia. In their view, the process of destructive frontier expansion in that area will decelerate for a variety of reasons, but difficult policy choices will have to be made and implemented if the area is to remain under forest cover into the more distant future. "Women and Human Rights in Latin America" by Elizabeth Spehar also gives some ground for optimism insofar as women's rights issues appear to be increasingly analyzed and addressed in the region. While Spehar views this as encouraging, she emphasizes that this is but the beginning, and that accommodation of women's rights will be an immense challenge in the 1990s. The important issue of informal settlements in the cities of Latin America is surveyed in the chapter by Yvonne Riaño and Rolf Wesche, who focus on "self-help" housing and the political and social organization of informal settlement residents.

In his survey of income distribution and poverty in the 1980s and discussion of prospects in these areas for the 1990s, Albert Berry presents a sobering analysis, unfortunately. Income maldistribution in the region has long historical roots and is highly resistant to change. In all of the countries analyzed, with the exception of Colombia, the economic contraction of the 1980s resulted in more inequitable distributional patterns. (In Colombia, the distributional pattern remained constant, while growth was exceptionally strong in the 1980s.) For the 1990s, Berry argues that reestablishing growth is of central importance for poverty alleviation, while well-targeted antipoverty policies are also crucial.

Of central concern in an exploration of the prospects for Latin America is the sustainability and improvement of democratization, which proceeded so successfully in the 1980s. Democracy, defined in terms of formal institutions, refers to a set of procedures for determining "who governs," and more specifically to a legitimation formula, namely that the "people rule"; that is, they are able to select their leaders and influence public policy. For democracy to be sustainable, a broad-based belief in the value of democracy or a democratic culture is required. However, a democratic culture is sustained by continuing processes of material exchanges. A number of the contributions in Part III of the book examine the relationship between what democratic institutions "deliver" and how they are valued by citizens.

In his chapter on democratic consolidation, Luis Roniger does not discount the possible recurrence of familiar patterns of social and political pressures and subsequent democratic breakdown. To avoid this, he emphasizes the need for a strengthening of institutional public trust and a shift toward greater political pragmatism to withstand uncertainties and the intense competition of demands placed on democratic regimes. A different type of analysis leads Julian Castro Rea, Graciela Ducatenzeiler, and Philippe Faucher to conclude that some of the larger countries of the region have returned or are returning to the older and familiar forms of "populism" and away from the difficult processes of building more genuinely democratic political systems and societies. Both of these general chapters as well as that of Jorge Nef and Remonda Bensabat are discouraging to those of us who have been highly optimistic with regard to the 1980s democratization process.

Turning to some of the country case studies, Nibaldo Galleguillos and Jorge Nef, who view the institutions of liberal democracy as unable to represent major interests in society, argue perhaps controversially that the 1988–90 Chilean redemocratization was really an institutionalization of the military's "counterrevolutionary" rules of the game. In his analysis of the Argentinian case, Alberto Ciria emphasizes that the weakness of democratic institutions and the strength of societal conflicts has undermined economic performance and resulted in a "rent-seeking system"—a hybrid of socialism without plan and capitalism without free markets.

The expansion of the "informal sector" in Latin America has interesting although still relatively unexplored political consequences. These differ significantly for the cases of Peru and Mexico in Maxwell Cameron's analysis. Informal-sector expansion has led to demands for institutional change in Peru, where political parties have responded by trying to change the structure of incentives that discriminate against the sector. In Mexico, on the other hand, institutional change in response to the informal sector has been less radical in challenging existing property rights.

In her chapter, Judith Teichman examines political implications of restructuring the parastatal sector in Mexico and concludes that this process has accentuated political polarization, reduced state capabilities at co-optation, and likely made the resolution of Mexico's economic problems more difficult.

Finally, in the chapter on Cuba—somewhat of an outlier in this volume, though perhaps appropriate to Cuba's distinctiveness in the region—Archibald Ritter argues that neither its political nor its economic systems are sustainable for long in view of their inherent weaknesses, the phase-down of implicit subsidization by the Soviet Union, and Cuba's imperatives to adjust to its new situation in the international community. A number of possible scenarios for political and economic change were discussed, but how Cuba evolves in the future depends significantly on two unpredictable factors: the role and durability of Castro and the character of the policy of the United States toward Cuba.

Although many of these authors would disagree on numerous substantive issues and although their approaches differ markedly, none of them is sanguine about the sustainability of Latin American democracy. While they tend to agree that existing systems inadequately represent social interests, they do not foresee dramatic political changes in the near future.

In summary, the authors whose chapters are included in this volume are, on the whole, not optimistic concerning the prospects for Latin America in the 1990s. The immense economic difficulties faced by the region will not be easy to overcome or even to manage. There is unanimous concern with respect to sustaining democracy in the region as well as improving it. Nor is there any guarantee that the equity of income distribution will be improved. Among the few positive prospects for the region envisaged by the authors are the hopes that improved economic policy evident in many countries will begin to achieve stronger positive results, that environmental issues—specifically in Brazilian Amazonia—will be handled more effectively, and that issues of women's rights will be increasingly incorporated into political processes and agendas. Admittedly these are rather slim rays of optimism for the coming decade. Let us hope that all the authors are pleasantly surprised by the year 2000 and that political sustainability, societal equity, healthy economic growth, and ecological sustainability are all more fully achieved than the authors expected when they conducted their analyses at the opening of the decade of the 1990s.

PART I

ECONOMIC PROSPECTS AND CENTRAL POLICY ISSUES

CHAPTER ONE

The Economic Outlook for Latin America in the 1990s

ENRIQUE V. IGLESIAS

As we near the threshold of a new decade, an effort to reflect on the direction and nature of certain central economic trends in Latin America would appear to be timely. It would enable us to identify the major shoals and dilemmas facing the economic authorities in those countries, as well as the future prospects for the region's development. The course of future events, as we well know, is predetermined to some extent by prevailing structural conditions and the inertial projections thereof. The varying effects of economic policy adjustments introduced by the national authorities and the mounting impact of the sweeping changes currently experienced by the world economy also play a part. The combination of all those conditions, both internal and external, makes for a considerable amount of uncertainty—which, far from serving as a brake, acts as a spur, inciting us to prudent action and heightened commitment.

Most of the Latin American countries found it singularly difficult to cope with the economic and social upheaval of the 1980s, unquestionably the most traumatic experience in the contemporary history of these peoples. In many instances, there was not only a standstill in production and employment, but a very real decline in the living standards of the great majority of the population and a serious worsening in these countries' potential for economic development as well.

That explains why the challenge currently facing the countries of Latin America is so decisive and so complex. On the one hand, we must lay the basis for a renewed economic growth process that will be sustainable in the long term, with a much greater degree of external openness and integration into the world economy. On the other hand, that development effort must be launched in a framework of distributive equity and societal participation, conditions that will allow the aggravated disequilibria of bygone years to be remedied and will stimulate the commitment for mobilization of all sectors in the common task of economic and democratic progress. We are confident that the region will be able to meet these challenges, supported by its vast reserves of natural resources, its history—rich in traditions of struggles and successes—and the might of its eminently young and eager population.

We are also optimistic over the new and more pragmatic attitude currently evinced by our countries' economic authorities, and the signs of a better understanding of the imperatives of world economic interdependence, permitting renewed faith in international cooperation and strengthening of its instruments. The years 1988 and 1989 appear to represent the turning point in the region's economic evolution, marking the transition from stagnation to recovery—which was achieved by dint of a relatively generalized and strenuous effort to implement internal structural reforms and greater trade liberalization.

In the internal sphere of Latin American economies, positive signs are perceived in the application of new stabilization and economic adjustment policies, as well as progress in long-term economic restructuring. In the external realm, we are gratified to note that Latin America's principal creditor countries are now increasingly aware of the need to remedy the problem of negative net transfers of resources from the region. Easing of the external debt burden and an injection of new financing represent a potentially very important contribution to this end. Additional relief for these economic woes came from the favorable effects of a certain recovery in world trade, coupled with a positive turn in raw material prices, which allowed the region to boost the value of its merchandise exports in 1989 to a level that even topped the figure attained in 1981, before the onset of the crisis.

ECONOMIC STAGNATION OF LATIN AMERICA IN THE 1980S AND PROSPECTS FOR RECOVERY

By the end of the 1980s, Latin America's development potential was bogged down by the combined weight of sharp internal and external disequilibria, which also sparked great social sacrifices. After two decades of rapid growth, when the overall gross domestic product (GDP) climbed at an annual rate of 5.6 percent in the 1960s and 5.9 percent in the 1970s, the region subsided into semistagnation in the 1980s, when production inched up only 1.3 percent a year. Concomitant rapid demographic growth pushed the $2,312 per capita product posted in 1989 back to the average level for 1978. This represented a cumulative decline of 8.1 percent from the figure achieved in 1980.

The crisis triggered multiple woes, in the social sphere as well as in the economy itself. First of all, it slowed the creation of new job sources, which were estimated to account for about one-fifth of the employment generated annually according to historical trends. As a result, open unemployment rose from 8 percent of the work force in 1977 to 10.7 percent in 1984, and gradually ebbed to about 8.4 percent in the last two years. But there are signs that the unemployment problem is more severe than those figures suggest. This would appear to be confirmed, for example, by the surge in employment by the urban informal sector, which rose at an average annual rate of 6.8 percent in the first half of the 1980s, swelling the sector's size to some 40 percent of all nonfarm employment during the period. That phenomenon may have become even more pronounced in the second half of the 1980s, particularly in the countries hardest hit by the economic crisis.

The crisis also brought a concomitant generalized decline in real wages, which dropped by an average of approximately 13 percent in the region during the 1980s, considerably exceeding the drop in the per capita product, and thus showing the high percentage of the economic adjustment borne by the workers' sector. Looking at a group of seven countries (Argentina, Brazil, Chile, Colombia, Costa Rica, Mexico, and Venezuela), which account for where 80 percent of the region's population is concentrated, average work income—a better barometer than the legal minimum wage—is seen to have plummeted in the course of the 1980s, when it dropped by approximately 28 percent between 1980 and 1987. In short, although these figures are by no means complete, they do point to a painful worsening of the economic status of Latin America's majority population segments, triggered by the crisis besetting the region in recent years. The Economic Commission for Latin America and the Caribbean (1990, p. 66) estimated that in the 1980s, poverty spread to 183 million persons—that is, 44 percent of the population.

A retrospective glance at economic developments in the decade now ending shows that the pattern of Latin America's historical development underwent a complete shake-up that was considerably more than mere adjustments to a recessive phase in a supposed economic cycle. The crisis pinpointed certain weaknesses and basic contradictions in the economic processes and traditional policies in place since the 1930s and World War II, which were substantially magnified by unusually adverse developments in the international economic picture. All this has brought the region face to face with the need for structural economic reforms and redefined guidelines for its future development strategy.

Despite the acknowledged and important differences from one country to another, the new development strategy is apt to include at least three essential policy components: (1) triggering of creative market forces by means of incentives to spur production and efficiency; (2) global reform of the role and purview of public-sector action that will remedy structural shortcomings and foster savings and productive efficiency; and (3) opening of the economies to international trade competition. There are cogent reasons for believing that the 1990s will find Latin America able to surmount present obstacles and embark on sustained long-term economic and social development. In the first place, there has been a fundamental change in the approach espoused by the region's economic agents and authorities, thus permitting a shift in the thrust and content of economic policy. Second, democratic coexistence has broadened and flourished despite economic troubles, thus making it possible to reach widespread social consensus in regard to the application of new policies. Third, there are very auspicious signs of a new and renewed political will on the part of the international community to strengthen economic cooperation with Latin America.

From the standpoint of economic prospects, moreover, forecasts for the first half of the 1990s, according to a study of projections drawn up by The WEFA Group (1990) point to gradual recovery of growth trends in the region. The average growth rate for the GDP would rise by close to 5 percent in 1991, then hovering at around an average 3.8 percent a year over the 1992–95 period. Along with restored productive activity, the general macroeconomic picture would tend to stabilize the present balance-of-payments deficit at an average annual level of about $10,700 million in 1990–93, accompanied by an easing of internal inflationary pressures. (All dollar figures cited in this volume are U.S. dollars.)

CAPITAL FORMATION AS A CRITICAL FACTOR IN ECONOMIC RECOVERY

A seminal factor in Latin America's economic stagnation and the decline in its potential for future growth is the drastic cutback in outlays for productive investment. Reflecting the recessive adjustment applied in many of the region's economies, particularly by means of a shrinkage in overall internal demand, investment expenditures as a share of the GDP dropped from 24 percent in 1980 to 16 or 17 percent in the last seven years.

The cut in investment spending was not limited to indefinite postponement or jettisoning of infrastructure projects in progress and the failure to launch new public and private investment programs. It also interrupted the absorption of new technologies that are not only necessary but indispensable for achieving production reforms, modernization, and heightened economic efficiency. The reduction in spending on productive investment has had a multiplier effect on current levels of the GDP and employment, at the same time depressing potential levels of economic growth and future social well-being in the region. Its restoration in the short term, to the point where it will regain—or even outstrip—the levels reached in the past, is therefore one of the greatest challenges facing domestic economic policy and international cooperation in forthcoming years.

Simply by way of illustration, it should be noted that the recovery of capital formation levels attained by Latin America in the past—in the early 1980s, for example—would entail an increase in 1990 investment spending amounting to about 45 percent more than the figure posted in 1989. This would be equivalent to additional investment outlays of about $75 billion. In order to sustain the upturn in production and employment, the corresponding increase would have to be factored into those figures.

⟨ In addition to the requisite volumes of investment, another item that is important—if not crucial—to formation of the economic and social development policies of Latin American countries in the next several years is an examination of the qualitative needs for investment and their allocation by productive or social sectors. Because of the difficult conditions under which the region's economy operates, this aspect of economic diagnosis can be addressed only in the specific context of each country's economy. It is nevertheless a vitally important analytical factor, not only for determining the extent of the savings mobilization effort that will have to be made by each country, but also for helping to guide international cooperation policies and programs for Latin America. As an example: Even if it were possible to reduce the negative net transfer of resources abroad to zero, Latin America would have to increase its internal savings by some $45 billion. Both conditions represent a formidable challenge to the region under present circumstances.⟩

EXPORTS AS THE ENGINE OF GROWTH

Perhaps one of the most valuable lessons Latin America has learned from the economic experience of the 1980s consists of the acknowledged advantages of an export-oriented development strategy, as compared with the limitations observed in the so-called import substitution model. The exacerbated skewing of the balance of payments in the late 1970s and early 1980s, cushioned by an unlimited supply of external financing—mostly with interest rates and financing terms incompatible with the capacity for servicing eternal debt—unleashed the financial crisis that led to the collapse of the economic growth model pursued until then by most of the Latin American countries.

A first reaction was adoption of an external adjustment policy designed to generate a mounting trade surplus, obtained largely by forceful suppression of imports. Statistics on expenditures of the GDP show that imports of nonfactor goods and services, at constant prices, dwindled at the rate of 2.5 percent a year over the 1981–88 period, as compared with the 8.1 percent increase posted in the 1970s. The balance-of-payment figures show that the current value of imports dropped from $103 billion in 1981 to slightly over $61 billion in 1983–86—that is, a decline of about 40 percent. The flip side of the coin consisted of a concomitant shrinkage of internal expenditures for consumption and investment, particularly in the latter category: the hallmark of the recessive nature of the adjustment policy followed by many Latin American countries.

The real value of exports, on the other hand, rose at an average annual rate of 3.1 percent during the 1980s—almost 2.4 times the growth rate of the

GDP, which was the most dynamic change on record in the structure of global Latin American demand. The aforementioned export push was largely offset, however, by an unusual and persistent sagging in the world market prices of raw materials. The unit value indicator of exported goods posted a 26 percent decline between 1980 and 1988. As a result, it was not until 1988 that current revenue from exports managed to climb above their 1981 level ($102.6 billion in 1988, as compared with $100.7 billion in 1981).

The region suffered copious losses owing to the downturn in prices. To illustrate that point, if the prices of Latin America's exports had remained constant between 1981 and 1988, foreign exchange revenue from that source would have amounted to nearly $160 billion in the last year of that period—that is, 53 percent more than the actual amount posted.

The vulnerability of Latin America's exports, which today include a high percentage of primary products—whose performance in world trade has gradually but significantly outstripped that of more dynamic manufactured items—is a very important argument for efforts to expand and diversify the region's export commodities. The goal was not only to achieve a wider array of products, with a larger local value added component, but also to secure better access to the markets of the industrial economies in the northern hemisphere and Asia. Some of the regional countries have already made important progress in that direction, but support will be needed to permit its consolidation and future expansion.

In short, the external adjustment of Latin American economies that was imposed by the debt crisis and the drying up of new external credit made it possible to generate a huge balance-of-payments trade surplus. As a share of the gross domestic product, it rose to 6.8 percent in 1985, compared with less than 4 percent in the 1960s and an equally unusual 2.5 percent deficit in 1980. The external adjustment experience has unquestionably been singularly severe, as shown very clearly by the swing of more than nine percentage points of gross domestic product, posted by the trade balance between 1980 and 1985. But the real challenge to Latin America is to change the nature of the process whereby the trade surplus is formed, based on better use of its producing and exporting capacity and heightened ability of the region's products to compete in world markets rather than the compression of imports that was experienced recently.

NET TRANSFERS OF RESOURCES AND THE EXTERNAL DEBT CRISIS

One of the factors that weighed most heavily on the balance-of-payments disequilibrium and the Latin American financial crisis was the negative net transfer of the region's savings to the rest of the world. The situation took on special features starting in 1982, when it was not only a way of siphoning off resources that might otherwise have sustained a better economic growth rate, but also constituted an obstacle to long-term regional development. When the drastically reduced inflow of new credits and foreign private investment was coupled with rapidly mounting outflows of interest payments and profits on foreign capital, the region suddenly became a net source of savings for the principal industrial country creditors. Over the 1982–89 period, the net capital inflow to the region totaled $78.2 billion—only 28 percent of the region's total payments to creditor countries for interest and profits. The net drain of Latin American savings that exited in this way thus amounted to a cumulative total of $203.1 billion over the nine years in question.

Almost all of the net transfer of funds from Latin American countries was covered by the trade surplus generated during the 1982–89 period, a cumulative total of $198.485 billion, equivalent to 98 percent of total net transfers of savings from the region to the rest of the world in those years. The remaining 2 percent had to be drawn down from those countries' international monetary reserves.

The net transfer of funds abroad and the buildup of a surprising trade surplus are two sides of the same coin, just as they are in highly developed countries. The counterpart of this mix of real (trade surplus) and financial (net transfer) resources is the recessive internal economic adjustment, which most of the countries had to undergo as their contribution to the stability of the international financial system and evidence of Latin America's commitment to maintaining external economic relations that it is hoped will be favorable to the region in the future. But two factors—the cutback in internal investment outlays, and the lack of opportunities for better export performance—had considerable impact on the standstill in production, the failure to make use of development potential, and deterioration of the overall economic climate in the region that have characterized the well-known "recessive adjustment" of Latin America's economy in recent years.

Another factor that aggravated the shortage of savings available for investment in Latin America is the so-called capital flight, which is as revealing of the lack of economic incentives in the region as of the unusually attractive rate of return offered to investors in some of the industrial countries. While it is virtually impossible to measure the true dimensions of capital flight from Latin America, some estimates put it at about $12 billion a year during the 1980s. This further drained the region's savings, triggering a sort of vicious circle in which the loss of that capital worsened Latin America's "economic climate" and further deepened the technological lag produced by diminished internal investment.

The setting of favorable macroeconomic conditions is thus a determinant requirement for increased savings and heightened foreign investment, as well as an incentive for the return of national capital invested abroad. The principles inherent in generation of a market economy are such that foreign and national investors have the same behavior pattern. Both seek profits and safety. "Capital flight" is a misnomer, a symptom rather than a root cause of the economic crisis. By the same token, repatriation of that capital should not be considered a condition of economic recovery policy but, instead, an indication that the desired climate of economic progress is settling in.

⟨ But improvement of Latin America's macroeconomic climate depends largely on progress made in the structural reforms undertaken by those countries and removal of the external trade and financial constraints that aggravate the balance-of-payments disequilibrium. In the financial order, we must recognize the development of new conditions that will help ease the foreign debt crisis. The Brady Plan made a very real contribution to the efforts to reconcile debtor country needs for savings to reactivate growth and institute reforms and restored confidence in the financial ability of those countries in capital markets. In particular, the financial arrangement secured by Mexico represents the first instance of actual easing of external obligations among the principal debtor countries. This has been a positive experience, and one that the international financial community hopes will be fine-tuned and utilized by other Latin American debtor countries. ⟩

ACCELERATION OF THE INFLATIONARY SPIRAL

Aggravated inflation was another symptom of—as well as a contributing factor in—the Latin American economic crisis of the 1980s. The scourge of inflation spread to more of the region's countries and in some cases reached unprecedented proportions, close to the worst inflation on record (examples from 1989 include Argentina, 3,079 percent; Brazil, 1,287 percent; and Nicaragua, 18,996 percent). To some extent this phenomenon represents a disease endemic to the region that has been around in one form or another for decades. Its causes are rooted in major structural disequilibria of the economies and the special features of the countries' institutions and social values.

But in the 1980s the economic and financial crises—accompanied, in some instances, by the perverse effects of some of the adjustment policy measures that were applied—put added pressure on prices. It is this mixture of basic conditions and episodic components that makes it so difficult to diagnose and to prescribe appropriate stabilization policies. That difficulty is occasionally compounded by a certain dose of dogmatism that places too much emphasis on simplistic solutions and purported panaceas. The experience with various attempts at stabilization in recent years, which resulted in resounding failures, are part of the legacy with which the region embarks on a new decade. There have also been some very favorable experiences in stabilization that allow us to consider not only the combination of necessary economic reforms and policy measures, but their sequence in time as well. Both the failures and the successes help us to face the challenges of restoring stable growth, with heightened pragmatism and confidence, in the years to come. A fundamental lesson is that the inflation crisis may entail a social cost so high that it will become the greatest political obstacle to the start of reforms and the necessary efforts at stabilization. This leaves us facing a formidable dilemma, and one that will require great courage and political resolve, plus an important measure of justice in distributing the social costs of the stabilization program.

CONCLUSIONS

Today the countries of Latin America are facing one of the greatest challenges in their history: the resumption of their long-term economic and social development, under conditions that promise a more equitable internal distribution of the fruits of progress and increasing worldwide economic interdependence.

The distinctive mark that the 1980s imprinted on the region was the monumental financial and economic tension it was compelled to face as a result of a complex combination of adverse internal and external factors. The domestic front saw a halt in production, a cutback in investment and employment, the spread and aggravation of inflation, the inability of inefficient production structures to compete, heightened risk and uncertainty, bankruptcy of commercial firms, and the insolvency of banks and other financial entities.

On the external side, Latin America was assailed by a strange combination of adversities, the backlash of a highly volatile international economic and financial climate, spawned by prolonged and stringent economic recession in the industrial countries, sharp exchange fluctuations, high real interest rates, persistently worsening terms of trade, and the shift from financial exuberance to a draconian shortage of external savings.

But the crisis was not confined to the negative economic balance and the alarming social cost of what we have agreed to term "the lost decade." Its legacy also included valuable lessons, which we must now use to our advantage. Perhaps the most important is the realization that there are no panaceas, no economic miracles, and no shortcuts to completion of the structural reforms on which the region has embarked. There is, in fact, a real consensus among the political leaders and economic authorities of our countries as to the need to direct our stabilization and development efforts to objectives that are both realistic and sustainable in time. Mobilization of the countries' development potential—especially the part that depends on the thrust of their human resources and internal savings—is a crucial factor in this process.

Most of the Latin American countries are making impressive efforts to achieve economic transformation and adjustment. The surprising trade surplus generated by Latin America suggests that external adjustment has been largely successful. Spiraling inflation and sluggish investment, however, tell us that internal adjustment is not yet in sight. Mighty efforts, with a large measure of social sacrifice and political commitment, plus the support of international economic cooperation, are needed. And it is here that multilateral financing organizations can play a highly strategic role, spurring effective progress in the reform processes and restoration of long-term development.

This is precisely the great task and solemn commitment of the Inter-American Development Bank, to which it pledges its vast experience of three decades of service to the region's development and renewed efforts to make more of its own resources available, along with the trust funds and parallel financing contributed by various industrial member countries of the Bank, especially Japan and Spain.

REFERENCES

Comisión Económica para America Latina y el Caribe (CEPAL) (1990). *Magnitud de la Pobreza en America Latina en los Años Ochenta.* Santiago, Chile: CEPAL.
The WEFA Group (April 1990). *World Economic Outlook*, Vol. 3. New York.

CHAPTER TWO

The Development of Latin American and Caribbean Countries in the 1980s and Prospects for the Future

GERT ROSENTHAL

Now that we are beginning the decade of the 1990s, what can be said about the Latin American and Caribbean development experience in the decade that just ended? So much has been said about the depth and duration of the recent economic crisis that it is difficult to add something original—at least in regard to its causes, scope, and consequences. Albeit, the ten-year time frame proffers an unusually fine vantage point for drawing up a short balance sheet and expressing a few ideas about future prospects, taking into account the legacy bequeathed to us by the decade that some describe as "lost" from the standpoint of development.

That description is not particularly appropriate, since it implies a retrenchment in all spheres and in every country. In point of fact, as we shall see further on, a certain amount of progress also occurred during the 1980s: partial and fragile in the economic arena, and considerable in the political domain (which is also part of the development experience). On balance, if changes in the region are measured by the most conventional and cumulative yardstick—evolution of the per capita gross domestic product—the adjective is not only warranted, but understated. Strictly speaking, the average per capita product in the region will be almost 10 percent below the level posted in 1980, thus paralleling the 1976 figure. Moreover, the phenomenon was generalized: in 1990, only three or four countries in the region will show any improvement over the early 1980s level in this indicator. When we recall the marked downturn in average income, it is all too apparent that the 1980s did, in fact, substantially erode the material well-being of the Latin American and Caribbean population.

But that is only one of the end results of the period, which assuredly will constitute a milestone—for better or for worse—in the economic annals of the region. The word "crisis" also characterizes the performance of most of the economies, as well as the many shortcoming and long-standing flaws disclosed by adverse world economic conditions.

In evaluating the decade, it must be remembered that the major trends observed did not affect all of the countries to the same extent, nor were they consistently present in any one country throughout the decade. Furthermore, they affected the different sectors, strata, and regions of each particular country in varying degrees. As noted above, there were in fact occasional bright spots in the generally gloomy scenario: firms that in every country improved their international competitiveness, even in the context of unfavorable conditions; communities that bettered their standards of living through heightened self-help; a general recognition of what worked and what did not; the spur to creativity implicit in various constraints; and in some cases—few thus far—relatively successful structural adjustment (although at a high social cost). Particular emphasis must be placed on the distinct trend toward democratization, accompanied by more pluralistic, tolerant, and participatory political regimes.

On balance, liabilities outweigh assets at the end of the decade. The following sections discuss four phenomena that summarize the major economic and social events of the period. All of them, of course, are interrelated and interact with each other.

LOSS OF DYNAMISM IN THE TRADITIONAL SOURCES OF GROWTH

In the first place, in varying degrees from one country to another, the chief sources of economic dynamism in the preceding three decades—an expanding export sector dependent on raw materials, and industrialization based mainly on internal demand—began to grow weaker or even ceased to be effective. In the exporting sector of most countries, the value (but not the volume) of external sales of traditional commodities dropped sharply owing to falling prices. In 11 of the 19 principal countries of the region, the value of overall exports stood still or even fell. Dwindling demand for basic commodities was apparently not due to the classic cyclical downturn alone: it also reflects important changes in the structure of such demand. According to the Economic Commission for Latin America and the Caribbean (ECLAC) calculations, a weighted index of real prices for 19 of the region's main export commodities other than oil indicates a decline of more than one-third between 1980 and 1988. When petroleum is included, the decline is of almost 50 percent.

Regarding industrialization, the value added of its production rose faster than GDP in periods of expansion; by the same token, it fell faster in periods of recession, at least in countries where output was geared mainly to supply internal demand. Industrial value added, as a share of GDP, tended to fall in most countries. For the region as a whole, it increased at an annual rate of only 0.5 percent, so that the average rate of industrial development in the region dropped from 25.2 to 23.8 percent between 1980 and 1988. Accordingly, the manufacturing sector helped to accentuate the recessive panorama instead of attenuating it.

The loss of dynamism of the two engines of growth immediately raises the question as to whether they can be restored; and, if the answer is in the negative, where the new growth stimuli of Latin American and Caribbean economies can be found in the future. The answer might be found in countries whose performance record improved in the last few years, which are precisely the ones that made headway in productive transformation. In some cases, the international competitiveness of manufactures increased. Their share of Mexico's exports rose from 12.7 to 44.5 percent between 1980 and 1988; Brazil posted an upturn from 56.5 to 71.3 percent in the same category for that period. In other countries, such as Colombia, heightened competitive success of manufactures was accompanied by the incorporation of new primary commodities in the export sector. In still others, mounting technical progress in primary-sector areas—vegetables, and marine and forestry products—triggered a sharp upturn in the export sector. This was the case in Chile, Costa Rica, the Dominican Republic, and Uruguay, for example.

THE INTRACTABLE NATURE OF MACROECONOMIC DISEQUILIBRIA

Both the characteristics and the consequences of the macroeconomic imbalances experienced by numerous countries of the region in the 1980s were marked by certain features that distinguish them from similar phenomena in earlier decades. Regarding their characteristics, they were much more pronounced than before. While many countries managed to adjust their trade balances to the new world economic realities, frequently by dint of recessive adjustment policies, very few of them were equally successful in fighting inflation and reducing external deficits while growing at the same time.

One of the factors that had the greatest influence on this situation was the impact of foreign debt servicing on the public-sector deficit and on the current account of the balance of payments. This phenomenon has been amply described in numerous documents and needs no further elaboration. Suffice it to say that the countries that were most successful in combining adjustment and stabilization efforts were those where there was a possibility of improving the financial position of the public sector. Accordingly, when the value of the exports produced by state enterprises rose (as in the case of Chilean copper), the balance of payments and fiscal accounts showed a direct and simultaneous improvement, thereby permitting faster growth and slower inflation. The converse is equally true: when the value of exports dropped (as was generally the case among oil exporters in recent years), the fiscal deficit tended to increase and external imbalance became more critical.

The economic disequilibria cited had a spin-off in the form of other consequences that are worth mentioning. One of them is the marked priority granted to short-term economic policy compared with medium- and long-term concerns: survival, one might say, instead of development. For the same reason, economic policy priorities tended to devote greater efforts to correcting imbalances and fighting inflation than to promoting growth and fostering change. Last, a reduced margin of maneuver in the execution of economic policy, which was imposed by the newfound scarcity of foreign exchange, considerably weakened the government's ability to act.

THE PLUMMETING OF INVESTMENT

The gradual loss of dynamism in Latin American and Caribbean output is closely tied to the sharp drop of net investment in many countries. In earlier decades, the expansion of productive capacity—for both exports and internal supply—was based on a relatively high and still growing level of public and private investment (between 22 and 25 percent of the GDP).

The scenario in the 1980s was very different. Worsening terms of trade and external debt service, usually accompanied by a reduced net inflow of foreign capital, made considerable inroads into the net resources available for investment use. The region's net investment ratio to GDP dropped from 22.7 percent in 1980 to 16.5 percent in 1988, and most—but not all—of the countries suffered as a result. The phenomenon also reflects the generally adverse evolution of public finances.

At the outset, tax collection declined as a result of the recession, and fiscal reforms were instituted to correct that downturn. It should also be noted that tariffs of public utilities tended to drop in the face of inflation. Current spending, on the other hand, rose, partly as a result of public debt-service payments, both at home and abroad. The financial burden of overseas payments, expressed in local currency, was magnified by successive devaluations and high international interest rates, while in most instances internal debt was affected by exceptionally high rates as well. The growing current-account deficits that characterized the decade resulted in reduced allocations to the areas considered to be the most expendable—public investment and social outlays—but the social cost was high.

In addition, different modalities for financing the fiscal deficit created negative expectations, impeded private investment, narrowed the public sector's room to maneuver in the financial sphere, and, in general, fueled the crisis. In some cases the availability of credit for the private sector was reduced by the imposition of forced savings mechanisms in a context of financial repression that encouraged capital flight. In others, public bonds were floated under circumstances that helped boost interest rates significantly, at the same time generating expectations of future taxes. There were also cases in which money was simply issued, thus stimulating demand, inflation, and exchange rate crises.

One of the many consequences of the phenomena described is that numerous countries are currently faced with increasing obsolescence of their productive plant and an alarming deterioration of their physical infrastructure.

THE DECLINE IN AVERAGE LEVELS OF MATERIAL WELL-BEING

While most of the economies stopped growing, the population did not. At the start of the 1980s, there were 362 million people in the region; by the end, the figure had reached 448 million. The demographic inertia of the preceding decades, plus the gradual absorption of women into the work force, pushed the economically active population level up by an annual 2.8 percent during this period. The data available generally show that although open unemployment increased—particularly in the urban areas—the rise was not proportionally equivalent to the curtailment in economic activity. The decline had been avoided at the cost of a spiraling downturn in productivity per worker and rapid growth of the informal labor market.

The sluggish economy, heightened unemployment and underemployment, the growing number of workers in the informal sectors (accompanied by a drop in real wages in most countries), and the constraints on public spending all contributed, in one way or another, to the swelling incidence of extreme poverty. Very rough calculations indicate that some 112 million Latin Americans (36 percent of the total) lived below the poverty line in 1980, and by 1985 that number had risen to 160 million and 38 percent. The great majority of countries saw the emergence of islands of modern production, usually associated with exports of nontraditional goods, which contrast with the panorama described in the preceding paragraphs. This suggests that the traditional segmentation of Latin American and Caribbean labor markets has become more pronounced in recent years, and that the gap between the higher and lower income groups has widened.

The marked decline in the quality of life of broad strata of Latin America's population has frequently led to social unrest. One of its many effects is the sharp increase in crime, particularly in the large urban centers. However, it would seem that enhanced efficiency in the use of current public outlays in the provision of social services has at times counteracted the effects of reduced expenditures. There is no evidence—at least thus far, and with few exceptions—of a clear decline in the indicators of health care and education. This situation will nevertheless be difficult to maintain where there have been no expenditures on health care and education facilities, or for training designed to improve nutrition and public health.

Finally, another effect of the economic and social erosion in the region is the rising level of Latin American and Caribbean emigration, particularly to the United States and Canada. That phenomenon is compounded by the exodus resulting from political and military conflict—as, for example, in the case of displaced persons and refugees in Central America, who have moved within the subregion or to other countries.

PROSPECTS FOR THE FUTURE

Based on the succinct balance sheet presented so far of Latin American and Caribbean economic and social performance in the 1980s, what can be said of the development prospects of the various countries in the region? Will the 1990s continue to be dominated by the recessive inertia and the onus of the considerable liabilities that will be carried over from one decade to the next? Or will the advances—at times hesitating and piecemeal—that have begun to be perceived in the last few years, at least in some countries, predominate? Will the trend toward ever-increasing differentiation continue, with the ability to grow restored in a handful of countries, while the rest remain in a secular state of virtual stagnation? Or will there be a generalized reactivation supported by the transformation of productive processes in the countries of the region?

It is obviously difficult to hazard any prognosis in this respect. It would probably be tautological to say that the outlook for the region's economies in the 1990s will depend on their success in overcoming the main restrictions of the 1980s—in other words, their ability to transform their productive systems and correct macroeconomic imbalances. That capability depends, in turn, on determinants of both internal and external origin. Any opinions on the scenarios for the next decade will thus have to be based, first, on hypotheses concerning the performance of the world economy; and, second, on certain assumptions regarding the possibility of domestic efforts to rectify macroeconomic disequilibria and transform production structures.

As to the first point, the evolution of the world's principal industrialized economies and their repercussion on monetary, financial, and trade systems in the context of the world economy will unquestionably play a decisive role in building alternative scenarios for the future of Latin American and Caribbean countries. The projected course of real interest rates in international financial markets, the path of basic commodity prices, and the denouement of the external debt drama are just a few of the imponderables that illustrate the difficulties and risks besetting the futurology profession today. There are, however, no signs on the horizon to suggest that the chief economies of the Organization for Economic Cooperation and Development (OECD), and perhaps some of the socialist economies, cannot maintain an acceptable and sustainable level of economic growth in the medium term. Obviously, it remains to be seen whether the developing countries will be given timely access to markets in the developed world, or if the protectionist pressures that have become stronger in recent times increase.

As to the second factor, the balance sheet for the 1980s suggests the expediency of exploring three decisive and interrelated variables, the evolution of which will determine future prospects. They are: the possibility of overcoming the macroeconomic disequilibria of the 1980s; the ability to transform productive systems as a means of achieving greater competitiveness in international markets; and the feasibility of mobilizing resources to finance sustained development. All too clearly, none of these variables is impervious to the way the debt service problem of countries heavily indebted to the international private banks is handled. And it is equally obvious that a resolution of this matter alone will not suffice to ensure sustained development.

The experiences of the 1980s taught us important lessons about how to achieve greater macroeconomic equilibrium, and particularly how to conduct a successful stabilization program. Two reasons foster the belief that progress will be made in this area in forthcoming years. The first consists of certain concrete experiences in the 1980s (for example, those of Bolivia, Costa Rica, and Mexico), which show that it is possible to conquer inflation, although painful measures are needed, along with a certain degree of access to external financing. The most successful cases were not limited to demand management; they included a simultaneous attack on supply, at the same time attempting to guide expectations and correct factors of structural origin (through "pacts" on wage and price policies). Reduction of the fiscal deficit played a decisive role throughout. The second reason is that hyperinflation conveys an eloquent warning about the high social cost of not making timely decisions to meet the situation. Antiinflation policy dominates the 1989 economic panorama precisely because of the fact that the creators of economic policy have become fully aware of the imperious need for it.

Insofar as the transformation of productive structures is concerned, there is also a new basis for hope. Even in the generally devastating scenario of the 1980s, some progress was made, although it differed in degree and scope from one country to another. The antiexport and antirural biases that characterized economic policy in earlier decades have gradually softened or are disappearing in almost every country. There is also today greater awareness about the fact that productive transformation calls for a complex array of activities in fields as diverse as macroeconomic policy, the removal of institutional and organizations restrictions, and the availability of human resources and physical infrastructure. This is not the place for an in-depth examination of such complex matters. It should be said, however, that inducing change in the productive structure is provenly possible, although it is a long-term undertaking, so that the results of applying such policies and strategies will not necessarily be apparent in the first few years of the decade.

Two burning questions remain. In the first place, how can we finance modernization of the productive apparatus and obtain greater social equity in the

future? There is a dangerous accumulation of unmet demands: physical infrastructure that urgently needs maintenance and rehabilitation; an increasingly
obsolescent capital plant; substantial gaps in the delivery of social services; mi-
nuscule allocations to technological research and its application to the productive process; the need for industrial restructuring; prevention of further
environmental deterioration; and many others. However, despite the persistence of certain activities in which there is extensive idle capacity in some
countries of the region, sustained development of supply will necessarily require an expansion of productive capacity.

It is not clear, however, where the funds to finance the necessary investment will be found. That is why it is so important to resolve the external debt
problem. This would not only make it possible to reduce the considerable portion of domestic savings that are being transferred overseas, but would also
provide at least the possibility of establishing a "virtuous circle" that would
make it easier to correct macroeconomic imbalances and reverse the transfer
of the approximately 4 percent of the GDP that Latin America is at present
sending abroad. In other words, if progress is made toward easing the burden
of debt service—and the first steps, however timid, announced by the Brady
initiative offer some hope in this respect—there would again be grounds to
face the 1990s with greater optimism. Needless to say, the multilateral financial organizations, particularly the Inter-American Development Bank, can
play a vital role in those endeavors.

In the second place, there is the question of equity. Latin American income
was most inequitably distributed before the 1980s, and, as stated, deteriorated
even more in the past decade. There is now the danger that the mix of economic policies needed to gain international competitiveness will not redress
this situation and could conceivably make it worse. Thus the objective of equity
will be very much on the minds of policymakers, not only due to ethical considerations, but also to consolidate democratic political systems.

To conclude, the prospects of the decade of the 1990s would improve if government and civil societies were to make better use of the potential offered
by economic integration. We must remember that the countries of the region,
considered individually, will have to face economic macroblocks that include
Europe without borders, the expanded market of Canada and the United
States, and the emergence of a new group of Pacific Rim countries. Why, then,
would it not be better to face these macroblocks jointly?

Subregional integration among Latin American and Caribbean countries and
the dynamic integration into the world economy do not necessarily enter into
conflict. On the contrary, they could be mutually reinforcing. The emergence
of new national development strategies based on liberalization, productive
transformation, and heightened ability to compete in international markets
suggests that regional markets may be conceived as sources of additional competition that can contribute to the systemic process of learning and undertaking technological innovation required for exporting to other markets.

Moreover, some sectoral efforts of a bilateral or trilateral nature have been made—with a strong dose of political support—in areas such as technology, capital goods, and agriculture, as shown by the agreement between Argentina, Brazil, and Uruguay. Similarly, the joint positions of the Central American countries vis-à-vis the international donor community, as a result of the progress made toward achieving peace in the subregion, have opened the doors to cooperation that could expedite the revitalization of intra-Central American trade and enhance existing interdependence in the areas of infrastructure and agriculture. Any progress in this respect would be grounds for greater optimism about the 1990s.

To sum up, the balance sheet for the 1980s itself provides certain clues to a possible scenario of increasing economic growth accompanied by improved well-being for the average Latin American. That scenario assumes that the international situation will undergo no important setbacks, and that the governments of the region, mindful of the harsh lessons of the 1980s, will advance, individually and jointly, toward removing some of the principal constraints on development.

Based on this assumption, and also assuming that financial constraints will be alleviated, the good news is that the economies can be reactivated, in contrast to what occurred during the preceding decade. The bad news, however, is that even with sustained annual growth rates of 4 percent in the first few years of the decade, most of the countries will be able to regain only the real per capita income level they had achieved as far back as 1980 by 1995. It also is not clear whether the benefits of this modest growth will "trickle down" to the majority of the population.

CHAPTER THREE

Hyperinflation in Latin America: The Search for Developmental Solutions

GARY McMAHON

The diseases of high inflation and hyperinflation have been widespread in Latin America throughout the twentieth century, but it is only in the early 1990s that they have reached plague proportions, infecting most of the countries of the region, often reaching levels never suffered before. As in virtually every other case of hyperinflation in this century, the illness intensified after the patient had to make large transfers of resources abroad. Until the mid-1980s the usual prescription to remedy both inflation and external deficit was a liberal dose of so-called orthodox policy, usually with a team of specialists from the International Monetary Fund (IMF) and/or World Bank overseeing the operation. For the most part this remedy failed to cure the disease—the doctor invariably blamed the patient for this result—but even when successful (partially or totally) the patient would suffer from the even more debilitating afflictions of unemployment and recession. Eventually the remedy would be postponed or discarded. In reaction to these failures, a number of economists have prescribed a more unorthodox approach.

Unlike the orthodox approach with its almost single-minded emphasis on restraining domestic demand, the heterodox approach attempts to bring down inflation by simultaneously attacking it on all fronts. The central assumptions behind this new approach are that (1) inflation is primarily an inertial response to expectations of the same, (2) inflation can be brought down without the economy going into a severe (or even moderate) recession, and (3) there are structural elements in the economy that will ultimately defeat an orthodox program. (The heterodox approach is usually associated with the Latin American neostructuralist school of economics.) Whereas the orthodox approach tries to break expectations by contracting the economy until the pressure on wages and prices to fall is too strong to resist, the heterodox strategy attacks them directly using income policies and price controls. The latter can (and usually does) contain elements of the former; in fact, some economists view orthodox policies as a subset of heterodox policies.

Since 1985 Argentina, Brazil, and Peru have all put a heterodox package into place to try to stop high inflation or hyperinflation without sending the economy into a recession. Each country initially enjoyed a period of success but ultimately—after one to two years—the policies failed disastrously. On the other hand Bolivia implemented an orthodox, IMF-supported program in 1985 that brought its inflation rate down to single-digit figures at the expense of a fairly mild recession, which was turned around in two years. The main purposes of this chapter will be to (1) analyze the reasons for the failure of the three heterodox programs, emphasizing whether the lack of success was due to the nature of the programs or the way in which they were implemented; (2) analyze the success of the Bolivian orthodox approach, emphasizing factors specific to Bolivia that made such an accomplishment more likely; and (3) determine whether the Bolivian success could likely be replicated in the other three countries or if their best hope lies in heterodox programs that are better designed and implemented.

The next section will examine the heterodox plan in each of the three countries. In the following section the Bolivian orthodox plan will be discussed. Before moving to the conclusions, the more recent stabilization attempts in Brazil and Mexico—the Collor Plan and PECE, respectively—will be briefly discussed. In the last section the common points and problems in the three heterodox plans will be compared. In addition we will try to determine the suitability of the Bolivian strategy for Argentina, Brazil, and Peru versus a different type of heterodox plan, taking into account the preliminary results of the Collor Plan and PECE.

THE HETERODOX CASES

In this section, Argentina, Brazil, and Peru will be analyzed from historical and theoretical points of view. For each country the reasons for the failure of their heterodox policies will be investigated in some depth. Finally we will speculate on alternative policies.

Argentina

While one would have to go back in time to uncover the roots of Argentina's inflationary problems, the problem became visibly apparent in 1975. After a long series of poorly designed or implemented economic policies, primarily of

an import-substitution nature, inflation accelerated in 1975 to three-digit figures and has rarely been otherwise since. Beginning in 1976 the foreign trade
regime was partially liberalized and capital flows totally freed. The exchange
rate was managed by a preannounced schedule of nominal devaluations in an
attempt to bring inflation down by slowing the rate of change of this key price.
In 1979 and 1980 there was a massive capital outflow as the exchange rate
was correctly believed to be seriously overvalued. It is worth noting that this
capital flight and the accompanying nationalization of private debt greatly aggravated (and perhaps even caused) the Argentine debt problem of the 1980s,
greatly increasing the difficulty of any domestic stabilization plan. Between
1980 and 1982, inflation increased owing to a large real devaluation and increases in public utility prices, the latter necessary to lower the fiscal deficit.
In 1984 the price level had another jolt when, in an attempt to recoup the large
losses the workers had suffered since 1979, widespread indexation was instituted by the new civilian government. With a monthly inflation rate of 24 percent in the first quarter of 1985 and a government deficit equal to 10 percent
of GDP, it was decided in April to introduce a heterodox program.

While the program per se did not begin until June 1985, some important preliminary steps were taken in April and May. These included real increases in
public utility prices and a real devaluation. The pillars of the Austral Plan were:
(1) across-the-board freezing of prices except nontradeables; (2) a standby
agreement with the IMF tied to strong fiscal adjustment; (3) a strong commitment not to finance the fiscal deficit by money creation; and (4) the introduction
of a new currency, the austral, to replace the peso, accompanied with a sliding
scale for the conversion of peso-denominated contracts in order that creditors
would not benefit from the expected large drop in inflation.

The plan was very successful on a number of fronts. In its first nine months
inflation fell to 1 percent and 3 percent per month for wholesale and retail
prices, respectively. Despite a fall in GDP of 2.5 percent in the first four
months of the plan, from September 1985 to September 1986 real GDP rose
by 8.8 percent. By January 1986 the fiscal deficit, exclusive of the central bank
deficit, had been brought down to 1.9 percent of GDP. (If the central bank deficit—the so-called quasi-deficit—is included, the figure is 3.2 percent.)

Ultimately, however, the heterodox program failed to meet any of its goals,
other than perhaps delaying the onset of a full-blown hyperinflation. In August
1986 the consumer price index rose by 8.8 percent, and it has been near or
above that level since. By December 1986 industrial production was back to
its preplan level and the fiscal deficit was back up to 9 percent of GDP. Despite
a series of new measures, the situation has continued to deteriorate up to the
present.

Two of the most important reasons for the failure of the plan are due to the
setting in which it was implemented. First, the combination of a large external
debt and a lack of access to new external financing seriously undermined the
program from the beginning. The successful European attempts to defeat hy-

perinflation in the 1920s were accompanied by widespread cancellation of reparation payments. Second, despite the popular acceptance of the price freeze, no serious attempt had been made to resolve the considerable social conflict that existed within the country before the plan was implemented. In fact, a precondition of the plan was that real wages could fall no further and, preferably, would be increased.

There were also a number of mistakes made in the design and implementation of the plan. One of the main reasons for its failure was that the "wrong" price vector was frozen at the beginning of the plan, although it is not clear as to how one chooses the "right" price vector. The increase in public-sector prices and imports preceding the plan were not allowed to filter through the economy, but of course this is a never-ending process. It is more likely that the neglect of the prices of nontradeables ruined any chance that the plan had of succeeding. Immediately after the plan was put into effect there was a large movement in the terms of trade in favor of flexible-priced nontradeables. As these items formed a large part of the workers' expenditures, wages rose. At first the large increase in labor productivity following the renewed stability absorbed these wage increases, but eventually industrial prices had to be increased. Moreover, the imbalance between flexible, controlled, and fixed prices grew greater as time went by. The relative prices of public sector goods fell dramatically and the fiscal deficit rose just as dramatically. The circle was complete and these prices were raised.

It was mentioned that the government made a strong commitment that the fiscal deficit would not be financed by printing money. However, with the absence of external financing and the enormous foreign debt, the government was forced either to increase taxes and public sector prices or print money, both of which would feed into inflation. Rodriguez (1988) points out that the government actually did increase the money supply in many nontraditional ways, most of which resulted in a large increase in the interest-bearing liabilities of the central bank. The end result was a large increase in the quasi-deficit and an increase in the monetary base of 180 percent from June 1985 to February 1987. Still, the government did not borrow directly from the Central Bank to finance its deficit.

Could a different Austral Plan have succeeded? The consensus seems to be that the external constraint was so severe that internal stabilization was nearly impossible. Unless massive budget cuts were possible, the government had to increase the prices of public goods or taxes. The oligopolistic and unionized structure of the Argentine economy (together with the increase in indexation that the civilian government had introduced) guaranteed that such increases would result in higher wages and prices, setting off yet another round of inflation. Perhaps with an increase in short-run external funds to finance a modest budget deficit, the government would have been able to moderate the increases in public goods prices and taxes as well as avoiding roundabout ways of increasing the money supply. A heterodox plan would then have had a fair chance of succeeding. Still, one could easily argue that without massive structural change there is little chance for sustained macroeconomic stability for Argentina.

Brazil

The wage indexation that had become widespread during Brazil in the 1960s resulted in large jumps in inflation during both the 1973 and 1979 oil shocks. In 1974 the inflation rate rose from 16 to 35 percent and in 1979 to nearly 100 percent. In 1983 an IMF-sponsored devaluation resulted in a further increase in the inflation rate to 200 percent (although the fiscal deficit was brought down from 8 percent of GDP to near balance). A combination of a severe drought and enormous pressure on the new civilian government to raise real wages led to another leap in the inflation rate in early 1986 to an annual rate of 450 percent. At the end of February 1986 it was decided to fight inflation with a heterodox program, the so-called Cruzado Plan.

Before we begin discussion of the Cruzado Plan, two important features of the Brazilian political economy are worthy of note. First, inflation was widely perceived as being predominantly of an inertial nature. Wage indexation would transmit any shock into a higher inflation rate. Then the economy would continue along at the new plateau until the next shock. Second, economic policy was very much circumscribed by the general election scheduled for November 1986. In fact, political expediency took precedence over economic rationality throughout the lifetime of the Cruzado Plan.

The main element of the Cruzado Plan was a widespread price freeze accompanied by the introduction of a new currency, the cruzado, to replace the cruzeiro. A number of formulae were used to convert old contracts, as in the Austral Plan (albeit in a more comprehensive fashion). Wages were also increased by 8 percent above the calculated level in order to restore to the workers some of the 20 percent loss in purchasing power they had suffered in the 1980s. In addition the indexation period was limited to one year—that is, it was illegal to have contracts indexed with a length of less than one year—but wages were put on a sliding scale of 20 percent. Every time the consumer price index increased by 20 percent, wages were increased the same. Monetary and fiscal policies were almost totally ignored in the Cruzado Plan, as inflation was seen as an inertial phenomenon.

The prospects for the Cruzado Plan seemed quite promising. Although the external debt was lurking ominously in the background, Brazil had a large current account surplus in 1985, industrial production had grown by 9.2 percent, and the fiscal deficit was about 1 percent of GDP. (There has been considerable debate on the legitimacy of this last figure, with some observers arguing that in reality there was a budget deficit of 3 to 5 percent of GDP.) Public support of the program was widespread, with daily reports of the "citizens' arrests" of storeowners who had raised prices and the total failure of a general strike called by the leaders of the largest unions.

At first the expectations of the plan were fulfilled. In the first three months inflation fell to the monthly rate of 1.4 percent. From March to October industrial production rose by 12.6 percent and inflation was only 11 percent. However, despite this apparent exceptional performance, by October the end was near.

A large part of the increase in demand was due to the existence of very low real interest rates, caused by a combination of excessive monetary expansion and the price freeze, and a growing fiscal deficit, although no one was very certain of its size. In August, in an attempt to moderate aggregate demand, the government put into effect some mildly restrictive monetary and fiscal policies, but they fell far short of what was necessary. By September there were severe shortages of imported raw materials and inputs, factors that were compounded by a drop in exports from $2.1 billion to $1.3 billion in October. By the end of October, queues were already a part of daily life. After the elections and the introduction of Cruzado II in November, inflation took off once again. In December inflation was 7.2 percent and in January 1987 it rose to 16.8 percent. In February interest payments on the debt were canceled and a new regime of quantitative restrictions was introduced. In 1987 GDP rose by 2.9 percent and inflation was 396 percent. In 1988 and 1989 GDP grew by -0.3 percent and 3.6 percent, respectively, while inflation was 693 percent and 1,287 percent.

Unlike the case of the Austral Plan, the Cruzado Plan may have failed simply because the government was not overly concerned with its success. Despite the enormous fanfare with which it was announced, the government consistently followed policies that ensured its demise. These policies were, however, consistent with Sarney being elected president. Still, it could be useful to investigate briefly the mistakes that were made.

A number of authors, including Modiano (1987), Carneiro (1987), and Ortiz (1988), have emphasized that the government tried to stabilize and redistribute income at the same time. However, as Modiano (1988, p. 226) points out, the 8 percent real wage increase at the beginning of the program was just enough to offset the real loss of the move to one-year indexation if inflation had hit its target level of 20 percent per year. It is likely that the public's stampede into consumer durables was a much more important factor. While this rush was aided by very low or negative real interest rates, it was likely brought on by a lack of confidence in the plan's success. This lack of confidence was due to the perception that the government was not about to do anything prior to the election that might endanger a recession or alienate workers. The extremely passive (if not permissive) nature of monetary and fiscal policy as well as the inclusion in the plan of the 20 percent sliding scale for wages almost certainly gave a large boost to this point of view. Eventually the spectacular increase in aggregate demand could not be matched by domestic production and the debt situation precluded any large increase in imports. Inevitably there were shortages and a new outburst of inflation.

Brazilian inflation was obviously more than an inertial response. While Brazil was constrained by its external debt, the recent strength of its economy gave it much more room to move. Our tentative response to the question of whether a different Cruzado Plan, one with full government support, could have succeeded is in the affirmative. Such a plan would have had to have waited until, as Modiano (1987, p. 247) argued, the economy had settled down to a new inflation "plateau," so that relative prices would be closer to some sort of "equilibrium." Our answer is tentative as the two subsequent stabilization attempts, the Summer Plan and the New Cruzado Plan, both failed. However, in both of these cases the initial conditions were quite different than in February 1986. The Brazilian economy was in a severe recession rather than a boom, the current account was not in such a strong position, and, perhaps most important, the population now had the experience of a failed heterodox plan.

Peru

Unlike most Latin American countries, Peru had no history of high inflation until 1974, when a series of discrete jumps began, each time to a higher plateau. The increase to 34 percent in 1974 was due to a large increase in aggregate demand, partially caused by monetary expansion. In 1978 a large devaluation gave rise to another jump to between 60 and 70 percent. Then in 1983 a severe drought in the south and flooding in the north, both caused by El Niño, led to inflation of 144 percent (even though the money supply increased by only 49 percent in the same period). A large increase in government-controlled prices coupled with an equally large increase in velocity sent inflation into the 200 to 300 percent range in 1985. From 1981 to 1985 at least four different IMF-sponsored stabilization programs had been attempted in Peru. All had failed at bringing down inflation, despite having some success in causing a recession. In August 1985 the recently elected APRA government of Alan García introduced a heterodox program to try to bring down inflation without the cost of a recession. For lack of a better name we will call this the APRA Plan.

Unlike the Austral Plan and much more than the Cruzado Plan, the APRA Plan had the simultaneous goals of macroeconomic stabilization and income redistribution. Moreover, this redistribution was not to be enacted primarily through government transfers or direct government ordinances (such as real wages will increase by x percent and everything else is fixed) but through profound restructuring of the economy. This restructuring, however, was not to be of the usual IMF export-orientation type. It was to be carried out by a rejuvenation of neglected areas of the economy (especially agriculture), the use of policies that would favor real over financial investments, decentralization, and the expansion of the internal market for low-wage goods.

The main details of the APRA Plan were: (1) There was a generalized price freeze (after an upward readjustment of public-sector and energy prices) and a long list of prices to be controlled by the state. In fact, pricing policies differed by sector, depending on the relevant price formation mechanisms. (2) There was a devaluation of the official and parallel exchange rates, the former of which was then frozen. (3) The salaries of less-favored sectors were increased by 13 percent and the minimum wage by 50 percent. (4) The nominal interest rate was reduced from 280 percent to 110 percent. Very little was said about monetary or fiscal policy, although in practice the latter was very cautious. In addition, unlike either the Austral or Cruzado plans, the technical aspects of the APRA Plan were ignored or not well worked out. (There has been some debate as to whether the APRA Plan should be called a heterodox plan, rather than a demand-led recovery with price controls.) Note also that the stabilization goal was moderate, not zero, inflation.

Despite the fact that it was introduced in the middle of a prolonged recession, the conditions for the stabilization program were favorable for a number of reasons: (1) the government of Alan García had strong popular support, and the people had suffered through a long experience of failed IMF policies; (2) indexation mechanisms were not widespread; (3) there was substantial idle capacity so that a large increase in demand could occur without putting pressure on the price level; (4) most exports were insensitive to the exchange rate, (especially cocaine); (5) the high inflation level was not caused by the fiscal deficit; and (6) given the small size of its economy, it was much easier for Peru to default on its debt payments, so this external constraint could be (and was) largely ignored.

At first, as in Argentina and Brazil, the program was successful. From August 1985 to December 1986 the monthly inflation rates hovered between 3 percent and 5 percent, versus 10 percent to 14 percent in the year before the plan. In 1986 the inflation rate was 63 percent and GDP increased by 8.5 percent. There was a large internal terms-of-trade shift toward agriculture and the informal sector, where prices were much more flexible. (The informal sector was the driving force behind the miniboom. However, its role is partly explained by the movement of formal-sector production to the informal sector in order to avoid price controls.) From July 1985 to July 1987 GDP rose by 17 percent, industrial output by 31 percent, real blue-collar wages by 48 percent, and real white-collar salaries by 34 percent.

However, a number of problems arose very quickly. First, the government failed to include many variables in the cost equations for the firms, ultimately resulting in either a number of tax concessions or business strategies to move products out from under the umbrella of the price freeze (such as inventing "new" products). Second, in an attempt to keep the prices of essentials down but the return to agriculture up, the government got increasingly involved in subsidy schemes financed by taxation or money creation. Third, the neglect of the export sector resulted in a rapid running down of reserves as early as April 1986. The lack of foreign exchange combined with the movement to full capacity set off large increases in inflation in early 1987. Fourth, while there were strong incentives for new investment, it never did materialize to any extent, contributing to the capacity problem.

The government reacted to the deteriorating reserve position by putting controls on capital flight, increasing tariffs, and bringing in new quantitative restrictions; that is, resorting to the usual mix of policies that result in a highly fragmented foreign trade regime. While a number of devaluations were attempted, they usually failed to keep up with the inflation rate. Finally, in July 1987, after further deterioration of the economy and little response to its investment strategy—partly due to a lack of public sector credibility but also due to a failure to legislate many of the promised provisions—the government announced a plan to nationalize the banks (which was only very partially carried out).

It is difficult to imagine a strategy that would have had more negative repercussions than the bank nationalization decision. The capital outflow speeded up, investment projects were paralyzed, there was a large increase in rent-seeking as the government lost its popular support and credibility, and, probably most important, the strong but always uneasy coalition between the government and private sector completely fell apart.

Since July 1987 the situation has gone from bad to worse. Inflation was 115 percent in 1987, 1,722 percent in 1988, and 5,836 percent in 1989. The public deficit was 8.7 percent of GDP in 1987, 5.1 percent in 1988, and estimated at 4.5 percent in 1989. After an increase of 6.7 percent in 1987, GDP declined by 9.6 percent in 1988 and 25 percent in 1989 (estimated). Could these devastating figures been avoided within the framework of a heterodox plan?

Thorp (1989) believes that the original framework contained the seeds of its own destruction by containing four partially erroneous assumptions. First, while excess capacity did exist in the industrial sector, this was not true of the rural sector. Moreover, the industrial sector still was dependent on imported inputs. Second, fiscal reform was necessary as the reactivation did not restore tax revenues. Third, the ability of the state to control prices was exaggerated. Fourth, limiting debt service was not enough to overcome the external bottleneck.

Schydlowsky (1989, pp. 28–31), however, believes that the plan could have been saved if action had been taken at the proper moment. While the García government had done a credible job of turning Peru around and starting the long-needed restructuring process, it was time to take care of the external sector and reintegrate the Peruvian economy with the international community. Given the rapid growth in the Peruvian economy in 1986 and 1987, there was now much more room to maneuver. In fact, in early 1987 Peru was in much the same position as Brazil at the beginning of its heterodox program, except with a much lower inflation rate and much less widespread wage indexation. A timely mixture of mild orthodox and heterodox policies may have spared the Peruvian people from the debacle of the last three years.

THE BOLIVIAN ORTHODOXY

Similar to Peru, Bolivia had no history of high inflation. From 1954 to 1973 the Bolivian fiscal deficit was funded by the U.S. Agency for International Development (USAID). When these funds were dramatically reduced in the early 1970s, external loans were quick to fill the gap. In the early 1980s the debt burden increased considerably, owing to the high real interest rates, but when the worldwide debt problem hit with full force in 1982, Bolivia was also cut off from outside funding. Due to the great difficulty in raising taxes in Bolivia—Morales and Sachs (1989, p. 65) point out that left-wing governments had no political ability to tax and right-wing governments no desire to tax—the deficit was financed by printing money. So began the first hyperinflation in the twentieth century that was not the result of war or revolution (Morales and Sachs 1989, p. 57).

Between 1982 and 1985 the government of Siles Zuazo introduced at least six different stabilization programs. The first was a heterodox program that failed owing to union resistance to wage controls and incorrectly administered prices. (The Zuazo government relied heavily on union support.) The next five programs were more orthodox, with the last two being IMF-sponsored. However, strong labor resistance to the IMF packages resulted in their early demise. By the time the government of Paz Estenssoro came into power in August 1985, the inflation rate was over 50 percent per month and GDP per capita had declined by 4.5 percent per year for five years. Estenssoro immediately introduced a very orthodox package of policy reforms.

Before we discuss the program we should first note that the Estenssoro government did not rely upon the labor unions for support, but on the business community and the small middle class. Moreover, given the chaos that existed in the economy, Morales (1988, p. 317) points out that most segments of the population were willing to give any new government a fighting chance. The main points in the orthodox program were the following: (1) The currency was devalued and, more important, the parallel foreign exchange market was stabilized by daily auctions held by the central bank. It should be noted, however, that if many of the other features of the program had not been successfully implemented, the government would not likely have had the foreign exchange necessary to stabilize this rate. (2) There was a great reduction in the fiscal deficit due mostly to a new hydrocarbon tax and the devaluation. The latter was important as the public sector was a large net creditor with respect to the rest of the world. Also of importance was the dismissal of 23,000 of the 30,000 employees at the public-sector tin mines. Civil servants also saw their real salaries fall by 60 percent. (3) There was widespread liberalization of markets, external and internal, including the labor market. (4) Capital flows were allowed to move freely. Most quantitative restrictions were removed and tariffs were lowered to an average level of 23 percent.

The results were highly successful with some very important reservations.

Inflation decreased very rapidly. In 1988 and 1989 it was 21 and 16 percent, respectively. After a downturn of 2.9 percent in 1986 (which may have been more a result of the collapse of tin prices than the stabilization program), GDP increased by 2.1 percent and 3.0 percent in 1987 and 1988, respectively—the first positive movements since 1980. The fiscal deficit has practically disappeared. The foreign debt obligations have been met or rescheduled, albeit with considerable help from the IMF and the U.S. government.

Whether the Bolivian success will continue in the long term is beyond the scope of this chapter, but we should point out a number of warning signals. First, part of the remedy has been due to a large repatriation of funds attracted by very high real interest rates. Most of these funds are in short-term instruments and could move out as quickly as they entered. The reduction in the fiscal deficit has relied primarily on cuts in public services, particularly education and health. These cuts and the deterioration of the quality of the civil service— the best people have mostly left owing to the large wage reduction—could have serious implications for long-run growth. It seems likely that the richer income classes will eventually have to pay higher taxes, something they have never been willing to do in the past. Finally, investment is at very low levels, only about 10 percent of GDP, suggesting that the private sector does not have full confidence in the government's ability to pursue its policies.

Which features of the Bolivian situation were most important for the success that was achieved? The severity of the inflation and the lack of an inflationary history certainly were important. Not only were people desperate for change, but, as organized labor was a very small segment of the population, wage indexation was rare. Moreover, the government was not dependent on the unions for political support. The small size of the Bolivian debt problem from an international perspective was also a key factor. The IMF, World Bank, and U.S. government were able to come to Bolivia's aid (and develop a much desired showcase) at a low cost, and Bolivia has been able to delay its debt payments to private creditors without causing an uproar. (In 1985 Bolivia's debt, although much higher as a percentage of GDP, was only $3.2 billion compared to Brazil's debt of $105 billion.) Bolivia also had a great deal of room to maneuver with regard to collecting taxes, given that tax collection had fallen to less than 2 percent of GDP by 1985. The almost total dollarization of the economy was also important, allowing policymakers to focus on the exchange rate.

RECENT INITIATIVES

This section will briefly discuss two more recent heterodox plans—the Pact for Stability and Economic Growth (PECE) in Mexico and the Collor Plan in Brazil. Although it is too early to come to any definite conclusions on either, these "second-generation" programs may be a better indicator of the future of heterodox stabilization plans than the first round.

PECE (or PASE as it was first named), activated in late 1987 after six years of instability in Mexico, including the failure of a major IMF initiative, culminated in an inflation rate of 160 percent between December 1986 and December 1987. PECE relied heavily on an income policy with the freezing of key prices, such as the exchange rate, public prices, and controlled prices. At the same time a tight monetary policy was followed and the government sped up the liberalization of the foreign trade regime. PECE is a pact in the sense that its most important features were arrived at through a consensus of political, business, and union leaders. The pact is renewed every year with changes arrived at through negotiations.

In the first year of the plan the inflation rate fell to 20 percent. Part of the reason for such a success was that the government used $10 billion of its $16 billion in keeping the nominal exchange rate fixed. A sliding exchange rate of 1 peso per day (or about 2 percent per month) was introduced in late 1988 in order to prevent a further deterioration of the exchange reserves. In June 1990 it was felt that the fight against inflation had been successful enough to lower the "slide" to 0.8 pesos per day. GNP grew by 1.4 percent in 1988 and 2.9 percent in 1989. While these figures are not very high, they should be compared against an average growth rate of 0 percent between 1982 and 1987.

The results obtained by Mexico's heterodox plan have to this point been very similar to the results obtained in the first two years of Bolivia's orthodox plan. Part of the success in both cases was due to debt relief. Though this was relatively much larger in the Bolivian case, Mexico received implicit compensation by the rise in oil prices just before the introduction of its plan. The big test for Mexico—and heterodox stabilization plans—will be to see whether it gets caught in a low-investment and low-growth stable equilibrium (which appears to have happened to Bolivia) or if it can truly achieve economic growth along with stability.

While it is not clear that Brazil's Collor Plan is really a heterodox plan—unless that label is applied to any program that departs from the IMF orthodoxy—it is still an interesting example of a stabilization plan. It was initiated on March 15, 1990, immediately after the inauguration of the new president, Fernando Collor. The plan had three main pillars: (1) There was a fiscal reform aimed at moving from a deficit of 8 percent of GNP to a surplus of 2 percent of GNP. The main tools would be attempts to reduce tax evasion and massive layoffs in the civil service. (2) There was the immediate freezing of most prices and incomes after a modest correction in public prices. (3) Most important, 80 percent of financial assets were frozen for 18 months and a new currency, the new cruzeiro, was created. This monetary reform was intended to greatly reduce the pressures of aggregate demand. At the same time the more orthodox policies of trade liberalization and privatization were also introduced to put downward pressure on prices and to reduce the government budget deficit, respectively.

Despite initial great public support, after just three months the plan was in serious jeopardy. The problems started owing to the large number of layoffs following the liquidity crisis that immediately shook the economy. Unfortunately, the frozen assets included both savings and quasi-money, the latter which was needed for bankrolling private firms. Moreover, many loopholes were soon found to get funds from the banks, and the government made exemptions for many firms and industries. This not only increased the money supply but created public resentment toward the plan. A hostile Congress also made things very difficult for the president and his team by blocking or stalling many of the provisions of the plan. This also reduced public confidence in the credibility of the plan, worsening their expectations with regard to future inflation. Finally, the ad hoc nature in which subsequent measures have been devised and announced has given rise to the general opinion that policies are being improvised on a day-by-day basis.

Despite the initial success in bringing inflation down to about 3 or 4 percent in April 1990, the increased liquidity caused by the loopholes and exemptions coupled with an easy money policy brought inflation back up to at least 10 percent in May as well as helped restore production to near its preplan level. By June the key indicators were heading back to where they had started. A poll taken on June 20, 1990, showed that support for the plan had fallen from 70 to 36 percent. The government's next step was to begin the layoff of an estimated 500,000 civil servants. It is likely that if this attack amounts to nothing, so will the Collor Plan.

A NEW LATIN AMERICAN ORTHODOXY?

Previously we saw that the three main heterodox experiments in Latin America during the 1980s all failed after relatively brief periods of success. We also saw that there were significant differences in the patterns of both their successes and failures. Moreover, except for the similarities of their inflation rates, the initial conditions were vastly different in the three countries. However, it still seems possible to pull out some common lessons from their experiences.

It seems clear that, even within the framework of a heterodox plan, fiscal and monetary policy must be given their due in any stabilization attempt. Although Brazil was in by far the strongest starting point of the three countries, its plan was also the biggest failure, primarily because the country ignored demand management policies. The Cruzado Plan may have succeeded if monetary expansion had been kept to the level necessary for remonetization of the economy and the fiscal deficit had been managed properly. Despite the constraints imposed by the large external debt, Brazil's large current account balance at the time provided a cushion between the fiscal and balance-of-payments deficits.

The Peruvian and Argentinean stabilization plans were implemented during severe recessions. It was necessary in both cases to get the economy moving again before relying heavily on fiscal and monetary policies to stabilize the price level. It is possible that both countries (especially Peru) could have succeeded with their stabilization plans if they had moved toward a more orthodox policy at the right moment; that is, once the economy had picked up and capacity constraints were being reached in industrial production.

A problem that all three countries faced was the race to buy consumer durables once stabilization had been achieved. In any country with prolonged instability it seems likely that this will occur. If there is some chance of supplying this demand by additional consumer imports, the inflationary pressures can be contained. However, all three of these countries had massive external debt, so once capacity utilization approached 100 percent, inflation was renewed. The somewhat longer lived success of Peru was probably due to its much larger amount of excess capacity. It seems likely that any heterodox plan is going to face this hurdle. Consequently, we are once again faced with the need for demand management policies at the proper time. (In Brazil's case the proper time may have been right at the beginning of the Cruzado Plan.)

All three heterodox plans faced the crucial problem of finding the right price vector to freeze. In addition it was necessary to decide what prices would be frozen or controlled and what rules would be used for changing controlled prices. The success of a heterodox plan depends to a large extent on how well this is done. When relative prices drift too far from their "market" values, the price stabilization aspect of the heterodox plan inevitably breaks down. If this occurs before inflationary expectations have been broken, the economy is likely to return quickly to the point it was before the plan was introduced. For a heterodox plan to succeed, it should be capable of keeping relative prices approximately in line until the point is reached where more orthodox policies can be introduced. Part of Mexico's success is likely due to the greater flexibility that was allowed for most prices, with a social pact being used to keep the general price level under control.

The last commonality we would like to mention is tied closely to the one just mentioned. That is, how does the government control public-sector prices. In all three cases a prime reason for the large increase in the fiscal deficit (after it had first been reduced) were the lags in the prices of public-sector and subsidized goods. In each case the government was afraid of sabotaging its plan by increasing these prices, but eventually the pressures caused by the growing fiscal deficits destroyed the plans in any case. The probable need to eventually raise these prices—which is precisely what the Mexican government did at the end of the first year of PECE—is another reason why governments should probably not aim for zero rates of inflation. Selowsky (1989, p. 9) emphasizes that without fiscal reform, any price guidelines will be short-lived. Without a major revision the government will either have to increase the money supply or its domestic borrowing. In either case there will be even more pressure on prices to rise.

Could the success of the Bolivian slash and burn orthodox experiment have been repeated in any or all of Argentina, Brazil, and Peru? This question must be answered on at least two different levels. The first is concerned with how the economic structure of these countries would have reacted to an orthodox program. The second has to do with the political feasibility of such a plan.

The thrust of an orthodox plan is that by liberalizing the economy at the same time as restrictive fiscal and monetary policies are implemented, the private sector will be able to pull up much of the slack in the economy. Eventually there will be large economic efficiency gains due to the greater reliance on the price system and private sector. There is a big debate on the length of time before the positive benefits of liberalization take effect to a significant degree. Of special importance for most developing countries is the response of the export sector to the large devaluation that is almost always part of a liberalization program. This is important partly so that the foreign sector will pick up some of the slack temporarily caused by the restrictive fiscal and monetary policies, but probably even more so because of the heavy reliance of most developing countries on imported intermediate and capital goods (and often raw materials).

Of our three countries Brazil seems to be by far the best choice for a slash and burn orthodox policy. Its economy was so buoyant at the time of the Cruzado Plan that a mild recession may not even have been noticed (assuming that the restrictive policy did not lead to a severe contraction). Its export sector has proven itself to be very responsive to the exchange rate, both before and after the plan, with a short response rate. In addition, its economy is much less dependent on imported inputs than the other countries. In 1985 shortages of crucial imported intermediate goods appeared only after industrial production had expanded nearly 20 percent in 18 months.

We are not optimistic about a full-fledged orthodox plan in either Peru or Argentina. The latter economy has been, more or less, in a destabilized state since the 1950s or perhaps even earlier. Given its heavy reliance on the state sector and a highly protected oligopolistic structure, restrictive policies would likely lead to a severe recession in Argentina. Moreover, the response of the export sector would almost surely be with a long lag, especially given that Argentina's main exports, beef and wheat, would face restrictions in the developed countries. (Ironically, a precondition for a recovery in Argentina may be the rapid development of Brazil, providing it with a large and expanding nearby market.) It does not seem likely that public confidence, especially that of investors, could withstand another recession at this time in Argentina. The out-migration of capital and skilled people would accelerate to even higher levels than at present.

Peru has a much more underdeveloped economic structure than either Argentina and Brazil, although not Bolivia. If Thorp (1987) is correct in her evaluation of the unresponsiveness of the Peruvian export- and import-competing sectors to the exchange rate, then it is unlikely that an orthodox program would succeed. Unlike Chile, for example, the agricultural sector in Peru is very undeveloped, having been neglected for decades owing to the high degree of centralization in Lima and the coast. On the other hand, unlike Bolivia, Peru does have a relatively large industrial sector, which, however, is very dependent on intermediate imports. It seems likely that a restrictive cum liberal policy coupled with limited access to foreign exchange due to the debt burden would be doomed to failure.

When we consider the political aspects of the problem the analysis changes somewhat. First, we should mention that the success of the Bolivian program depended to a large extent on the help of the IMF and U.S. government. (Similarly, the Mexican plan benefited from some debt reduction and higher oil prices.) We have argued that the Brazilian economy may have been able to withstand an orthodox program without any or much new external financing, but the same was not true of Argentina or Peru. Of these two the magnitude of the funds would have been much less for Peru, making it a much better candidate for an IMF showpiece. While this was not about to happen with the ideological APRA government, in the future it should not be ruled out. The difficulty here is that the internal restructuring problems, especially the neglect of the Andean area, might then be shoved to the back shelf. At best this would retard the development of the country; at worst it would heighten the hinterland's reliance on the cocaine trade and lead to intensification of the war with the Shining Path.

When the prospects of an orthodox plan in Brazil were discussed, two important facts were neglected. The first is the strength of the unions and the widespread, institutionalized wage indexation. The second is the very unequal income distribution. An orthodox plan is likely to lead to price increases in the short run owing to the exchange devaluation and the restriction on credit. These increases would be directly transmitted to wages, sending inflation to even higher levels. (In Bolivia wage indexation was so uncommon that this transmission mechanism was of minor importance.) It is not likely that the unions or the public would long stand behind a policy that increases prices and reduces production, no matter how temporary a period of time, especially as the poor will be expected to bear most of the short-run burden of the program. (The recent developments in the Collor Plan give support to this view.)

In this chapter we have looked at heterodox and orthodox programs in a number of different countries from a number of different angles. It is our belief that there is no one good plan that is universally applicable, including the usual IMF plan. We believe that it is much more likely that there is a sequence of policies that, roughly speaking, will have widespread applicability. There is a growing body of literature, mostly from Latin America, that emphasizes the sequencing of new policies or lines of attack. For example, Schydlowsky (1989) has argued that the main policy mistake made in Peru by the García government was not to realize when it was time to change tack until it was too late. Some may argue that this new type of fine tuning is as difficult as the economic tinkering that has been tried in some high-income countries. However, we are not speaking about small policy changes but broad policy strokes, kept as transparent as possible, the intentions of which will be to catch and retain the confidence of the public and business sectors until the recovery of sustainable long-run growth. The recent developments in Mexico have shown that a well-run heterodox program can succeed in bringing economic stability to a country. It still remains to be seen whether it can bring sustained economic growth.

REFERENCES

Bruno, Michael, Guido Di Tella, Rudiger Dornbusch, and Stanley Fischer (eds.) (1988). *Inflation Stabilization: The Experience of Israel, Argentina, Brazil, Bolivia, and Mexico.* Cambridge, Mass.: MIT Press.

Carneiro, Dionisio D. (1987). "El Plan Cruzado: Una Temprana Evaluación Después de Diez Meses." *El Trimestre Económico,* 14, pp. 251–274.

Modiano, Eduardo M. (1987). "El Plan Cruzado: Bases Teóricas y Limitaciones Prácticas." *El Trimestre Económico,* 14, pp. 223–250.

——. (1988). "The Cruzado First Attempt: The Brazilian Stabilization Program of February 1986." In Bruno et al., pp. 215–258.

Morales, Juan A. (1988). "Inflation Stabilization in Bolivia." In Bruno et al., pp. 307–346.

Morales, Juan A. and Jeffrey D. Sachs (1989). "Bolivia's Economic Crisis." In Sachs, pp. 57–80.

Ortiz, Guillermo (1988). "Comments on Brazil." In Bruno et al., pp. 298–302.

Rodriguez, Carlos A. (1988). "Comment on Argentina." In Bruno et al., pp. 202–209.

Schydlowsky, Daniel M. (1989). "The Peruvian Debacle: Economic Dynamics or Political Causes?" Mimeo. Boston University.

Selowsky, Marcelo (1989). "Preconditions Necessary for the Recovery of Latin America's Growth." Mimeo. Washington, D.C.: World Bank.

Thorp, Rosemary (1987). "La Opción del APRA en el Perú." *El Trimestre Económico,* 14, pp. 351–368.

CHAPTER FOUR

Global Income Redistribution: An Alternate Perspective on the Latin American Debt Crisis

MYRON J. FRANKMAN

International income redistribution is a fact of economic life. Income is redistributed through each change in the terms of trade, through the pricing policies of multinational corporations, through the action of cartels, through changes in the London Interbank Offer Rate, through nationalization of assets, and, rather minimally by comparison, through foreign aid programs. Income is not redistributed internationally in a systematic, predictable, progressive way at present. Income redistribution resulting from the transactions of private and public actors has on balance not favored global equity. Indeed the last time global equity was even heard about with any regularity was during that brief period of euphoria following the passage of the United Nations resolution on a New International Economic Order in the mid-1970s. But words and deeds are two distinct matters: The absence of meaningful acceptance of the goal of global equity led to an "I'm all right Jack" response to the impact of the oil crisis on oil-importing LDCs (less developed countries). Little was done to cushion the shock that they experienced.

Debt has been a great reallocator. It has transferred income and wealth from the less developed to the more developed countries, it has transferred income regressively within Third World countries, and it has transferred the attention of some of the best brains from even thinking about the shaping of a new global order to the pursuit instead of schemes to mitigate the debt crisis. Were one to have a dollar for each student paper, thesis, and dissertation written on debt in the universities of North America alone in the past decade, one would no doubt have a most substantial sum. Were one to receive instead an amount equal to the minimum wage for each hour devoted to these labors, one could probably retire in an opulent manner and still be able to leave a nest egg to one's heirs.

In Albert Hirschman's (1965, p. 305) words, debt has been the privileged problem, the focal point of attention—a continuation of the years when balance of payments crises (without major indebtedness) were the object of near exclusive preoccupation. In the crisis-based choice of research and policy concerns, merely being destitute does not suffice: It is the big debtors that matter most to the survival of the international financial system. It is not quite a case of the devil take the hindmost, but basic needs and the situation of the poorest of the poor no longer have the priority that they did during the 1970s.

THE END OF PROGRESSIVE REDISTRIBUTION?

Sayre Schatz (1983) described in 1983 a process that he referred to as socializing adaptation—somewhat akin to John Kenneth Galbraith's notion of countervailing power. In Schatz's view, this phenomenon of long-standing at the local and national levels can now be observed in its manifold variations at the level of the global economy. A stereotyping of this concept, which is consistent with Schatz's presentation, is that concessions to economic justice are introduced in the interests of keeping the world safe for capitalism:

To be successful socializing adaptations need not be generous or freely accorded or sufficient to meet minimal human needs. Changes can be grudging, mean-spirited and stingy responses to problems that have become too painful to ignore. However, if they suffice to mollify dissatisfaction that jeopardizes the viability of the system, they constitute successful socializing adaptation (Schatz, 1983, p. 4).

In a world undergoing structural change, in which firms, confronting stiff global competition, are rethinking their relationships with their home countries, the earlier, more generous outcomes of socializing adaptation—local and national welfare programs—appear to be threatened and magnanimity at the international level seems extremely remote. For example, the OECD countries as a group were closer in the 1960s to the goal of allocating 0.7 percent of gross product to official development assistance (ODA), than at any time since then. Not only has aid stabilized at about 0.35 percent of the product of the OECD countries, but terms of the lending have deteriorated for all borrowers except those in low-income Africa. We have witnessed instead limited responses: among them the Baker and Brady plans, expansion of IMF compensatory financing facilities, and variations in structural adjustment lending.

The 1970s were filled with rhetoric about the poorest of the poor and targeting aid to provide basic needs, but that is no longer the dominant thread running through discussions of development. Making markets work is the name of the game; while there is much to be said for removing egregious distortions, that strategy must be complemented by socializing adaptation to attend to the negative effects of economic forces. Solutions to the debt problem as such do not address the problems of the poorest of the developing countries. The recent calls for "adjustment with a human face" represent an attempt to *mitigate* the effects of budget reductions on the most vulnerable members of society. In calling for resistance to expenditure cuts in priority areas, countries are being asked to try valiantly to make the best of what has become a nearly impossible situation. Chile tried to discriminate in favor of the vulnerable when making cuts in social expenditures in the 1980s, but as Dagmar Raczynski observes, "selective social policies, regardless of how effective they are, will always be ineffective when implemented in a context of economic policies that create poverty" (Cornia et al., 1988, p. 87).

Within the industrialized countries we see regressive changes being paraded as tax reform. Very much muted in these discussions is the notion of progressivity. Is it a characteristic of our age that we lose sight of the big picture and focus instead on the details of specific proposals? Has the overhanging threat of international migration of production, with associated losses in jobs and tax base, effectively killed notions of progressivity and of equity? In one country after another we are witnessing tax competition to attract and hold investment, with a consequent reduction in tax progression. The existence of threats to the survival of northern welfare states in a nonwelfare international capitalist system does not augur well for a more enlightened treatment of the South.

THE IMMATURITY OF "MATURE" DEBTORS: REVERSE TRANSFERS

The earliest formulations relating capital flows and the trade balance spoke of the transition from the status of immature debtor to mature debtor. This was presumed to occur after the borrower had received sufficient real resource transfers to bring about desired structural change, and it was identified as corresponding to a shift from a positive to a negative trade balance. Today we have the specter of countries still in need of real resource inflows making major transfers to the industrialized countries. Net aid receipts and net direct private investment in Latin America and the Caribbean in recent years have been greatly overshadowed by interest payments on external debt alone, which, as Table 4.1 shows, were sufficient to exceed gross disbursements in every year from 1983 through 1989. For those countries of the region that report on their indebtedness to the World Bank, net outward transfers associated with long-term debt amounted to $143.8 billion over the period 1983–88, of which three-quarters were recorded transfers from Argentina, Brazil, and Mexico. When voices were first raised calling for massive real resource transfer, no one could have anticipated that they would be from South to North, rather than from North to South.

Table 4.1
Latin America and the Caribbean: Selected Data on Capital Flows,
1983–90 (billion U.S. dollars)

	1983	1984	1985	1986	1987	1988	1989[a]	1990[b]
Total debt stocks	361.1	377.3	389.4	409.2	445.4	427.5	434.1	416.2
Gross disbursements	37.6	32.5	23.3	23.7	26.8	28.7	30.4	27.2
Principal repayments	15.5	16.4	19.3	22.1	19.3	22.3	24.4	20.3
Interest payments	34.4	34.8	34.6	29.8	28.2	33.3	33.7	22.9
Net transfers	-12.4	-18.7	-30.6	-28.2	-20.6	-26.9	-27.6	-16.0
Argentina, Brazil,								
Mexico	-12.0	-14.8	-25.2	-20.5	-15.4	-21.3	-19.5[c]	-11.7

[a]World Bank projections of payments due on existing debt, including
undisbursed.
[b]World Bank projections (as above), excluding IMF.
[c]World Bank estimates, including IMF.

Sources: World Bank, World Debt Tables: External Debt of Developing Countries.
I. Analysis and Summary Tables, 1989-90. I. Analysis and Summary Tables (1989),
II. Country Tables (1989) and First Supplement (1990).

The hope for a restoration of inward resource transfers to the LDCs has led
to a search for economic surpluses. Covetous eyes have been turned in the
1980s to the Japanese payments surpluses, just as in the 1970s the focus was
on the OPEC surpluses. Writers such as Paul Streeten (1988) have singled out
the Japanese surplus as a key element for relieving the capital shortage in the
LDCs. Streeten argues that Japanese capital would find more secure and profitable outlets in the Third World than in the United States. Suffice it to say,
that would appear not to be the predominant perception in Japan. The focus
on the Japanese, while not misplaced, is yet a further example of the insistence
on voluntarism and on piecemeal approaches to debt. Dealing with debt requires that the public finance function be globalized. In a world in which, to use
the words of Charles Morris (1989, p. 52), "bank deposits surge around the
world in nanoseconds," in which it no longer makes sense to speak about Japanese, European, and American firms given the web of production locations, ad-
mixtures of ownership, and proliferating joint ventures, global public finance
cannot be left to voluntarism. The creation of international institutions in the
1940s was the product of many visions of a better world. That framework
paved the way for the globalization of markets, but it left out the public finance
function as such, although those writing at the time called for its development.

THE COSTS OF ADJUSTMENT

Yet somehow the chilling injustice of what is happening is escaping our attention, passing by our windows on the smooth flow of economic analysis, disguising itself in the respectable clothing of the financial vocabulary. We are intermittently told that we are muddling through, a repayment rescheduled here, a debt written down there, masking from our view the closed clinic, the empty desks at school, the unvaried diet, the anaemic mother, the child who never puts on weight (UNICEF, 1990, p. 11).

We have come to expect many economic indicators to be at our disposal on either a quarterly or even monthly basis. By and large, however, these are not the data that can tell us anything directly about the distributional consequences of adjustment to the debt burden. We may be able to surmise, but insistence on strict statistical standards would require that one stand idly by in the face of obvious distress.

Even those researchers with privileged access to data at the IMF, the World Bank, and UNICEF, *inter alia,* who have been trying to assess the social impact of either the debt burden or of structural adjustment programs, have run into major gaps in the information they need. The lack of data to forcefully substantiate what is readily apparent to the informed observer is a recurrent theme in UNICEF's *The State of the World's Children* for 1988, 1989, and 1990. Peter Heller and Jack Diamond in a study of government expenditure published by the IMF in April 1990 conclude with this caution: "For making judgements on the quality of an expenditure pattern, one must clearly dig more deeply than a simple sectoral aggregation. How money is spent within the health or education sector matters far more than the fact of its allocation to one of these sectors."

The quality and availability of data is a chronic problem that is exacerbated by budget stringency. Suffice it to say that such numbers as are at our disposal have not painted an encouraging picture of developments in Latin America in the 1980s, which is being spoken of as "the lost decade." Most indicators of social development showed regular, marked improvement in the countries of Latin America throughout the 1960s and 1970s, despite rapid population growth and even more rapid urbanization. This was not the case in the 1980s.

While comprehensive and up-to-date social data are unavailable, much of the financial data of debt is abundant, by now quite familiar, and easily accessible. The data in Table 4.2 have been chosen to provide a slightly different perspective and, in doing so, to shift attention away from Argentina, Brazil, and Mexico, whose total debt represents a proportionately smaller national burden than that of Guyana, Nicaragua, Jamaica, Bolivia, Chile, and others. The reader may well be surprised to discover that 10 countries in the region have a debt/GNP ratio in excess of 80 percent. These same 10 countries accounted for 27 of the region's 49 debt restructurings and reschedulings during the period 1983–89 (IMF, April 1990, p. 31).

Table 4.2
Latin America and the Caribbean: Debt/GNP (1988) and Exchange Rate
Ratio (1982/1989)

	Debt/GNP	Exchange Rate 1982/89		Debt/GNP	Exchange Rate 1982/89
Guyana	521.8	11.0	Belize	51.4	1.0
Nicaragua⁼	247.5	3796.0	Uruguay*	50.1	23.8
Jamaica*	154.1	3.6	Trinidad	50.1	1.8
Bolivia*	135.5	14900.0	Barbados	47.7	1.0
Panama	126.0	1.0	Peru*	47.3	2693.1
Ecuador*	113.3	19.6	Colombia*	46.5	6.2
Costa Rica*	100.0	2.1	Paraguay	42.8	9.0
Chile*	96.6	4.0	Haiti	37.5	1.0
Dom. Rep.	96.1	6.3	St. Vincent	34.3	1.0
Honduras	81.9	1.0	Guatemala	33.2	3.5
Argentina*	60.5	370103.1	El Salvador	32.2	2.0
Mexico*	58.5	27.4	Brazil*	30.7	45432.0
Venezuela*	57.7	10.0	Bahamas	7.4	1.0
Grenada	51.7	1.0	Region total	48.9	

Notes:

⁼Debt/GNP for 1987.
*Denotes the 12 Latin American countries which are included in the World
Bank's 1989-89 list of 17 Highly Indebted Countries (Baker 15 plus Costa
Rica and Jamaica).
"Debt" refers to total reported external debt, long and short term, public
and private, guaranteed and unguaranteed.
End of year U.S. dollar market exchange rates used.
For Cuba, which does not report to the World Bank, total debt represented
21.0 percent of its gross social product in September 1987. A.R.M. Ritter,
"Cuba's Convertible Currency Debt Problem," CEPAL Review, No. 36 (Dec.
1988), 117-40.

Sources: I.M.F., International Financial Statistics, various issues and
World Bank, World Debt Tables: External Debt of Developing Countries. I.
Analysis and Summary Tables, 1989-90 (1989), II. Country Tables (1989) and
First Supplement (1990).

In lieu of recent and reliable data on income distribution and living conditions, we must fall back on inferences. The very weight of debt to national
product, by itself, would suggest distributional consequences. Each major exchange rate change (see Table 4.2) that has accompanied adjustment to indebtedness has brought with it a shock to those dependent on wage goods imports
and fuel imports, to mention but two categories of imports. The needs of debt
service may well have moved many Latin American countries from chronically
overvalued to seriously undervalued exchange rates. Suffice it to note that the
current dollar value of Latin American imports had fallen in 1985 by 38.6 percent relative to 1981 (IMF/IFS, 1986). In countries dependent on imported
capital goods for economic expansion, large devaluations have a dampening effect on investment and formal-sector growth. As Alejandro Portes (1989, p.
33) has noted, the formal and informal sectors expand and contract together:
as formal-sector growth has waned, urban poverty in Latin America has expanded. There were said to be 89 million urban Latin Americans living in absolute poverty in 1985 (UN ECOSOC, 1989, p. 86).

A NEW BRETTON WOODS?

In light of exchange rate volatility, rising protectionism, and the crushing burden of Third World foreign debt, there have been many voices urging that there be convened a new conference comparable in focus to the 1944 Bretton Woods meeting, which led to the creation of the International Monetary Fund and the International Bank for Reconstruction and Development. Some of those who have issued the call envision a difficult, but limited, agenda: a return to fixed exchange rates and the creation of an international lender of last resort, perhaps by expanding the functions of the International Monetary Fund. Some would have debt as part of the agenda for such a gathering. But one searches in vain for a call to include global public finance per se. Instead there is a general call for an increase in real resource flows to the developing countries.

Greatly expanded functional federalism should be at the top of the agenda at an urgently needed new Bretton Woods conference. The new Bretton Woods must treat not only economic matters, but must give precedence to the social and the environmental. Topping today's agenda must be jurisdictional spillovers, global distribution, as well as survival of life on this planet. With organization and forethought, this could even be a time when the grass roots could finally exercise a prior influence on state decisions. The elements that I believe to be essential to a resolution of our present dilemma are in the domain of greatly expanded international cooperation, including, in particular, international income redistribution.

International income redistribution will require the development of international taxes. There is no lack of proposals ranging from taxes on international trade and travel to taxes levied in proportion to a country's GNP. These schemes, which date back at least to the work of James Lorimer in 1884, need merely to be taken off the shelf, dusted carefully, and updated for our current circumstances (Frankman, 1989). For the poorest countries of the Third World, no other viable option is open.

OUR COMMON HERITAGE

The notion of the common heritage of mankind may well hold the conceptual key to the introduction of global taxation and income redistribution. Not, however, the 1970s version of the common heritage, which was limited to *res nullius*—the property of nobody. The common heritage idea was used in the discussion of global sharing of the proceeds from the extraction of seabed resources. In the very forum in which the notion of common heritage was being frequently invoked in those years, a great sea grab took place, assigning resources not in proportion to need, but rather in proportion to length of coastline and the richness of the resources located there (Cline, 1979). As long as one's thinking about our common heritage is limited to what is no country's land, then that which is left as the common heritage is what little remains after all else is appropriated.

Let us take the next logical steps: a moment's reflection would tell us that virtually the entire world we live in today is based on a common heritage: written and spoken language, the food we eat, the clothes we wear, the very thoughts we think, not to mention the technological building blocks in the machines that surround us. The notion of a common heritage was doubtlessly applied primarily to seabed resources as a domain over which prior claims of sovereignty and property rights had not yet been established. But property rights themselves are part of our common heritage. The historical accident of national boundaries having been drawn should not justify denying to the bulk of the world's population a share in the monetary gains resulting from the harnessing of our common heritage.

Once the perspective is broadened, our common heritage appears to be ubiquitous: international public goods, among which are peace, freedom of the seas, and an open trading system, can be spoken of as part of our common heritage (Kindleberger, 1986, pp. 7–8).

If we accept the notion of the common heritage, then we may come to agree that a share of the profits derived from the application of our "joint stock of knowledge" should be redistributed internationally. International income redistribution is merely hinted at in the 1975 United Nations resolution on a New International Economic Order, which timidly reaffirmed the target of 0.7 percent of gross national product to be devoted to official development assistance. That document called for the expeditious consideration of other means of transfer of real resources, which are predictable, assured, and continuous. It is only likely to be through the distribution of the proceeds of international taxation that needy countries will ever receive adequate financial inflows.

THE NATIONAL ANALOGY

Transfer payments both to individuals and regions are part of the economic landscape of each nation-state. It would be hard to imagine what the four maritime provinces of Canada would be like without transfer payments from Ottawa. Historical accident entitles those provinces with their 2 million inhabitants to total annual transfers that exceed by a very wide margin the net disbursements of ODA received from all sources by India, the world's major aid beneficiary with its population of 800 million. The amount of aid per capita to the Maritimes is 500 times that to India.

Historical accident entitles regions to transfers; historical accident and mental blinders deny entitlements to nations. Consider for a moment the rhetoric and mind-set associated with transfers to regions as opposed to aid to nations. No one seriously suggests that it is about time that the Canadian maritime provinces pay their own way. No one is suggesting that they should turn increasingly to international capital markets for their needs. No one is suggesting that, given their relatively developed state, it is appropriate to reduce significantly the grant equivalent of public assistance they receive. No one is suggesting that the Maritime wage level or welfare system should be radically different from that in the rest of Canada in order to increase their export earning capacity. And certainly no one is proposing that they could get their prices right if only they had a separate currency that they could devalue as regularly as clockwork.

We plot Lorenz curves and calculate Gini coefficients for individual countries. A periodic examination of these is a rough gauge of how well we have met our obligation to the poorer members of our (national) community. I have yet to see a first approximation to a Lorenz curve for the world in which individual incomes would be arrayed on the horizontal axis irrespective of country of residence. When data are grouped by countries, the developed market economies, which had 16.6 percent of the world's population in 1987, accounted for 69.1 percent of the world's GDP (UN ECOSOC, 1989, p. 82). My guess is that at least 90 percent of the residents of the OECD countries would be in the top quintile of the global distribution and that any household with an annual income over $50,000 is likely to be in the top 5 percent.

Such an exercise would probably reveal that some of the welfare recipients in the industrial countries are, from a global perspective, among the elites of the world. We are reasonably comfortable with socializing adaptation within the nation-state: in the United States and Canada, the notion of local community responsibility has, in effect, been extended from the Atlantic to the Pacific. A century or two of conditioning in North America, longer for others, occasions that sense to stop short at national boundaries.

In the last few years contributions have been pouring in to various groups that are working to preserve endangered species or to save the Brazilian rain forest. What changes would be necessary for us to feel a meaningful concern for Brazil's poorest citizens as well? The environment has joined the ranks of privileged problems; once we truly begin to think of the world as a single unit and once we fully appreciate the linkages between poverty and environmental decline, concern for the poor of the world may grow into support for extensions of global socializing adaptation.

CONCLUSION

Just as the roots of the debt crisis can be traced to insufficient global social adaptation, so its resolution can be looked for in righting this imbalance: that is, putting a formal system of income redistribution on the agenda for a long-overdue new Bretton Woods conference. So-called solutions to the debt problem insist on the needs of both lenders and creditors: Most of the literature tries to resolve the problem within that box, much like the problem of putting four straight lines through nine points arrayed in a square, without lifting one's pencil. Approaches to the debt problem that go beyond the limits of the box are those that have emphasized growth in either the MDCs (more developed countries), the LDCs, or both. But if the debt crisis was born of inadequate public financial flows to LDCs and insufficient capacity on their part to respond to various shocks—among them oil price increases, the fall of commodity prices, a decline in MDC demand for their exports, and increases in interest rates— then it seems clear that an institutional arrangement to increase the flow of funds to developing countries is the only certain way to change the parameters within which the LDCs must operate.

If we are serious about mobilizing some portion of the global surplus for investment in the Third World, then it must be through the cooperation of sovereign states in building a system of international progressive income redistribution. Without a formalized system of income redistribution, the developing countries will for many decades to come continue to be prey to the vagaries of market forces. Try as some of them may through tax incentives and suppression of wage levels, they are likely to still find foreign investment and bank lending heading for more profitable shores.

It is clear that much of what has been applied in dealing with the debt crisis thus far has involved muddling through—case-by-case "solutions," which at best give brief respites, but no clear road ahead. The problems of debt (and other disorders of the global economy) require instead a change in world view—a paradigm shift. These problems need to be put in a broader perspective. A recent editorial in *Le Devoir* (Juneau, 1988, p. 8) observed that everyone is singing the tune of sustainable development, but few are drawing the political implications. The same can be said of the globalization of economic activity. A major implication of the globalization of markets is the need for global income redistribution. Global social adaptation that falls short will assure that we will continue designing palliatives for successive crises as poverty spreads.

The change in perspective that comes with an acceptance of progressive global redistribution might provide a lasting solution for the Latin American sovereign debtors. Jeffrey Sachs (1989) has spoken of two debt crises: the financial crisis and the poverty crisis. The title of a recent article puts it most starkly when it speaks of "Paying Interest in Human Life" (*World Watch*, 1989, pp. 6–8). The almost limitless writings on the debt crisis tend to focus exclusively on the financial crisis. In looking for a solution to the debt problem, I would suggest that the approach differs significantly if one emphasizes the poverty crisis and keeps that aspect paramount in the search for solutions. The debt problem, per se, may require continuing case-by-case arrangements, but these must be within a context in which the nations of the world make a commitment to systematic income redistribution.

REFERENCES

Cline, William R. (1979). "Resource Transfers to the Developing Countries: Issues and Trends." In William R. Cline (ed.), *Policy Alternatives for a New International Order: An Economic Analysis*. New York: Praeger, pp. 333–353.

Cornia, Giovanni Andrea, Richard Jolly, and Frances Stewart (eds.) (1988). *Adjustment with a Human Face*, 2 vols. Oxford: Clarendon Press.

Frankman, Myron J. (May 1989). "The Idea of International Income Redistribution: Intellectual History and Status Report." McGill University, Department of Economics Working Paper no. 9/89.

Heller, Peter and Jack Diamond (April 1990). *International Comparisons of Government Expenditure Revisited: The Developing Countries, 1975-86.* IMF Occasional Paper No. 69.

Hirschman, Albert O. (1965). *Journeys Toward Progress.* New York: Anchor Books.

IMF (April 1990). *International Capital Markets: Development and Prospects.*

———. *International Financial Statistics* (IFS), various issues.

Juneau, Albert (October 27, 1988). "La 'vertu' de l'écologisme." *Le Devoir*, 79, p. 8.

Kindleberger, Charles P. (1986). "International Public Goods without International Government." *American Economic Review*, 76, pp. 1–13.

Lorimer, James (1884). "Book V. The Ultimate Problem of International Jurisprudence." *The Institutes of the Law of Nations: A Treatise of the Jural Relations of Separate Political Communities.* Edinburgh: William Blackwood and Sons.

Morris, Charles R. (October 1989). "The Coming Global Boom." *The Atlantic*, 264, pp. 52–64.

Portes, Alejandro (1989). "Latin American Urbanization During the Years of the Crisis." *Latin American Research Review*, 24, pp. 7–44.

Sachs, Jeffrey (Summer 1989). "Making the Brady Plan Work." *Foreign Affairs*, 68, pp. 87–104.

Schatz, Sayre (January 1983). "Socializing Adaptation: A Perspective on World Capitalism," *World Development*, 11, pp. 1–10.

Streeten, Paul (1988). "Surpluses for a Capital-Hungry World." In Paul Streeten (ed.), *Beyond Adjustment: The Asian Experience.* Washington: IMF, pp. 256–261.

UN Children's Fund (UNICEF) (1990). *The State of the World's Children 1990.* Oxford: Oxford University Press.

UN Economic and Social Council (UN ECOSOC), Commission for Social Development (1989). *1989 Report on the World Social Situation.*

World Bank (1990). *World Debt Tables: External Debt of Developing Countries. 1989-90.* Washington, D.C.: World Bank.

World Watch, 2 (July-August 1989).

CHAPTER FIVE

Trade and Industrial Policy in Latin America: Issues for the 1990s

DAVID GLOVER

This chapter looks at recent experience with trade and industrial policy in Latin America and extrapolates from it to highlight some issues that are likely to increase in importance in the 1990s. The chapter emphasizes industrial *policy*—that is, the range of instruments that have been used by governments to influence the industrial sector. It does not deal extensively with characteristics of the industrial sector, its structure, performance, technology, and so on. The chapter provides a broad overview, so it unavoidably involves many generalizations and stylized facts.

The chapter starts by looking at some general characteristics of industrial policy in the 1980s and then turns to two sets of issues that are likely to increase in importance during the next ten years: those related to trade, industrialization, and growth; and those related to the implementation of industrial policy.

INDUSTRIAL POLICY IN THE 1980S

Trade and industrial policies in the 1980s have been characterized by greater liberalization and simplification, partly as a response to World Bank/IMF conditionality. Prior to the 1980s, most Latin American countries followed a well-known model of import substitution. The Latin American model, based on generalized protection for local industry, is in contrast to the targeted strategic protection provided by some of the successful Southeast Asian newly industrialized countries (NICs) and to the reliance on public enterprises in Sub-Saharan Africa.

This pattern of protection involved quantitative restrictions, high average tariffs with a high rate of dispersion (in other words, a wide range between the highest and the lowest tariffs), and the use of many other policy instruments that directly or indirectly, consciously or unconsciously, provided incentives or disincentives to industry. These instruments include credit policies, exchange rates, fiscal policy, minimum wages, and others. The overall structure of incentives provided by these policies often became extremely complex (Corbo and de Melo, 1987). For example, in Ecuador the number of lines of credit provided to industry by the public sector between 1972 and 1981 increased from 26 to 58, with nominal interest rates covering a range from 2 to 15 percent (Abril and Urriola, 1988). Similar ranges could be found in some of the other macro prices affecting industry such as exchange rates, tax rates, and so on.

The use of multiple incentives probably reflects in part the structuralist orientation of many of the technicians in the state apparatus. This is insufficient explanation in itself, however. The baroque complexity and frequent lack of internal consistency in these incentive structures probably reflects as well a lack of coordination among the agencies responsible for fiscal policy, trade policy, exchange rates, and the like; in part the differing interests among semiautonomous agencies; and in part the process by which economic agents react politically to changes in policies.

To illustrate the latter, imagine a scenario in which the Central Bank devalues the local currency. A firm whose profits are negatively affected by devaluation then petitions the Central Bank to revoke the decision. Alternatively, depending on where the firm can most effectively exert its influence, it may petition instead for a change in taxes or tariffs that will compensate for the damage done by the change in the exchange rate. The next step will be for firms that favor the devaluation to counterreact through a similar variety of channels. In this way a complex structure of incentives is established and expanded. The sectoral and related macro policy measures employed in this process are simultaneously incentives to industry and mechanisms to compensate those negatively affected by policy changes.

The effects of this complex incentive structure are several. First, the structure of incentives loses its transparency. No one really knows what the net effect of various incentives on a particular industry or a branch really is, and so incentives lose their effectiveness for strategic planning. Second, because so many compensating incentives are provided as a result of the lobbying process, everyone gets an "incentive." If everyone gets an incentive, then no one gets an effective incentive and one ends up with generalized rather than targeted protection. Third, because the incentives are provided as the result of lobbying by established firms, they tend to create barriers to entry to new firms. This is particularly true of quantitative restrictions and licenses (Tower, 1986).

As the complexity and obscurity of these incentive structures increased over time, this and other weaknesses of the import substitution strategy were starting to be recognized by policymakers in the latter part of the 1970s. In addition, when the debt crisis hit in 1982, the World Bank and IMF assumed an enormous amount of influence over the trade and industrial policies of debtor countries through the conditions imposed in Bank/Fund programs. The elements of the trade and industrial policy recommended by the Bank and Fund are fairly well-known. They involve simplification of the incentive structure and moves toward freer trade. Quantitative restrictions are to be replaced in the first instance by tariffs; tariffs are to be lowered and the dispersion or range of tariff levels is to be narrowed. Ideally, the average tariff should be zero in the long run, but a uniform rate of 10 percent seems to be acceptable. Uniform tariffs are supposed to provide a neutral trade environment, a "level playing field" in the jargon, which allows comparative advantage to operate with full effect.

The time allowed for implementation of these measures is typically quite short. The Bank prefers "shock treatment" in which many macro and sectoral policies are changed immediately and simultaneously—partly, the Bank says, to increase the credibility of the program and disallow time for lobbying against the measures. These policy changes are supposed to increase the incentives provided to the tradable rather than nontradable sectors and to increase exports, particularly nontraditional exports.

Several side issues could be noted here. One is that the overriding goal of most of these measures is to improve a country's balance-of-payments position; longer term growth issues don't get much attention. Second, resulting from the last point, macroeconomic policy has assumed a position of supremacy in the policy hierarchy, and so have the agencies related to macro policy, such as the Central Bank and the Finance Ministry. Sectoral ministries and the interest groups that affect them have less influence than they did in the past, and this has obvious implications for the kind of lobbying process described before. A third point is that LDC trade policy is now largely negotiated with the Bank and the Fund. While developing countries make some efforts in bilateral negotiations with governments or within the General Agreement on Tariffs and Trade (GATT) to obtain better access to developed country markets, domestic aspects of a country's trade policy—its degree of openness, export-orientation, levels of protection (in fact many of the things that can be used as concessions in bilateral or multilateral negotiations)—are all included in Bank/Fund adjustment policies and are largely determined a priori.

What have the results of the new trade and industrial policies been? Certainly incentive structures have become less complicated. In the Ecuadorian example given earlier, the number of lines of credit and dispersion of interest rates has been reduced considerably (Abril and Urriola, 1988). The export performance of most Latin countries in terms of both volume and diversification of products has been impressive. Countries that have wholeheartedly adopted

the shock treatment approach, notably Chile, have undergone some deindustrialization. In spite of massive adjustments and net capital transfers from the
South to the North over the last several years, there has been no appreciable
reduction in the stock of debt. Nor have there been many major concessions
by developed countries on trade or market access outside specific initiatives
like the Caribbean Basin Initiative.

ISSUES FOR THE 1990S

There are several reasons to believe that the trade and industrial policy
agenda for the 1990s is going to shift somewhat from that of the previous decade. One reason is the only partial success of the adjustment process. While
the record on specific indicators such as export performance is fairly good,
overall performance has been less positive. Second, the old arguments about
declining terms of trade for primary commodities, though not completely resolved, now seem to be more persuasive than they once were (Singer, 1988a).
The levels and stability of prices for primary commodity exports are not encouraging and the need for industrialization is more obvious than ever. Third
is a general acceptance of the principle that growth is a legitimate, necessary
objective in structural adjustment packages. Fourth is recognition of the very
high costs of structural adjustment through shock treatment, particularly in
terms of growth and employment.

It is likely that many elements of the 1980s approach will continue, particularly the emphasis on the private sector, on export orientation, and particularly
the diversification of exports. It is interesting to observe the political debates
in Chile, for example. While there is strong opposition to Pinochet's social policies, the major political parties have accepted many of the current government's economic policies and will likely maintain a very open export-oriented
economy. There is little or no serious discussion in Latin America about returning to import substitution.

However, it is likely that some aspects of trade and industrial policy that
were neglected in the 1980s will receive much greater attention in the 1990s.
The first of these is the relationship between trade, industrialization, and
growth. Although there is some relatively academic World Bank research on
trade and growth, at the operational level, the Bank's principal justification for
trade liberalization within structural adjustment programs is still to improve
a country's balance-of-payments position. (Tariff reductions reduce the import
costs of export industries; macro policy reduces domestic aggregate demand
for both imports and exportables; and devaluation increases the incentive to
export.) However, the Latin American debt problem is no longer a short-term
crisis but a semipermanent phenomenon. It does no good to export a higher
percentage of a shrinking pie. More generally, it is crucial to know what the
implications of a more open economy are for economic growth.

As the pendulum swings away from short-term balance-of-payments issues toward longer term growth concerns, several kinds of research will be needed. First, comparative statistical research needs to be much improved. The kinds of correlations drawn, for example, in the 1987 *World Development Report* between outward orientation and growth are weak and the direction of causality unclear. Adequate measures of "outward orientation" are lacking and much of the assessment is based on highly subjective qualitative criteria (Singer, 1988b). Second, more empirical case studies carried out within a comparative framework are needed on the process of growth in the industrial sector as it is affected by trade policies (Helleiner, forthcoming). The textbooks tell us that the direct effects of freer trade on growth tend to be very small—less than 5 percent of GNP. At the same time, we have seen spectacular growth in the trade-oriented Southeast Asian NICs. Clearly something is happening there that we need to understand better. Is the direction of causality from growth to export performance rather than the reverse? Are the chief benefits of trade in the area of learning effects, x-efficiency, or technical change?

This leads to a third area of research that requires more conceptual work. It seems that much of the onus for the statistical and empirical work proposed above rests with those who advocate trade liberalization so strongly. The principal counterargument to trade liberalization from those who favor some protection is dynamic comparative advantage (DCA), an elaboration of the traditional infant industry argument. While the liberalizers' case for free markets and static comparative advantage (SCA) is weak empirically, the structuralists' case for DCA is weak conceptually. Few would disagree that considerations of dynamic rather than static comparative advantage should guide trade and industrial policy. However, unless economists can insert some analytical content into this concept and provide guidance about how to achieve it, there is a danger that DCA will become a mere slogan used indiscriminately to justify protectionist policies.

In fact, economists have never developed an effective methodology to identify SCA a priori. Today we are all apostles of something infinitely more subtle—DCA—without ever having resolved the methodological problems associated with its predecessor. This is not so much a criticism as an indication of where increased effort could be put. For example, there is considerable opportunity for cross-fertilization between those who study industrial organization and firm behavior and those who study trade policy (Krugman, 1986). What precisely is DCA? What criteria does one apply to select industries in which a country has DCA? What determines it? Can it be created, encouraged, controlled? If so, how and at what cost?

The management of a development strategy based on DCA is also important because while the approach presents many opportunities, it also has dangers. DCA is by definition temporary; international markets contain many short-term opportunities that can disappear rapidly with changes in demand and technology and the entry of new competitors. Unless the economy develops the capacity to adjust rapidly to changing demand conditions or unless the revenue from DCA-based industry is well managed, the result could be cycles of boom and bust equal in severity to those derived from reliance on the export of raw materials. In other words, an industrial strategy based on the promotion of DCA should not focus exclusively on technology policy. It will require a well-trained labor force, particularly in product design, engineering, and marketing. It should probably emphasize the ability to shift within product categories (e.g., from basic to designer clothing) rather than attempting to shift across highly dissimilar products. And it requires careful management of revenue, employment, fiscal policy, and other measures relevant to export orientation.

A second area that will probably receive more attention in the coming decade is the implementation of trade and industrial policy. Although there does appear to be some consensus in Latin America about the desirability of a somewhat more export-oriented, diversified, and open economy, there is considerable disagreement about how to achieve it. As mentioned above, the World Bank and IMF favor the rapid and simultaneous reduction of tariffs to a low common level. This approach assumes that prices are the most effective instruments that policymakers can manipulate and that economic agents will respond to them rapidly. An alternative view is based on structuralist assumptions that rigidities in Latin American economies impede a smooth response to market signals and can even result in perverse results (Ffrench-Davis, 1988). Free market and structuralist approaches may not be conceptually incompatible; one could propose that an optimal industrial strategy is one that permits the transmission of market signals, particularly from the rest of the world, but intervenes selectively to remove or compensate for rigidities that prevent an appropriate supply response.

The elements of the structuralist approach to implementation are basically three: the use of a wide range of policy instruments, the sequencing of policy changes, and the use of the nonprice interventions. Each of these are discussed in turn below.

The structuralist argument holds that the state should use the full range of instruments at its disposal (e.g., fiscal policy, tariffs, subsidies, quantitative restrictions, credit, exchange rates) because while the same net effect on a given firm's profitability could be achieved with the use of any single instrument, the effects on intervening variables and on the government budget may be quite different. Some instruments have different effects on market structure, employment, capital intensity, use of local material, interindustry linkages, and so on. Some instruments also cost the government much more in direct expenditure or foregone tax revenue than others and are therefore the least feasible in the short run.

The second element of this approach is the sequencing of policy changes. The principal argument in favor of shock treatment seems to be political—that the gradual implementation of policy changes will generate opposition from groups negatively affected. There are reasons to believe that shock treatment is technically inefficient and even counterproductive and that the political argument is in many cases not valid. It could be argued that phasing in policy changes in a particular sequence may produce a more sustainable reform process both economically and politically.

For example, evidence from many countries suggests that it is extremely difficult to try to stabilize the economy (e.g., reduced hyperinflation) and at the same time liberalize trade (Selowsky, 1989; Bruno et al., 1988). Stabilization is probably a necessary precondition for improved trade performance. Similarly, liberalizing financial markets at the same time that the real side of the economy is undergoing adjustment may simply lead to capital flight, as it has often done in the Southern Cone (Cortazar, 1988). Finally, within trade policy one can't assume a priori that the import and export responses to devaluation will be identical in timing or magnitude. Some research is being done on this through the World Bank and one study even suggests an optimal sequence as follows (Choksi and Papageorgiou, 1986): first, apply fiscal discipline; second, free up the labor market—that is, allow real wages to drop; third, liberalize trade; fourth, liberalize domestic financial markets; and finally, liberalize the external capital account.

Costa Rica is a country that carried out a sequenced trade policy reform in spite of objections from the World Bank. It provided export incentives before it lowered tariff barriers, allowing time for export revenues to accrue and producers to shift from import competing to export industries. Gradual phasing of the program also allowed time to build consensus behind it (E. Rodriguez, 1989).

A third area for increased attention is the role of nonprice interventions by government in support of the industrial sector. Some evidence (M. Rodriguez and Schydlowsky, 1987) suggests that industrial exports may not be particularly sensitive to changes in the exchange rate. Potential exporters may be hampered by lack of market information and market access, poor communications media, insufficient lines of credit, and the like more than by overvalued exchange rates (Schydlowsky, 1988). These traditional structuralist arguments are increasingly being supported by empirical data. They seem to indicate that getting the prices right is at most a necessary but not sufficient condition.

At the same time, even a casual observer can notice a dramatic difference between the size and efficiency of the services sector in Southeast Asia and Latin America (banks, telephones, telex, postal service, airports, frequency and reliability of flights, etc.) There appears to be a correlation between a strong services sector and a strong export-oriented manufacturing sector (Sieh Lee Mei Ling, 1988). Which of these is the chicken and which is the egg is harder to say. Research may support the hypothesis that strengthening services and ancillary industries is a more effective way of supporting manufacturing than heavy reliance on the manipulation of macro prices. If so, governments could look for ways to improve the flow of information within the economy and to link firms in formal and informal sectors. The experience of the Philippines in establishing "clearinghouses" for industrial subcontracting would be worth investigating.

The observations made above imply a fairly specific research agenda for those who would wish to revive a structuralist approach to trade and industrial policy. The agenda would have to pay considerable attention to political as well as economic factors, since much of the attractiveness of the neoclassical approach is its alleged political-administrative feasibility and simplicity rather than its technical efficiency. The steps in mounting a convincing argument (for alternative policies, or at least for the right to more pluralism and experimentation) would seem to be the following:

First, one needs to buttress the arguments for selective, strategic industrial policy with better empirical research. Where have infant industry policies succeeded? How have governments been able to pick winners? What growth effects, learning, x-efficiency, and so on have occurred?

Second, one would need to present credible arguments that a nonuniform tariff structure would not succumb to pressure from local lobbies and degenerate into the baroque and internally inconsistent incentive structures of the past.

Third, much more needs to be done to identify "rigidities" that justify structuralist interventions. At present, references to these "rigidities" tend to be very general and at times they degenerate into pessimism and even tautology. The rigidities most frequently named are land tenure patterns, concentrated market structures, and low savings rates. Surely there are other bottlenecks and surely many of these are susceptible to policy interventions. Many economists have done modeling exercises in which they simulate the effects on the stock of external debt of small changes in various elements—for example, a 1 percent increase in the savings rate or a 1 percent decrease in the capital-output ratio. The result, not surprisingly, is that if very little changes, very little will change. Yet we know from comparative studies of Japan and other countries that the savings rate, for example, is not innate or culturally determined. It can be affected by the availability of savings institutions, changes in income distribution, pension plans, taxation of mortgages, and many other factors (Fajnzylber, 1988). The purpose of structural adjustment is to change the structure of the economy. A neostructuralist approach to economic policy should not be predicated on the assumption that structural rigidities are immutable and can only be compensated for by adding more and more distortions.

A fourth step would be to prepare arguments about the optimal pace and sequencing of liberalization, an area in which the Bank and Fund seem to be receptive. Optimality would be political as well as economic; a particular sequence may successively neutralize opponents and strengthen supporters in such a way as to permit the implementation of the overall package.

Finally, one would have to demonstrate the government's capacity to implement a selective, fine-tuned, and sequenced policy package. This is no small task. Alan García's package for Peru, in many ways a structuralist one, seems to have failed in part because of inadequate administrative capacity and lack of coordination among government agencies (Schydlowsky, 1989). For this reason, the desire to use a wide range of policy instruments rather than a relatively simple and transparent incentive structure is probably the most unrealistic element in the neostructuralist argument.

A final issue that may reappear in new forms in the coming decade is regional integration—a subject that provided material for countless Ph.D. theses in the 1960s and 1970s but virtually faded from sight in the 1980s. There are several reasons why this issue has been dormant recently. One is that the problem was probably subjected to as much economic analysis as it could bear. The economic costs and benefits are probably fairly well-known; the extent to which integration has not taken place probably results more from a lack of political will than from a failure to recognize possible benefits. A second reason is the decline in domestic import substitution policies; regional integration is to a large extent import substitution writ large and interest in it has correspondingly diminished. A third reason may be a tendency of such agreements as the Andean Pact to freeze the pattern of industrial production, impeding flexible response to changing opportunities. Once Country A agrees to produce refrigerators and Country B computers, it is difficult to change the agreement without long and difficult negotiations. This is a particularly serious drawback during a period of rapid and accelerating change in the world economy.

In spite of this we have seen some revival of interest in regional integration in the last couple of years. Interest is high in the members of the Central American Common Market, and the Argentina-Brazil trade bloc is apparently functioning quite well. In the 1990s, the prospects for regional integration are likely to remain limited but there is some possibility for export-oriented cooperative production schemes. In such schemes, individual countries would bear responsibility for producing various components of a product according to their comparative advantage, for eventual assembly and export. The most promising region for such ventures may be Central America in the context of the Caribbean Basin Initiative.

CONCLUSIONS

The challenge for policymakers in the 1990s will be to learn from the experience of Latin America and other regions over the last 20 years in order to design selective and pragmatic industrial policies for the future. There is a clear need to encourage flexibility and to think beyond the short-term objectives of stabilization and generation of export revenue to long-term growth and the development of dynamic comparative advantage. This will require the use of some targeted, selective policy instruments; neither the generalized protection of the import substitution period nor the across-the-board liberalization of the 1980s are likely to achieve the kind of success for which Korea is so widely cited.

The design and implementation of such a policy framework will require changes in Latin American political culture: greater attempts to forge consensus on national development goals; greater emphasis on flexibility and a willingness to share the risks and costs associated with it; deliberate sequencing of policy reforms; and the capacity to combine technical efficiency with political feasibility in policy design.

The need for effective policies is greater than ever—the balance-of-payments problems that plagued the region in the 1980s will be compounded in the 1990s by greater competition from powerful trading blocks in Asia, Europe, and North America. Latin America's industrial sector has great potential. The 1990s may well prove to be the decisive decade in achieving that potential or falling farther behind in a race led by increasingly powerful competitors.

REFERENCES

Abril, Galo and Rafael Urriola (1988). "Fomento industrial y desarrollo económico en el Ecuador: una evaluación de la Política de Incentivos, 1972–1986." In Rafael Urriola, ed., *Políticas de Industrialización en América Latina.* Quito.

Bruno, Michael, Guido DiTella, Rudiger Dornbusch, and Stanley Fischer (eds.) (1988). *Inflation Stabilization: The Experience of Israel, Argentina, Brazil, Bolivia, and Mexico.* Cambridge, Mass.: MIT Press, 1988.

Choksi, A. and D. Papageorgiou (eds.) (1986). *Economic Liberalization in Developing Countries.* Oxford: Basil Blackwell.

Corbo, Vittorio and Jaime de Melo (1987). "Lessons from the Southern Cone Policy Reforms." *The World Bank Research Observer,* 2, no. 2.

Cortazar, Rene (ed.) (1988). *Políticas Macroeconómicas: Una Perspectiva Latinoamericana.* Santiago, Chile: CIEPLAN.

Fajnzylber, Fernando (December 1988). "Competividad internacional: evolución y lecciones." *Revista de CEPAL,* No. 36.

Ffrench-Davis, Ricardo (April 1988). "An outline of a neo-structuralist approach." *CEPAL Review,* No. 34.

Helleiner, G. K. (Forthcoming). "Trade Strategy in Medium Term Adjustment." *World Development.*

Krugman, Paul (ed.) (1986). *Strategic Trade Policy and the New International Economics.* Cambridge, Mass: MIT Press.

Rodriguez, Ennio (1989). "A Path in the Maze: Costa Rica, Cross Conditionality and Development." Mimeo.

Rodriguez, Martha and Daniel Schydlowsky (September 1987). "The Effectiveness of Devaluation to Achieve Industrial Competitiveness in Latin America: A Simulation Analysis." CLADS Discussion Paper No. 72. Boston University.

Schydlowsky, Daniel (1988). "La política industrial frente a las brechas del desarrollo económico." In Abril and Urriola.

———. (1989). "The Peruvian Debacle: Economic Dynamics or Political Causes?" Mimeo. Boston University.

Selowsky, Marcelo (June 1989). "Preconditions for the Recovery of Latin America's Growth." Mimeo.

Sieh Lee Mei Ling (1988). *Services in Development.* Ottawa: IDRC.

Singer, Hans (January 1988a). "The World Development Report 1987 or the Blessings of Outward Orientation: A Necessary Correction." *Journal of Development Studies,* 24, no. 2.

————. (1988b). *Rich and Poor Countries: Consequences of International Disorder,* 4th ed. New York: Unwin-Hyman.

Tower, Edward (January 1986). "Industrial Policy in Less Developed Countries." *Contemporary Policy Issues,* 4, No. 1.

World Development Report (1987). Washington, D.C.: World Bank.

PART II

Society, Economy, and Ecology: Toward Equity and Sustainability

CHAPTER SIX

Distribution of Income and Poverty in Latin America: Recent Trends and Challenges for the 1990s

ALBERT BERRY

As the Latin American economies progressed during the 1960s and 1970s, it appeared that poverty might be more or less eradicated, albeit belatedly, through a process of "growth without redistribution"—that is, growth within the context of an unchanged and extreme level of income inequality. Given the higher average income in Latin America than in many other parts of the Third World, poverty, at least in its more physical manifestations, could have been pushed to fairly low levels by another decade or so of "growth with inequality." Alternatively, there were some grounds for hope that a number of countries were just around the corner from an end to their labor surplus condition and thus about to undergo a significant tightening of the labor market. The rapidly increasing levels of education also seemed to bode well for the evolution of the income levels of the poor, as well as others (Berry, 1983). Kuznets' (1955) celebrated proposition that a frequent pattern during the process of development involves income distribution first worsening and then improving also provided grounds for optimism in Latin America, since it was reasonable to presume that inequality had peaked in these countries and would have a tendency to fall in future.

The generally robust growth of the 1970s was cut off by the international debt crisis and the economic recession of the early 1980s, with the result that the 1980s are often referred to as a "lost decade" in Latin America. For the region as a whole the rate of growth of per capita income (absorption) fell from 3.4 percent per year in 1965–80 to –1.1 percent in 1980–89 (World Bank,

1990, p. 160). Most of the countries suffered serious or even hyperinflation, stop-and-go cycles of economic activity, seriously reduced rates of investment, sharp declines in real wages during the economic downturns, and mounting public dissatisfaction, which in most countries now expressed itself through some more or less democratic process. There has of course been some variability in the performance across countries, from the drastic crisis of Peru compounded by inappropriate policy to the relatively acceptable growth in Colombia. Several countries were already undergoing serious macroeconomic problems during the 1970s, while most of the region continued to grow at decent rates, albeit at the cost of large buildups of foreign debt. But for the region as a whole, the beginning of the 1980s marked the onset of the crisis.

It goes without saying that, in one important sense, the poor have been the big losers from the "lost decade." The fact of being poor means that income declines or lost opportunities to achieve gains hurt more. Many observers have also argued that the poor have suffered greater percentage declines in income than have other groups in the society, further aggravating the crisis they have had to face. Others have argued that the bigger percent losers have been certain middle-income groups—for example, the paid blue- and white-collar workers employed in the modern sector. No very powerful theory is available to guide one's expectations on this matter, and the empirical evidence is very partial and imperfect. Inevitably, the nature of the challenges facing the region during the 1990s is greatly affected and determined by the problems of the 1980s, so it is important to get as precise a reading on them as possible.

RECENT TRENDS IN INCOME DISTRIBUTION AND POVERTY

The extreme income inequality found in Latin America is of long standing and quite resistant to change. Powerful mechanisms in the economy, the polity, and the society conspire to perpetuate those patterns. Unequal land distribution, once a major determinant of income concentration, fed over time into the extremely unequal access to education and nonagricultural capital. Such major events as the revolution in early twentieth-century Mexico did not appear to greatly alter the degree of income inequality, although the Cuban Revolution certainly did.

As of the 1960s and early 1970s, all of the Latin American countries had very high levels of inequality by the standards of other less-developed countries, with the exceptions of Cuba (by then a centrally planned socialist economy), Argentina, and Uruguay; somewhat less inegalitarian than those but still better than the regional average were Chile, Costa Rica, and probably Venezuela. [1] The most common explanations of the lower inequality in the Southern Cone included their greater level of development (e.g., farther along in the Kuznets cycle) with associated development of social security systems, wage protection, and so on, and their greater racial homogeneity, which more or less removed lack of sympathy between the dominant racial group and the others as a source of inequality.

Given their high levels of per capita income and low inequality relative to the region as a whole, the Southern Cone countries suffered lower incidence of poverty than the rest of the region; somewhat comparable poverty lines suggest 1970s incidence of under 20 percent for the Southern cone cases, of somewhere between 20 and 30 percent for Costa Rica and Venezuela, and of over 40 percent for all of the other countries (see Table 6.1). [2]

What do the data reveal about trends in the degree of inequality during the severe macroeconomic crises of the last 10–15 years? While any regionwide trend toward either improvement or worsening in the income distribution seems unlikely, [3] the experience has varied significantly across countries. In

Table 6.1
Growth of Per Capita GDP, Incidence of Poverty, and Income Distribution, Latin American Countries, Recent Decades

Country (Ranked by GDP)	GDP per Capita in 1980 (1975 dollars)	Growth Rate of GDP per capita (annual average)		Incidence of Poverty[c]			Gini Coefficient[d] (Circa 1970)
	1980	1950–1980	1980–1989[b]	1970	1980	Mid-1980s	
Brazil	2,152	4.2	0.0	49	43	40(1987)	0.537
Mexico	2,547	3.0	-0.7	34	29	30(1984)	0.545
Argentina	3,209	1.8	-3.0	8	8	13(1986)	0.431
Colombia	1,882	2.3	1.5	45	43	38(1986)	0.539
Venezuela	3,310	1.5	-3.1	25	24	27(1986)	0.531
Peru	1,746	2.1	-3.1	50	49	52(1986)	0.591
Chile	2,372	1.8	1.0	17	16		0.504
Uruguay	3,269	1.4	-0.8			15(1986)	0.449
Ecuador	1,556	3.1	-0.1				0.576
Guatemala	1,422	1.8	-2.2			68(1986)	
Dominican Republic	1,564	2.6	0.2				0.493
Bolivia	1,114	1.3	-3.4				
El Salvador	899	1.3	-2.1				0.536
Paraguay	1,753	2.4	-0.4				0.441
Costa Rica	2,170	3.3	-0.7	24	22	25(1988)	0.557
Panama	2,157	2.9	-2.1	39	37	34(1986)	
Nicaragua	1,324	2.3	-4.4				0.612
Honduras	1,031	1.4	-1.4	65	64		
Latin America[a]		2.7	-1.0				

a   Except Cuba and Haiti.
b   1989 figures are preliminary.
c   Note that the poverty indices are not comparable for the same country over time.
d   The figure presented is an average of those reported by Kakwani (1980) and by Lecaillon et al. (1984) where both are available, and with the exception of Venezuela, where the Lecaillon figure was chosen on the grounds that it was more in accordance with other sources.

Sources: For GDP and its growth, Summers and Heston (1984) and ECLAC (1989). For the incidence of poverty in 1970, Altimir, (1982), for 1981, Molina, (1982), and for the mid-1880s, CEPAL (1990, p. 39). The Gini coefficients are from Kakwani (1980) and Lecaillon et al. (1984); the data from the two sources have been combined in the way indicated in footnote d.

the interpretation of that experience, it is useful to distinguish several types of factors that may have affected the observed trends in distribution during the crisis and its aftermath. First, trends already in evidence before the onset of the crisis in the individual countries may have extended into the period under discussion. Although most countries in the region did not witness major shifts in distribution during the 1970s, some underlying patterns of structural change hinted at possible changes in the not-too-distant future. Thus the sharp increase in real wages of lower skilled workers in Brazil during the "economic miracle" of the late 1960s and early 1970s, and the less dramatic increase in real wages in agriculture and some other sectors of the Colombian economy, suggested that these two economies might be on the verge of a tighter labor market and continuing wage increases, especially among those lower skilled workers. Second, the crisis was presaged in most of the countries by a period during which absorption was markedly higher than production, an usually unsustainable condition whose end might imply certain types of changes in the income distribution. Third, the crisis stabilization episodes that occurred, again in most of the countries of the region, may have had significant distributional effects. Finally, the "structural adjustment" that followed on the stabilization, and that involved increases in the relative incentives to exports, a pattern of privatization, and financial deregulation of various stripes would be expected to have some distributional effects. Needless to say, one would not expect to be able fully to sort out these various factors in the empirical record, but it is nevertheless helpful to have them in mind in the course of the discussion.

The timing of the economic crises varied somewhat, with the Southern Cone countries already in difficulties of one sort or another by the mid-1970s, whereas for most of the others the onset was signaled by the international debt crisis of the early 1980s. Particularly severe short-period (2–4 years) declines in per capita income were suffered by Costa Rica, Chile, Peru, and Venezuela, while GDP per capita fell by over 30 percent during the 1980s in Argentina, Venezuela, Peru, Bolivia, and Nicaragua. The trends in other welfare indicators are of special interest, since they have not fully paralleled those of per capita income or consumption.

Although not all of the crises/slowdowns began around 1980, it is convenient to compare per capita income levels and economic structures as of that year. The highest GDP per capita was found in Venezuela, Uruguay, and Argentina at about $3,000 1975 dollars. A middle range included Mexico, Chile, Panama, Brazil, and Costa Rica, roughly in the $2,000–2,500 range. Between $1,500 and $2,000 came Colombia, Peru, Ecuador, Paraguay, the Dominican Republic, and (at a little below $1,500) Guatemala (see Table 6.1). Of the first group of three countries, only Venezuela had a high poverty incidence, the result of a somewhat higher level of income inequality than found in the other two. In the next group down, poverty incidence was moderate (under 25 percent, according to the criteria underlying the figures of Table 6.1) in Chile and Costa Rica, where inequality was of below average severity. All the lower income countries had high levels of poverty.

Considerable uncertainty surrounds the evolution of income distribution during the crisis and adjustment periods in most of the countries of Latin America. Usually the most useful and reliable information comes from household income surveys, but their main defect is the systematically weak reporting of nonlabor incomes. When there is no reason to believe that the labor share has changed markedly or that the distribution of capital income has been altered, this underreporting is unlikely to bias greatly the estimated trends. During the 1980s, however, there *is* reason to believe that the capital share has risen, as the result of higher interest rates, on government domestic debt among other things (Felix and Caskey, 1989). During the crises themselves, a common pattern was government borrowing abroad or locally to shore up the exchange rate; this facilitated massive capital flight. Governments (e.g., those of Chile and Ecuador) essentially socialized private foreign liabilities, which are the domain of the rich; the Chilean Central Bank, pushed by the international banks to act as guarantor of private nonguaranteed foreign loans, subsidized debtors to the tune of about 4 percent of GDP over the period 1982–85 (Meller, 1989, p. 111). Later, when the crises had passed and structural adjustment had begun, high interest rates remained the order of the day as part of the new financial orthodoxy. Our understanding of the net effects of the various impacts on capital incomes during this period is not adequate to say with certainty that the capital share has risen by enough to imply an overall trend to worsening since the onset of the crises, but that possibility must be borne in mind. In the rest of this discussion, however, we will draw essentially on the survey information.

In the group of countries for which we have some usable information, and of which all but Colombia suffered significant declines in per capita income (by a total of say 5 percent or more over periods of 2–4 years), the broad record on trends in inequality since their economic crises/slowdowns began appears to be as follows. Distribution clearly worsened in Argentina and Chile; probably improved in Colombia; and probably changed little in Brazil, Peru, Venezuela, and Costa Rica, unless a significant increase in the capital share occurred, as discussed above. (Unfortunately, credible data are not available for Mexico, one of the most interesting cases.) A first rough reading of the evidence suggests that the onset of the crisis per se did not lead systematically to a worsening of distribution, though of course it increased poverty in all cases, using per capita income as the indicator thereof. In the case of Chile, it seems likely that the worsening, which did arrive with the crisis, had mainly to do with the conservative policies instituted; in Argentina the interpretation is less obvious, which will be discussed later. In Colombia the improvement may be interpretable as the latter stage in a Kuznets cycle, involving a tightening of the labor market among other things.

It seems clear that the variety of distributional experiences across countries would not be diminished by the successful incorporation into our account of what was happening to capital incomes. If distribution did worsen in countries like Costa Rica, Brazil, and Peru, it would nonetheless remain true that at the heart of the crisis the poverty-increasing effect of worsened distribution would be much less than that of falling per capita income itself. The exceptions to this would be Argentina and Chile, where the increases in inequality were marked. Of course poverty was initially (and still is) less prevalent in these countries (especially Argentina) than in the others of the region. We now turn to a consideration of the experiences of several individual countries.

Brazil

The experience of Brazil is of particular interest and importance, given its large population and extreme inequality, which possibly exceeds that of any other country whose data are of comparable reliability. It is widely accepted that distribution worsened somewhat between 1960 and 1970; between 1970 and 1980 any overall shift was minor, as a clear worsening in the rural areas was partially or wholly offset by a decrease in the urban/rural income differential (Denslow and Tyler, 1984).

Between 1980 and 1983, per capita income fell by about 15 percent, after which it recovered fairly strongly through 1986, then slipped again such that by 1989 GDP per capita was about 5 percent below the 1980 level and consumption per capita a little farther below. Annual data available since 1979 indicate virtual constancy, at least through 1987, in the distribution of income among Brazilian households (ranked by total household income); the reported Gini coefficient never moved outside the range 0.584–0.597, while the share of the bottom 50 percent of the population fluctuated within the range 12.2–12.9 percent (Hoffmann, 1989a, 1989b). Distribution in each of the four major regions of the country showed a comparable stability. The distribution among income recipients was less stable; the Gini coefficient ranged from a low of 0.572 in 1981 (the year of the sharpest income decline) to 0.603 in 1987. The share of the bottom 50 percent had fallen from an average of about 14 percent for the 1979 and 1981 observations to an average of 12.6 percent over 1985–87. That the household income distribution did not become more skewed when the distribution among income recipients *was* moving in that direction may have been due to an increase in participation in the labor force by secondary workers, which tends to increase the skewness of distribution among workers while possibly diminishing that among households. During the abrupt income decline (21 percent in mean and 17 percent in median income) recorded between the household surveys of 1980 and 1983, the fall was sharpest in the rich Southeast (25 and 24 percent, respectively) and least in the poor Northeast (15 and 7 percent, respectively) and in the also less industrialized Centerwest (16 percent and 7 percent, respectively). If the August 1980 minimum wage is used as a household poverty line, Hoffmann's figures indicate that incidence rose from 20.8 percent in 1981 to 26.5 percent in 1983, then fell back to somewhere around 22 percent by 1986. Fox and Morley (1990), who rank households by per capita income, report a sharper increase in poverty between 1980–81 and 1983, a sharper decrease over 1983–86 and a marked jump again in 1987, whose estimate, however, remains provisional.

Some social indicators continued to advance, albeit less rapidly than before, during the period of crisis in Brazil. World Bank data on life expectancy, infant mortality, food production per capita, and the share of the population with access to electricity all show improvements between 1980 and 1987, whereas the share with access to safe water fell. Some improvements may be the result of past investments; in such cases low levels of current investment will take their toll in the future. And some of the data may simply be inaccurate.

Public-sector "social expenditures" (i.e., those directed to education, health, housing, and social security) have been criticized as strikingly ineffective in contributing to poverty reduction in Brazil. Food and nutrition, water supply, and sanitation programs take only a small share of these expenditures (usually about 5 percent), while social security, with a dramatically regressive distributional impact, took 42 percent as of 1986 (McGreevey et al. 1988).

Argentina

Argentina's tradition of relative income equality gives particular interest to its experience of the last 15 years. Since 1974 the country's growth performance has been singularly weak; GNP was only 4 percent higher in 1988 than in 1974, while population had grown about 20 percent in the interim. GNP fell particularly sharply, by 13 percent, over 1980–82. Accompanying this macroeconomic failure has been an increase in income inequality of proportions seldom seen in such a short period, with the Gini coefficient among income earners in greater Buenos Aires rising from 0.365 (1974–75 average) to 0.46 (1987–88 average).

Such an increase calls for an explanation. After rising by about 28 percent between 1962 and 1965 to a peak in 1973–75, the real wage fell dramatically to 16 percent below that 1962–65 level by 1985–87 (Sanchez, 1989, p. 5). One interesting hint that international trade policy and the management of the real exchange rate may play a role comes from the short-run inverse relationship that exists, over 1970–87 at least, between the real exchange rate (Argentine currency per dollar) and both the real wage and the ratio of the real wage to per capita income (Berry, 1990a, p. 31). That ratio is related, in turn, to the distribution of income; periods when the ratio was lowest (1976–79 and 1986–89) have been characterized by sharp drops in the income share of the middle (in both cases) and lowest (in the second case) deciles.

It is plausible, given the prominence of wage goods among Argentina's exports, that an increase in the real exchange rate (through devaluation, for example) would, ceteris paribus, lead to a decrease in the real wage rate and a worsening of the distribution of income. But it is clear that the decade-plus worsening of the income distribution cannot be fully explained by this link with the real exchange rate, since net worsening occurred even over periods (of several years) when there was no net increase in the real exchange rate. Other factors must have been at work. Possibly the informal sector was expanding while the gap between formal- and informal-sector wages was widening. Possibly structural changes wrought by the change in trade policy (e.g., increased concentration in manufacturing) worsened inequality.

Unlike Chile, Argentina's experience at this time was not characterized by a destruction of the power of the unions or by high levels of unemployment. The rights of the worker against dismissal remained strong. It may be that under the conditions of macroeconomic stress and stagnation that characterized the country at this time the maintenance of union power not only contributed to the economic stagnation but also to the marked worsening of the distribution of income. It is also probable that the very large capital flight from the country played a role, by lowering the amount of capital available to complement the labor force. Other factors were no doubt at work too.

Chile

Chile's recent economic experience has some similarities with Argentina's, but several key differences as well. There have been two severe recessions since 1970, the first associated with Allende's overthrow as GDP fell by 23 percent over 1972–75, and the second associated with the international debt crisis, as GDP fell by 14 percent between 1981 and 1982. After each collapse, growth resumed quickly and was rapid, but the impact of the recessions was still to hold average growth over 1970–88 to only 2.4 percent.

As of the late 1960s, inequality was a little lower than in most other Latin American countries, albeit significantly greater than in Argentina. Since 1973 the economy has undergone the most radical "reforms" of any Latin nation. The income distribution data for greater Santiago suggest that there may have been a slight worsening trend prior to the Allende years, when a sharp improvement occurred; by 1976 household inequality had reached a level both markedly worse than before the Allende government and no longer superior to the levels observed in most other Latin countries. Paradoxically, the data on distribution among income recipients, while showing the same cycle as for the household distribution, do not indicate that the level of inequality was greater in the late 1970s than in 1970. This anomaly, still to be fully explained, does not greatly diminish the likelihood that household distribution did worsen significantly. Certainly a number of the policy steps taken by the Pinochet regime would be expected to foster inequality under the conditions of the Chilean economy.

The extensive privatization, mainly carried out during the severe recession of 1972–74, led to acute concentration of ownership and the formation of large conglomerates (Meller, 1989, pp. 24–25). Curtailment of agricultural credit to small farmers led to land concentration as well. Preferential financing to small entrepreneurs was also cut back. Perhaps most important was the reform of the labor legislation, which relaxed worker dismissal regulations, suspended unions (to 1979, when they were again authorized to operate, but with many restrictions), greatly reduced the social security tax paid by the employers, and reduced other nonwage costs as well. After the second crisis (1981–83), wage indexation was abolished, replaced by a real wage "floor," specified to be the real wage prevailing in 1979. Wealth and capital gains taxes were eliminated, profit tax rates substantially reduced, and public employment greatly cut back. Unemployment rates rose to unprecedented levels in the neighborhood of 25 percent. Although the ratio of real wages to per capita income or per capita absorption was sharply lower in the immediate post-Allende years than in 1970, it did not remain systematically lower in later years, even though household distribution seemed to have changed discretely for the worse. As distinct from the case of Argentina, the pain and poverty through which these reforms undoubtedly forced many Chilean families to go has at least been followed by a period of sustained growth from 1984 on, such that GDP per capita in 1989 had risen by 27 percent to surpass its 1980 level by 10 percent.

Some estimates indicate a dramatic increase in poverty between 1970 and the early 1980s in Chile; thus Meller reports an increase from 17 percent in 1970 to 45 percent in 1985 with poverty lines not more than 6 percent apart. While this may somewhat exaggerate the trend, it is true that both per capita income and per capita absorption were about 20 percent lower in the latter year and that the share of the bottom quintile or two of the distribution of income among households had fallen by about 10–15 percent. The increase in poverty was due importantly to both the decline in average income and the worsening of its distribution. The high incidence of television sets (over 70 percent), refrigerators (49 percent), radios (83 percent), and bathrooms (74 percent), even in the lowest quintile, throws some question on the 45 percent figure, though it is true that some of these items probably became much more prevalent owing to the low prices that came with the import liberalization around 1980.

Another special and interesting feature of the Chilean experience was the combination of make-work policies for low-income groups and targeted poverty redressal, which seems to have helped to limit the most serious poverty impacts of the negative income trends just discussed.

Costa Rica

Costa Rica brought a tradition of social and political stability to the trials of the 1980s, and came off a strong postwar economic performance in which average GDP growth exceeded 6 percent over 1950–80. A good social service system gave the country the highest life expectancy in Latin America, with the possible exception of Cuba, and the absence of an army saved it money. Growth in the 1970s was fragile, however. Threatened by recession after the oil price hike of 1973, the government pursued an expansionary monetary and fiscal policy that did work in the sense of restoring growth (aided by the fortuitous increase in coffee prices in 1976–77 and the continued high share of investment financed by foreign savings), but which also caused a serious buildup of foreign debt and facilitated a continued expansion of public-sector employment (Gindling and Berry, 1991). The second oil price hike, rising interest rates, and the world recession brought a sharp 14 percent decline in GDP over 1980–82, a 23 percent fall in income per capita, and a 25 percent cut in real wages.

At the depths of the trough a new president with ties to labor and (through his party) to previous social legislation took office, buoyed by a high level of public support and confidence. Over the next few years a strong adjustment program was put in place, including tax increases, weakening of the power of unions (union strength had lain mainly in the public sector), privatization, and incentives for exports, especially nontraditional ones. It has been relatively successful in reestablishing a decent growth performance. Policy changes were less extreme, more gradual, and less erratic than in Chile, and much more successful than in Argentina.

In contrast to both those cases (especially Chile), real wages did not long remain low, as the indexing mechanism that linked nominal wage increases to past inflation was left in place with only mild modification, so that when tightened monetary and fiscal policy brought inflation quickly to heel, real wages moved back to or near their previous peak in only three or four years. The national unemployment rate also moved quickly back to its normal range around 5 percent. Income distribution, less unequal than in most Latin countries, does not appear to have altered significantly in the course of the crisis, though there is some possibility that some concentration has occurred in the subsequent recovery. Overall, however, this must be counted one of the most successful adjustment performances in the region, in the sense of reestablishing growth without a sustained higher level of poverty than before.

Colombia

Colombia has a special place in this discussion as the one Latin country where a fair case can be made that distribution has improved over the last couple of decades. Londoño's (1989) detailed analysis suggests a marked decline in the Gini coefficient between 1971 and 1978, from 0.532 to 0.481 and essentially no change from then until 1988, when the figure stood at 0.476. [4] If these figures present a reasonably accurate picture, they suggest an experience somewhat similar to that in neighboring Venezuela in that distribution improved during the years of fast income growth in the 1970s, then stabilized during the slowdown (in the case of Colombia) or decline (in the case of Venezuela) in the 1980s (Berry, 1990b).

LESSONS, CHALLENGES, AND IMPLICATIONS FOR THE 1990S

For most countries of Latin America, the 1980s (and in a few cases part of the 1970s) were lost from a growth perspective. Some other indicators of welfare did continue their upward trend from before, albeit more slowly. At the same time, frustrations could only mount, as expectations built up over the course of several decades of good growth were dashed. Several implications and lessons seem to emerge from this very unhappy experience.

1. It is essential to reestablish healthy growth if poverty alleviation is to pick up where it left off in the 1970s. Although no one would argue that the typical Latin pattern of economic expansion with extreme inequality is anywhere close to ideal, growth of that sort is certainly better than no growth at all when it comes to poverty alleviation. It is hoped that more equitable growth can be achieved at some point in the future, but in the meantime growth of any sort must be welcomed. Indeed, the experience of several Latin countries suggests that if growth could continue on its earlier course, distribution might fairly soon improve. A positive trend appears to have taken shape during the 1970s in Venezuela and Colombia, and the sharp increase of unskilled real wages in Brazil during the "economic miracle" of the late 1960s and early 1970s similarly suggests that fast growth may have a large "trickle-down" at the stages where these economies now find themselves. One tempting hypothesis is that several of them are approximately at a "turning point" to labor scarcity; every year that their achieving that point is delayed by weak macroeconomic performance can have a heavy cost in terms of poverty not alleviated. If such a labor-market-based interpretation of improvements in income distribution is valid, it becomes evident that the slowing of population growth remains a matter of high priority, even though its impact on distribution is delayed. Although considerable advance has been made in this direction, the economic slowdown has raised the premium on further reduction in the growth of population. To the extent that rising levels of education remain a major factor in slowing population growth, the continuing advances in that field of social development are to be applauded, not only for the other benefits they bring but also for their contribution along these lines.

2. The at-the-time reasonable confidence with which Latin American leaders viewed the future of their countries ten or so years ago has of course evaporated in the trauma of the last decade. It is no longer defensible to assume that growth will by itself reduce poverty at an adequate rate. Poverty redressal and income support systems must be studied with care and implemented where promising. The above-cited Chilean programs made an important difference in that country; several other countries have made interesting innovations in recent years, ones that deserve close attention and in some cases replication elsewhere. The evidence on the inefficiency, at least from the perspective of poverty alleviation, of "social" expenditures in Brazil could probably be repli-

cated in most of the other countries; the message is that it is not necessary to greatly increase spending in this area to achieve much more favorable outcomes.

3. The economic crises from which the countries are trying to extricate themselves have, partly via pressure from international agencies and creditors and partly from changes in their own perceptions of what policies are needed, led to a series of trade policy "reforms" to achieve greater outward orientation and success in the international market, privatization to improve productivity and cut fiscal deficits, and decreased government controls in the financial markets to raise savings and improve resource allocation. In none of these cases are the income distribution implications clear on the basis of theory or prior empirical work. But there is plenty of scope for their application to occur in such a way as to have negative impacts, as was noted in the case of the privatization program in Chile during the 1970s. Clearly it will be a challenge both to design and to carry out necessary reforms in such a way as not to have significantly perverse effects on income distribution. The record in Costa Rica is encouraging in this regard. Severe steps were taken and union power was reined in, but existing wage-setting institutions prevented the drop in the real wage from lasting. If the severe wage repression that has taken place in Chile has had a positive impact of economic performance, it is not apparent in a comparison of the records in Chile and Costa Rica.

4. An important consideration when the labor market is slack due to poor macroeconomic performance is that the employment- and income-generating potential of the small- to medium-scale sector of the economy be fully taken advantage of. Some progress has been made with respect to the microenterprise or informal sector, with the concerned assistance of nongovernmental organizations of both national and international origin. Less attention has been directed to the fairly small but not microlevel firms; there is some concern that the policy reforms will be applied in ways not conducive to the success of this group, whose potential is little understood and whose interests receive very little attention from the key policymakers in most countries of the region.

5. Latin America has seen a considerable shift toward democratic regimes and the correspondingly greater public participation during the last couple of decades. While this is a source of much hope, the need for more openness, more accountability, and recognition of the interests of a wider range of economic groups has tested and will test the political acumen of national leaders; it is not surprising that some of their concessions to group interests seriously hamper growth, worsen distribution (often in less than obvious ways), or both. The experience of Argentina since the early 1970s fits broadly into this category; although the government was not democratic for most of this period, its attempts to reconcile the demands/interests of labor and of other groups turned out to be severely counterproductive.

6. The "real story" of how the trauma of these past years has affected distribution in Latin America and whether it will leave a permanent imprint on that

distribution in the future cannot be told or assessed until there are better data on the distribution of capital incomes. It is conceivable, though not likely in my own judgment, that the capital share has risen regionwide by enough to suggest worsening distribution in nearly all of the countries. This issue has obviously become one of high research priority.

NOTES

1. Altimir (1987, p. 154) has made systematic adjustments to the available data for several countries to achieve maximum comparability, and he reports a much lower level of inequality for Venezuela than for the other four countries for which evidence is presented.

2. Although figures are not available for all of the countries in Table 6.1, data on per capita incomes and reasonably firm evidence on distribution make it highly unlikely that in any of the missing cases poverty incidence would be under 40 percent.

3. As traditionally measured by the decile distribution of private income among household units, ranked either by total household income or by household income per capita.

4. In this Colombian case a complicating factor is the presumed failure of the figures to pick up most of the income generated in the illegal drug trade. Its inclusion would probably raise the estimated inequality somewhat.

REFERENCES

Altimir, Oscar (1982). *The Extent of Poverty in Latin America*. World Bank Staff Working Paper. Washington, D.C.: The World Bank.

————. (1987). "Income Distribution Statistics in Latin America and Their Reliability". *Review of Income and Wealth*, Series 33, no. 2, (June).

Berry, Albert (1983). "Predicting Income Distribution in Latin America During the 1980s." In Archibald R. M. Ritter and David H. Pollock (eds.), *Latin American Prospects for the 1980s: Equity, Democratization and Development*. New York: Praeger.

————. (1990a). "Economic Performance, Income Distribution, and Poverty in Latin America: The Experience of the 1980s," Mimeo, University of Toronto.

————. (1990b). "The Effects of Stabilization and Adjustment on Poverty and Income Distribution: Aspects of the Latin American Experience," Mimeo, University of Toronto.

Comisión Económica Para America Latina y el Caribe (CEPAL) (1990). *Magnitud de la Pobreza en America Latina en los Años Ochenta*. Santiago, Chile: CEPAL.

Denslow, David Jr. and William G. Tyler (1984). "Perspectives on Poverty and Income Distribution in Brazil." *World Development*, 12, pp. 1019–1028.

Economic Commission for Latin America and the Caribbean (ECLAC) (1989). *Yearbook of Latin American Statistics, 1989*. Santiago, Chile.

Felix, David, and John P. Caskey (1989). *Baker to Brady to Chance? Tinkering With the Latin American Debt Crisis*. Washington University Economics Department, Working Paper No. 140.

Fox, Louise and Samuel Morley (1990). "Who Paid the Bill? The Impact of Brazil's

Macroeconomic Policies on Poverty in the 1980s." World Bank background paper to the *World Development Report 1990*.

Gindling, Timothy H. and Albert Berry (1991). "Labor Markets and Adjustment in Costa Rica." In Dipak Mazumdar and Ravi Kanbur (eds.), *Labor Markets in an Era of Adjustment*. Washington, D.C.: World Bank.

Hoffmann, Rodolfo (1989a). "Evolucao da Distribucao da Renda no Brasil, entre pessaos e entre familias, 1978-86." In Gulherme Luis Sedlacek and Ricardo Paes de Barros (eds.), *Mercado de Trabalhoe e Distribucao da Renda*. Vina Coletanea.

———. (1989b). "A distribucao da renda no Brasil em 1985, 1986 e 1987." *Revista de Economia Politica*, 9, no. 2, (April–June), pp. 122–126.

Kakwani, Manek (1980). *Income Inequality and Poverty: Methods of Estimation and Policy Implications*. New York: Oxford University Press.

Kuznets, Simon (1955). "Economic Growth and Inequality." *American Economic Review*, 45, no. 1 (March).

Lecaillon, Jacques et al. (1984). *Income Distribution and Economic Development: An Analytical Survey*. Geneva: International Labour Office.

Londoño, Juan Luis (1989). *Income Distribution in Colombia 1971–88: Basic Estimation*. Report to the World Bank.

McGreevey, William et al. (1988). *Brazil: Public Spending on Social Programs: Issues and Options*. World Bank Report 3 7086-BR.

Meller, Patricio (1989). "Economic Adjustment and its Distributive Impact: Chile in the 1980s." Mimeo. Santiago, Chile: CIEPLAN.

Molina, Sergio (1982). "Poverty: Description and Analysis of Policies for Overcoming It." *CEPAL Review*, No. 18.

Sanchez, Carlos (1989). "Labor Markets in an Era of Adjustment: Argentina." Cordoba: IEERAL, Fundacion Mediterranea. Mimeo.

Summers, Robert, and Alan Heston (1984). "Improved International Comparisons of Real Product and its Composition: 1950–1980." *Review of Income and Wealth*, 30, no. 2, (June), pp. 207–262. World Bank (1990). *World Development Report, 1990*. New York: Oxford University Press.

CHAPTER SEVEN

Brazilian Amazonia: From Destruction to Sustainable Development?

ROLF WESCHE AND MICHAEL SMALL

"Decade of Destruction" is the apt title of Adrian Cowell's series of documentaries that portrays the environmental decay and related social problems in Brazilian Amazonia in the 1980s. During this decade the cleared area increased from 2.5 percent to more than 10 percent (Fearnside, 1990; Mahar, 1989) of Legal Amazonia (see Figure 7.1). The image of accelerating destruction obscures, however, substantial contextual and policy changes during the 1980s, particularly since Brazil's return to democracy in 1985. A retrospect in 2000 will likely reveal that the 1980s saw both the peak of a largely destructive process unleashed by military governments since 1964 and the beginning of a new mode of pragmatism and moderation that could keep the larger part of the Amazon forest intact well into the twenty-first century.

The general nature and implications of the post-1964 mode of Amazonian "development" have been widely examined (e.g., Binswanger, 1987; Branford and Glock, 1985; Bunker, 1985; Hecht and Cockburn, 1989; Mahar, 1979, 1989) and are increasingly part of popular knowledge. Generally the forest has been burned after highly selective extraction of lumber and replaced with low-grade pasture or short-lived crop agriculture. Large numbers of Amazonian *caboclos* (the Portuguese-speaking peasantry derived from earlier labor imports, racial mixing, and acculturation [Parker, 1985]) and native Indians were displaced, if not decimated. With them declined their environmental know-how. Soil decay, water pollution (mainly due to placer gold mining), air pollution from burning, changed rainfall regimes, and flooding are increasingly observed

Figure 7.1
Legal Amazonia

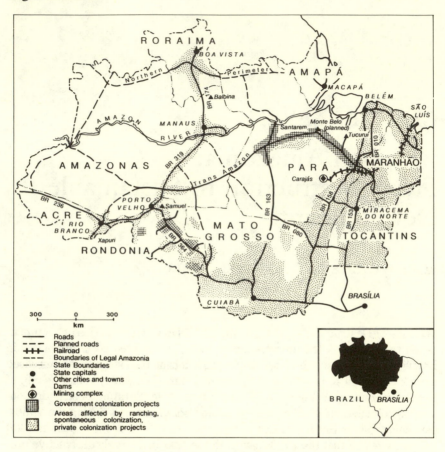

at local and regional levels. The impact on global warming and rainfall regimes is beyond doubt.

At the surface level the causes of destruction are readily identified. On the one hand, population growth, poverty, and speculative entrepreneurial greed propel the rush to the frontier. On the other hand, typical conditions during the pioneer stage of settlement frontiers in market economies normally produce extensive, disorderly, and relatively destructive land use. These conditions include cheap and abundant land; high risk; competitive disadvantage in remote external markets and limited local demand; the underdeveloped state of infrastructure, services, and public administration, and inadequate adaptation of settlers and available technology. In the case of the Amazon, early frontier problems are compounded by predominantly poor soils and a difficult, fragile environment.

However, a fuller understanding of the forces that have shaped and will shape Brazil's approach to the Amazon requires a political perspective. Accordingly, this review is organized in three parts. The first selectively synthesizes the major forces that distorted Amazonia's resource development during the military regime (1964–85) whose legacy continues, as does the military's influence in Amazonian development. It seeks to explain why the process of Amazonian "development" has been so abnormally destructive. The second part identifies promising new departures toward more rational resource use that were initiated or took shape during the Sarney administration (1985–90). A speculative final part attempts to forecast the challenges for the future of Amazonia faced by the Collor government.

THE MILITARY GOVERNMENTS (1964–85): OPERATION AMAZONIA

The Amazon has witnessed several historical cycles of occupation that failed to integrate it effectively into Brazil. The current cycle took shape as the project of a series of military governments, mainly allied with South-Central Brazilian business interests, which took power, and effectively increased the power of the national government, in 1964.

It was formally unveiled as "Operation Amazonia" on December 3, 1966, in essence a federal government-led occupation, along military lines, of the country's seemingly "empty" resource periphery. Conveniently downplayed was the fact that the Amazon was already largely occupied by caboclos, as well as a less-numerous Indian population.

The stage of the post–1964 occupation was "Legal Amazonia" (Fig. 7.1), a planning region favored with regional development incentives that had already been outlined before the advent of military government. It comprises almost 60 percent of Brazil, including the Amazon rainforest proper, as well as open forests (*cerradao*) and savannas (*cerrado*), which are mainly located on the region's southern and eastern fringe.

An understanding of the nature of the occupation process is best reached through the explicit as well as implicit objectives that guided government action. These can be grouped in three broad and overlapping categories: geopolitical, economic, and social.

The Geopolitical Imperative

An overarching geopolitical vision for Amazonia (e.g., Silva, 1967; Meira Matos, 1980) was natural for generals ruling a nation with a tradition of manifest destiny. The urgency of strategic occupation by friendly forces, mainly modern South-Central Brazilian enterprises and secondarily homesteaders, to counter external and internal threats to national sovereignty in the Amazon became the rationale of Operation Amazonia. This rationale had some historical foundation (Hecht and Cockburn, 1989) but limited current plausibility, particularly because the military government soon proved open to multinational investment, and because it could identify only a small guerilla movement in Northern Goias (now Tocantins, Figure 7.1) and Indian populations of questioned loyalty as internal threats.

Doubtlessly more important was the unstated objective of opening up the continental interior in order to project influence over Brazil's lesser neighbors. Furthermore, the generals saw the conquest of the Amazon as a vehicle to legitimize the military government, as a symbol of the nation's march toward world power status around which to galvanize the national self-confidence and entrepreneurial spirit, and as a target onto which to deflect the nation's attention from pressing internal problems.

It is evident that this amalgam of largely intangible objectives was not compatible with conventional cost-benefit analysis of public expenditures in the Amazon. Nor was there scope for serious public debate of the Amazon venture under a dictatorship that suppressed the internal opposition while portraying foreign criticism as a challenge to national sovereignty, and that promoted its chauvinist futuristic vision of the Amazon through an astute media campaign.

This context, combined with easily available international funding and a booming economy during the period of the "Brazilian miracle," led to the premature expansion of the Amazon frontier. It occurred well before earlier frontiers to the south and east had been effectively integrated, let alone developed. It also encouraged a relatively dispersed, geostrategic occupation of space, rather than the systematic, deliberate, contiguous advance and consolidation of the frontier.

A far-flung, low-quality road network, intended to reach the international boundaries, became the main instrument in the occupation of the Amazon. It exposed large areas of the Amazon to speculators and settlers well before the preconditions of intensive resource use existed. Among the roads, those providing a link to the country's South-Central core area (i.e., BRs 153, 158, 165 and 364 [see Figure 7.1]) proved most important as economic and settlement corridors. The Trans-Amazon Highway, intended to drain the population surplus of the Northeast and eventually to link the Atlantic with the Pacific, met neither objective. The Northern Perimeter Highway, which was to establish a *cordon sanitaire* of settlers along the international boundaries, remained largely incomplete.

The Economic Imperative

An economic imperative was intertwined with the foregoing geopolitical considerations: the bulk of Amazonia's resources were to be allocated in large properties to modern, South-Central Brazilian enterprises, which were to play the leading role in the region's economic development. A lavish set of fiscal incentives (i.e., tax write-offs) was devised to promote this objective under the direction of SUDAM, the Amazon regional development agency, and BASA, the Amazon regional development bank. Economic policy was increasingly influenced by the São Paulo-based Association of Amazon Entrepreneurs (Pompermayer, 1979, 1984). Among its members, Brazil's major construction companies were key promoters and beneficiaries of infrastructure projects in the Amazon. Besides roads, these projects notably included the Carajas mining and railroad complex (Hall, 1989) and the Tucuruí, Balbina, and Samuel hydropower dams (see Figure 7.1).

The heady combination of cheap land, generous subsidies, and expectations of rapidly advancing infrastructure induced large enterprises to rush into land development. They soon learned that extensive ranching, marginally profitable if not subsidized, was the most practical instrument to implant de facto ownership and to access fiscal incentives in anticipation of speculative gains and an improving environment for modern growth (Hecht, 1985). Large ranches became the main destroyers of the Amazon forest.

The Social Safety Valve

A third major objective, propagandized during the Medici administration (1970–74) under the slogan "lands without men to men without land," was the use of Amazonia as social safety valve. The military had come to power in a climate of agitation for land reform and had passed a progressive agrarian reform law in 1964. Rather than implementing the law, however, the government was encouraging an unprecedented expansion of large property in the Amazon. Incongruously, Amazonia also was to serve as a substitute for land reform through colonization projects directed by INCRA, the National Institute of Colonization and Agrarian Reform.

These projects were supposedly designed to create a class of capitalist family farmers on standard 100-hectare lots. Initially targeted for the rural surplus population of the traditional Northeast, which in 1970 suffered one of its recurring droughts, it was targeted again in 1972 to encompass migrants displaced by agricultural modernization and land concentration in South-Central Brazil.

The government's invitation to both big enterprise and rural surplus population was uttered in a highly ambiguous land tenure context. Not only was the government inconsistent in its own position regarding the land tenure issue, it furthermore failed to clarify the preexisting tenure structure in Amazonia before opening the floodgates to new settlers.

Government-directed colonies were primarily established in Rondônia, Pará and along the Trans-Amazon Highway. Ultimately they accommodated only a minority of settlers, mainly owing to funding shortfalls and faltering government commitment. Private colonization schemes became increasingly important as a substitute. For the majority of migrants, however, squatting on unused public and private lands was the only available outlet other than joining the landless in a land dominated by large landowners.

Recipe for Destruction

Combined, the objectives and policies outlined above proved a recipe for destruction. Hastily conceived and imposed in pursuit of national priorities rather than addressing regional needs, they vastly accelerated and magnified a wasteful frontier occupation process that had already started when the military assumed power.

In this process large areas, once under the sustainable use of native Amazonians, were transferred to the destructive approach of newcomers. The spatial overextension and discontinuity of the frontier accentuated the constraints and resource-wasting consequences associated with the pioneer stage of frontier development. In the case of large enterprise, artificial subsidies compounded the problem by stimulating land clearing for pasture. Inadequate government support for the majority of small farmers encouraged shifting cultivation and conversion to pasture.

Worst of all, land tenure confusion and the government's inconsistent stance regarding the land tenure issue contributed to a veritable land war in which the clearing of forest serves as the tool with which to assert property claims, displace the opponent by removing his livelihood, or, in the case of the squatter, to wrest compensation from the encroaching "landlord."

This selective review of forces leading toward destruction does not intend to suggest that the military government failed to implement constructive measures aimed at controlling the process. It did from the beginning, and increasingly as the evidence of destruction mounted. These measures included a stipulation that 50 percent of each property remain under forest, gradual regularization of land tenure and delimitation of Indian and forest reserves be maintained, as well as a reduction of the fiscal incentives program. In general, however, remedial measures were poorly funded, implemented in lackluster fashion, and occasionally counterproductive. Nor did they frontally challenge the essence of the development model that had unleashed a process running largely out of control.

THE SARNEY GOVERNMENT (1985–90): SHIFTING GEARS

When José Sarney took office on March 15, 1985, as the first civilian president of the new republic, Amazonian development rated close to the bottom of his priorities. By the time he left power five years later, it had become one of the "hottest" issues, domestically and internationally, on the Brazilian government's agenda. Over this five-year period—slowly at first but then picking up speed by late 1988—there was a rapid change in the gears in Brazil's Amazonian policy.

Military Occupation of the Amazonian Borders

The Sarney government's first Amazonian policy was a refinement and continuation of the geopolitical "Operation Amazonia" model inherited from the military regime. Known as Calha Norte, or the Northern Watersheds project, it was launched in September 1985, under the direction of the National Security Council, attached to the presidency. Formally, Calha Norte consisted of a program to build a series of forward bases along Brazil's sparsely populated northern borders with Colombia, Venezuela, Guyana, and Surinam. Under Calha Norte, the military had a coordinating role for the delivery of all government services and agencies operating within the *faixa de fronteira*—a 150 kilometer strip back from the border.

Closely linked to Calha Norte was a new land demarcation policy of the federal Indian agency (FUNAI), intended to create "indigenous colonies" that restricted Indians' exclusive rights to small "colonies" around their existing areas of settlement—opening up wider areas of traditional land to other uses, for example, by classifying them as "National Forests." This policy, as formulated by the National Security Council, which approved all Indian land claims, implicitly involved a bargain. More "acculturated" Indians would be "liberated from FUNAI's tutelage" by being granted access to a wider range of government services, if they relinquished the extensive land claims based on the need to protect their traditional life-styles. Less acculturated Indians would have their land demarcated in larger traditional reserves, but the only public services they would receive would be channelled through FUNAI. Significantly, the first region where this policy was implemented was with the Tikuna tribe near the Calha Norte post at São Gabriel de Cachoeira, in a region with major proven mineral reserves. Critics of Calha Norte from the church and the civilian Left accused the government of using both programs as means of opening up land for new colonization projects along the Amazon frontier—a goal that, if actually held, was still unrealized by the end of the Sarney administration.

Calha Norte exemplified the way in which Amazonian policy for the Sarney government remained: fundamentally a security issue over which the military retained its control. In the traditional vision of the Brazilian military, the ultimate goal of security policy is to increase national strength through economic and social development. Thus the ability of the state to maintain control over technology and natural resources, as well as over its territory, are important security issues. Under the Sarney regime, the principal guardian of the government's security policy was the National Security Council—a council of economic and military ministers, presided over by the chief of the president's Military Cabinet, General Bayma Denys. The secretariat of the Council was the most powerful policy-setting body in the government. Attached directly to the presidential palace, and with a majority of its roughly 400-person staff as military officers, the Council operated under conditions of military secrecy. Significantly, when the Council was reformed under the 1988 constitution, and renamed as the Council of National Defense (or SADEN), the government successfully lobbied in Congress to give it a constitutional mandate to "propose criteria for the preservation and exploitation of all types of natural resources"; and to "propose criteria for the use of all areas considered indispensable to national security, especially the *faixa de fronteira,* 150 kilometres around the nation's borders" (Constitution of Brazil, 1988, Article 91).

The Environmental Movement

However, three new forces emerged after 1985 that began to exert growing pressure against the Sarney government's Amazonian policy. The first was a national environmental movement that arose under the conditions of democracy. This movement had many different personalities and agendas but, broadly speaking, it broke down into environmental NGOs (nongovernment organizations) based in the cities of South-Central Brazil; Indian-rights NGOs, both religious and secular, again based in São Paulo, Rio, or Brasília, but with field offices in a number of Amazonian cities; and the various rural workers' unions representing small farmers, and particularly rubber tappers, from municipalities at the frontier of development in Pará, Amazonas, Rondônia, and Acre. The National Council of Rubber Tappers, based in Rio Branco, the capital of Acre (see Figure 7.1), served to connect many of these unions. At the beginning of the Sarney administration, these subgroups formed part of a broad coalition of popular movements from "civil society," which sought to use Brazil's newly restored democratic institutions to recoup the losses of the preceding 21 years of military rule.

The 19-month exercise of drafting Brazil's new constitution, from March 1987 to September 1988, gave every economic interest group in the country a chance to entrench its own privileges, or overturn those of their competitors. Ranching interests did well in emasculating the text of the land reform provisions in the constitution—in part due to very effective lobbying by the right-wing UDR (Democratic Rural Union), which represented many large rural landowners. This was a major blow to the "progressive forces" in the Assembly from the left wing of the PMDB (Brazilian Democratic Movement Party) and the PT (Workers' Party), which placed land reform at the top of their constitutional agenda.

Surprisingly, two of the most successful issues on the "progressive agenda" for the constitution were the rights of Brazil's Indians and the protection of the environment. In the former case, the coalition of pro-Indian NGOs used the active support of the Catholic Church to build coalitions with right-wing congressmen to draft a clause giving broad constitutional recognition to Indians' traditional land rights, and defeating the government's attempts to entrench a distinction between the rights of acculturated and unacculturated Indians. In the case of the environment, a multiparty "Green coalition" of congressmen, largely from urban areas in the South-East of Brazil, was assembled by Deputy Fabio Feldman. Feldman's political base lay in the São Paulo environmental movement that emerged in the late 1970s in opposition to the building of new nuclear power plants. The environmental chapter of the constitution that was drafted by Feldman established broad public rights to a healthy environment, which could be backed up by civil suits against the state, and identified the Amazonian forest, along with certain other ecosystems, as "national patrimony. The use and development of their natural resources are to be undertaken within conditions, determined by law, that assure the preservation of their environment" (Constitution of Brazil, 1988, Article 225).

While these congressional victories did not change the effective control over Amazonian resources, they demonstrated that the small well-organized lobby groups could use the new powers vested in the Congress to acquire political legitimacy and to create a countervailing source of federal power against the landed regional elites in the Amazon.

Meanwhile, the rubber tapper movement that began under church tutelage in the state of Acre in the mid-1970s found in the mid-1980s a new political strategy, in the concept of "extractive reserves," and a strategist, in the person of Chico Mendes, president of the Sindicato dos Trabalhadores Rurais of Xapuri. The extractive reserve concept applied the idea of a collective traditional land entitlement, taken from the law dealing with Indian land claims, and adapted it to the circumstances of rubber tappers, living in loose communities (known as *seringais*), and working overlapping trails through a jointly exploited area of forest. Chico Mendes, like many of the other *seringueiro* leaders, always considered himself a trade unionist, and was an active member of the PT—a party that otherwise had a slender political base in the Amazon. His particular genius, however, lay in his realization that the rubber tappers could build a broader alliance beyond PT lines in the environmental movement, by portraying extractive reserves as a proven model of sustainable development in the Amazon. He established an informal coalition with Indian rights activists in the Amazon, notably Ailton Krenak of the Union of Indigenous Peoples (UNI), under the rubric of the Alliance of the Forest Peoples. Through his contacts with British and American environmental activists who were documenting the growth of the rubber tapper movement, Mendes was able to find allies far beyond the Amazon.

Fiscal Constraints on Amazonian Development

A second force was the increasing fiscal crisis of the Brazilian state, which eliminated the capital for the past policies of megaproject investment that had fueled the Operation Amazonia phase of development. Brazil entered its protracted debt crisis in late 1982, and its cumulative effect over the rest of the decade was to drastically lower growth rates, increase inflation, reduce both public and private investment, and reduce inflow of foreign investment. The government's infrastructure budget, which had been one of the motors of rapid growth in the 1970s, particularly suffered when the state could no longer borrow freely on foreign capital markets. By the end of the decade, the effects of declining investment in the road network became especially visible in the Amazon, as many of the highways carved out of the forest in the 1970s either broke up into potholes (e.g., the Porto Velho–Manaus Highway) or disappeared in places altogether (e.g., stretches of the Trans-Amazon). Four major infrastructure projects in the Amazon were completed during the Sarney government: the Tucuruí, Balbina, and Samuel hydro dams; and the Carajas mine/ highway/railway complex, but no new projects were begun.

Even more important, the fiscal incentives for cattle ranching in the Amazon administered by SUDAM and the subsidized credit for other types of agriculture offered by the Bank of Brazil and BASA were drastically reduced. The quiet realization that many of the past investment strategies (e.g., the cattle ranching subsidies) had failed to achieve even their own narrowly defined objectives (e.g., creating productive ranches) encouraged central planners in Brasília to eliminate them in the name of economic efficiency. Two of the more important subsidies that encouraged deforestation—below-market agricultural credit and the plantation reforestation incentives program—were both eliminated in 1987 as part of the government's deficit cutting under the Bresser Plan.

The one organization that could have picked up some of the slack in infrastructure investment was the World Bank. But the Bank had a horrendous experience with its first large Amazon development loan, the $455 million Polonoroeste regional development project in Rondônia and Mato Grosso approved in 1981 (Mahar et al., 1981; Price, 1989). The loan was intended to rationalize the pell-mell occupation of Rondônia, which had begun in the early 1970s, principally by promoting the development of perennial tree crops (coffee and cocoa) that would fix small farmers on the plots the government had awarded, thus reducing the rapid cycle of deforestation through slash-and-burn subsistence agriculture. Fifty percent of the loan was allocated to the costs of paving the BR364 highway through the state and expanding a network of feeder roads. By 1985 it became apparent that the project had almost tripled migration into the state; deforestation soared, from just 3 percent in 1980 to 24 percent of Rondônia by 1988 by the World Bank's own estimate (Mahar, 1989). At the same time, the attempt to encourage tree crop agriculture was largely a failure, due to the high risk factor for small farmers compared to the guaranteed returns from deforestation for ranching or land speculation.

These disastrous results were documented in detail in a series of hearings held by the U.S. Senate Committee on Finance, chaired by Senator Robert Kasten and instigated by the Washington-based lobby group, the Environmental Defense Fund. By mid-1985 the World Bank felt compelled to suspend disbursements on the loan, citing the failure of the Brazilian government to complete the demarcation of agreed Indian land and forest reserves and to remove squatters from already demarcated reserves. These conditions were met and the remainder of the loan was disbursed a year later. However, the international environmental NGOs scored a David-versus-Goliath victory through the Kasten hearings, with profound repercussions for the World Bank's public image. While the Bank responded by restructuring and upgrading its weak environmental department, an international network of NGOs launched a standing campaign across many Western countries of closely monitoring the environmental impacts of major Bank projects and lobbying of creditor governments to increase the Bank's accountability. After this experience, the Bank became much more cautious about financing new projects in Brazil with potentially negative environmental impact in the Amazon.

The Rise of Public Awareness

The third force that affected Brazil's Amazon policy was the growing world concern over the disappearance of tropical rain forests and the public "discovery" of the threat of global warming. Brazil's development policies in the Amazon served as a locus for criticism on both of these issues. Throughout the 1980s, international conservation groups began to target their public information campaigns away from protecting individual species and toward protecting entire ecosystems. Tropical forests, which may contain up to 90 percent of all the world's species, were singled out for the greatest attention—and Brazil, which has 30 percent of the world's tropical forest, became a focal point for ecologists' concerns.

However, what turned a slowly rising tide of international public opinion into a flood was the discovery of the impact of Amazonian deforestation on global warming. The long hot summer of 1988 in North America coincided with a wealth of new data from scientists arguing that the earth's temperature had already begun to rise, in response to the enormous increase in man-made release of "greenhouse gases." In June 1988, Alberto Setzer of INPE, the Brazilian Space Research Institute, released the first results of his study of areas burned in the Amazon in 1987. Using data from the American weather satellite NOOA-2, Setzer estimated that 200,000 square kilometers of Legal Amazonia had been burned in 1987, of which 80,000 square kilometers represented newly cleared forest. This estimate was more than triple previous official estimates of annual deforestation rates in the Amazon. More strikingly, Setzer estimated that the CO_2 release from burnings on this scale equaled the entire CO_2 release of the city of São Paulo for the past 34 years. 1990 estimates from World Resources Institute based on Setzer's data showed that deforestation in the Brazilian Amazon in 1987 equaled the entire CO_2 output of the United States through burnings of fossil fuels and cement production. In the words of one of the senior Brazilian Forest Department officials that commissioned Setzer's study, his data had the impact of "a veritable atomic bomb" on public opinion, both inside and outside Brazil.

By the autumn of 1988, the $500 million Second Power Sector loan to Brazil was ready to come before the World Bank's Executive Board. The project was critical, not only for the modernization of the power sector, but for Brazil's overall balance of payments, because the June 1988 commercial bank rescheduling agreement tied part of the "new money" from the private banks to a comparable volume of new World Bank loans to Brazil. Capitalizing on the mounting public concern in Europe and North America over Brazil's management of the Amazon, environmental NGOs in these countries mounted a highly successful public campaign to pressure their Executive Directors to reject the loan. The September joint World Bank/IMF meetings in Berlin were the scene of unprecedented public protests from environmentalists, heavily focused on the Bank's lending record in Brazil.

The Government Respsonse: Nossa Natureza

The risk of foreign NGOs using Brazil's environmental policy in the Amazon to threaten its balance of payments finally prompted the National Defense Council to take decisive action. On October 16, just before his departure on a state visit to Europe and the USSR, President Sarney announced the launching of a major environmental review, to be called Nossa Natureza, "Our Nature." Staff were pulled together from all over the federal government to develop the plan, under the supervision of SADEN. INPE was asked to do a major new baseline survey of deforestation in the Amazon.

In addition, the weak and competing former Environment Secretariat (SEMA) and the Forestry Institute (IBDF) were combined, along with two smaller units, to produce a unified environmental agency—IBAMA, nominally under the Ministry of Interior but operating with financial autonomy under the leadership of Sarney's former press spokesman Fernando Mesquita.

Throughout the spring of 1989, international media scrutiny of Brazil's Amazon policies became more intense. The assassination of Chico Mendes on December 22, 1988, by local cattle ranchers in his home in Xapuri received worldwide publicity. President Sarney announced that the Bush administration had tried to persuade the Japanese government not to finance the paving of an extension of the BR364 across Acre—in the absence of concrete evidence that the Japanese were intending to fund such a project in the first place. Sarney also fulminated publicly against the suggestion that Brazil could accept any form of "debt-for-nature" swap that might infringe its sovereign control over the Amazon. A group of Kayapo Indians, led by young chief Paulinho Payakan, staged a media spectacle in the small Amazonian town of Altamira against plans to build a major new dam on the lower Xingu River (to be financed in part by the Second Power Sector loan). Altamira attracted over a thousand Brazilian and international media representatives and celebrities in a mass demonstration of support for these new-found "guardians of the rain forest." Meanwhile, the World Bank's Power Sector loan quietly foundered, owing to an insuperable disagreement between Brazil and the Bank over Brazil's insistence that its nuclear power program be included in the sector loan.

Finally on April 6, the results of Nossa Natureza were released in a major press conference in Brasília by President Sarney as an indigestible package of 54 separate administrative decrees, draft laws, and interministerial memoranda—which then took weeks to be published and ultimately another three months to be passed in Congress. Nossa Natureza effectively achieved its main purpose—which was to signal a change of course in Brazil's Amazonian policy and to stifle foreign criticism. Its actual policy impact was more muted. Its most publicized accomplishment was to end all remaining fiscal incentives for cattle ranching administered by SUDAM. A second result was to initiate a process of macroeconomic zoning for the Amazon, in order to allocate Brazil's future development efforts rationally, by dividing the region up into 28 subunits based on watersheds and municipal boundaries. Other measures created six new national parks, banned the export of round logs, restricted the legal use of fire to clear land, licensed chain saws, and required forest landowners to register separately the size of the 50 percent reserve of forest they were required by law to maintain on their land.

In hindsight, the importance of Nossa Natureza lies not in its actual measures but in the official diagnoses of the failures of past Amazonian policy contained in its main policy document. The main conclusions drawn by its architects and endorsed by SADEN were that:

1. The government-led occupation of Amazonia since the 1960s had been disorganized, conducted without any understanding of how to exploit the natural resources of the region, and consequently had been destructive to the environment.

2. The "empty spaces" of Amazonia have traditional inhabitants—the Indians and extractive populations—whose interest had been ignored in this occupation process.

3. A strategic decision had to be taken to use the land-reform process and other fiscal measures to reduce the pressures of out-migration from the coastal areas of Brazil and to use the Center-West region, rather than Amazonia, as the catchment area for these populations in the future.

4. In Amazonia there was a clear linkage between the protection of human rights, the peaceful resolution of political conflicts, and the defense of the environment.

5. An incremental process of macro zoning (*ordenação territiorial*) would have to be undertaken to rationalize the existing occupation of Amazonia—without attempting to roll back patterns of occupation that had already emerged.

6. The existing underdeveloped or undeveloped areas of Amazonia should not be exploited at least until more is learned about how to use them rationally as a renewable natural resource; and that at least for the meantime, these areas should remain the domain of existing extractivist populations—rather than the target of new occupation plans.

In effect, Nossa Natureza signaled an official recognition by the Brazilian government of the real "limits to growth" in the Amazon, imposed by the region's ecology, and the political rights of its existing inhabitants. It also represented the high-water mark for environmental initiatives by the Sarney government. By the time the legislation was passed in July, the administration had already descended into a preelectoral state of political paralysis.

In its final months, the only force inside the Sarney government still pushing for environmental reform was Fernando Cesar Mesquita, the new president of IBAMA. In the face of considerable initial scepticism, Mesquita proved himself to be a skilful publicist for the cause of increased environmental protection and he traveled constantly around the country dramatizing the struggle of his department to enforce environmental regulations—particularly those against burning cleared forest land. Mesquita's personal example sought—and obtained—an unprecedented degree of cooperation for the overworked IBAMA inspectors (*fiscais*), from the state and federal police, the military, local fire brigades and even commercial airline pilots. One of his most successful moves was to persuade the government that IBAMA could keep the fines that it levied and funnel them back into further law enforcement. In one week in late August, his newly inspired officers levied over $10 million in fines. Combined with a much wetter "dry season" period, from May through October 1989, these increased enforcement efforts were reckoned to have produced at least a 30 percent drop compared to 1988 in the total area burned in 1989.

The Sarney government's final Amazonian initiative came two days before it left office. After months of internal lobbying on behalf of the rubber tappers by Mesquita, the government made the dramatic announcement that 1.6 million hectares in new extractive reserves in Acre would be decreed *terra devoluta*—including all of the remaining forest land in the municipality of Xapuri—to be named the Chico Mendes Extractivist Reserve. These decrees represented a culmination of ten years of struggle by the rubber tapper movement in Acre—and the beginning of a wholly new set of responsibilities to prove that the extractive reserves they had fought for could work.

CONCLUSION

President Fernando Collor de Mello assumed office on March 15, 1990, and promptly appointed one of Brazil's best-known environmentalists, José Lutzenberger, as his new secretary of environment. The Collor government and its successors now face a new problematic in the formulation of Amazonian policy. The old "Operation Amazonia" policy of state-sponsored occupation and integration of the region has come to an end. The Sarney government shifted the gears of Amazonian policy from forward to neutral, by ending the deliberate infrastructure subsidies that encouraged new migration into the Amazon, and the fiscal incentives to landowners that encouraged deforestation. Lutzenberger has announced his desire to shift the gears now into reverse—toward a sustainable development strategy for the Amazon.

There are reasons to expect that in the coming decade the process of destructive frontier expansion will be slowed. First, the areas on the southern and eastern periphery of Legal Amazonia, dominated by open forest and savannah that are best suited to agricultural settlement, are already largely occupied or claimed. These areas have the best market access, contain patches of good soils, and have a strongly seasonal climate that facilitates burning and modern agriculture. In these areas, modern agriculture is starting to consolidate and will absorb most of the future public investment in support of Amazonian agriculture. By contrast there has been a notably decreased enthusiasm for agricultural development in the rain forest proper on the part of the government, entrepreneurs, and settlers.

Second, the economic choices for future infrastructure investment in the Amazon are now clearer, on the basis of experience and information on the region's natural resource endowment. Generally, they favor spatially selective investment in support of mineral and hydropower development. Spatial selectivity will continue to be reinforced by funding constraints.

Third, the constitutional and legislative reforms that occurred in the last half of the Sarney administration, and the creation of an environmental alliance within Brazil with strong international links, will exercise a countervailing force against further deliberate destruction of the Amazonian forest.

The most pressing challenge for the Amazon policy of the new Collor government will be to find a development strategy for forest lands in the Amazon that offers sound economic reasons to keep the land under forest cover. No amount of land use regulations from Brasília, backed up by macro zoning plans, will have any impact if the owners of the forest see no long-term value in keeping the land that way. The only model so far developed to address this challenge is the concept of extractive reserves—and its economic viability has yet to be proven in practice (Hecht and Schwartzman, 1989). Extractivist models will have to be developed for the extensive zones of Amazonian forest without rich concentrations of rubber or Brazil nuts and for other rural populations besides rubber tappers. Various strategies of agroforestry and selective sustained yield logging would seem to yield the most promising results. The challenge will be to develop strategies that the large absentee landowners as well as small subsistence colonists will be motivated to pursue. Although the events of the last five years have given Amazonia's traditional inhabitants new official respect and a new political voice, they will most likely continue to be minority shareholders of the land in Amazonia.

NOTE

Much of the information contained in the section on the Sarney government is based on private conversations in Brazil from 1986 to 1989 between Michael Small and, in particular, the following individuals: Mary Allegretti, Sergio Amaral, General Bayma Denys, Philip Fearnside, Steve Schwartzman, Fabio Feldman, Willem Groeneveld, Susanna Hecht, Richard House, Maritta Koch-Weser, Jose Carlos Libanio, Peter May, Francisco (Chico) Mendes, Brent Millikan, Juan de Onis, Luciano Pizzato, Alberto Setzer, and Carlos Alfredo Texeira.

REFERENCES

Binswanger, H. P. (1987). Report ARU 69, "Fiscal and Legal Incentives with Environ-
    mental Effects on the Brazilian Amazon." Washington, D.C.: World Bank.
Branford, S. and Glock, O. (1985). *The Last Frontier: Fighting Over Land in the Ama-
    zon*. London: Zed Books.
Bunker, S. G. (1985). *Underdeveloping the Amazon: Extraction, Unequal Exchange,
    and the Failure of the Modern State*. Urbana: University of Illinois Press.
Fearnside, P. M. (1990). "Deforestation in the Brazilian Amazonia." In G. M. Wood-
    well, (ed.), *The Earth in Transition: Patterns and Processes of Biotic Impover-
    ishment*. New York: Cambridge University Press.
Hall, A. (1989). *Developing Amazonia: Deforestation and Social Conflict in Brazil's
    Carajas Programme*. Manchester: Manchester University Press.
Hecht, S. (1985). "Environment, Development and Politics: Capital Accumulation and
    the Livestock Sector in Eastern Amazonia." *World Development* 13, no. 6, pp.
    663–684.
Hecht, S. and Cockburn, A. (1989). *The Fate of the Forest: Developers, Destroyers and
    Defenders of the Amazon*. London: Verso.
Hecht, S. and Schwartzman, S. (1989). "The Good, the Bad and the Ugly: Extractivism,
    Colonist Agriculture and Livestock in Comparative Perspective." Submitted to
    Interciencia.
Mahar, D. J. (1979). *Frontier Development Policy in Brazil: A Study of Amazonia*. New
    York: Praeger.
———. (1989). *Government Policies and Deforestation in Brazil's Amazon Region*.
    Washington, D.C.: World Bank.
Mahar, D. et al. (1981). *Brazil: Integrated Development of the Northwest Frontier*.
    Washington, D.C.: World Bank.
Meira Matos, C. de (1980). *Uma Geopolitica Pan-Amazonica*. Rio de Janeiro: J.
    Olympio.
Parker, E. P. (ed.) (1985). "The Amazon Caboclo: Historical and Contemporary Per-
    spectives." *Studies in Third World Societies*, 32, pp. 1–317.
Pompermayer, M. J. (1979). "The State and the Frontier in Brazil: A Case Study of
    the Amazon." Ph.D. dissertation, Stanford University.
———. (1984). "Strategies of Private Capital in the Brazilian Amazon." In M. Schmink
    and C. Wood (eds.), *Frontier Expansion in Amazonia*. Gainesville: University
    of Florida Press, pp. 419–38.
Price, D. (1989). *Before the Bulldozer*. Cabin John, Md.: Seven Locks Press.
Silva, G. C. (1967). *Geopolitica do Brasil*. Rio de Janeiro: J. Olympio.

CHAPTER EIGHT

Women and Human Rights in Latin America: Challenges for the 1990s?

ELIZABETH SPEHAR

The subject of "women and human rights in Latin America" may require some initial explanation. After all, is it not redundant to speak of *women* and *human* rights? Logically, don't "human rights" already include women as well as men? The answer appears to be "not necessarily."

For some human rights organizations within and outside of Latin America, the term "women and human rights" refers to cases concerning female victims of traditional human rights violations such as illegal detention, disappearance, or torture, or to the particular role of women in the defense of human rights.

For some feminists and the women's groups they work with, the concept of "women and human rights" refers to the specific violations to which women are subjected owing to their very condition as women, and which are not generally included in the scope of traditional human rights concerns. Their position is that current definitions and concepts of "human rights" do not adequately cover women's realities.

In Latin America and around the world, the promotion and defense of human rights and of women's rights have habitually been two separate areas of activity. Human rights organizations such as Amnesty International deal with "classic" human rights abuses, while women's organizations—nongovernmental or governmental bodies—concentrate on the specific needs of women. What is particularly interesting now is the growing recognition among leading feminists and women's groups in Latin America of the need to bring together the issues of "women's rights" and "human rights" in their work. Similarly, some human rights and social NGOs are beginning to review their traditional vision of human rights as it relates to the specific concerns of women.

The apparent willingness of some human rights-related organizations in Latin America to expand their traditional roles to include the specific situation of women and to collaborate with women's groups on such issues, as well as the growing strength and maturity of the women's movement in its promotion of rights, could mean a promising beginning for arriving at a fuller, more comprehensive definition of human rights. Without being overly optimistic about immediate results, such developments increase the chances for a more just response to the needs of all Latin American citizens in the protection and enjoyment of their rights.

In an attempt to explore the above concept, the first section of this chapter will provide a background on the meaning and implications of "women and human rights" from a feminist perspective, as interpreted by some of today's leading Latin and North American feminists. The second section will provide an overview of how women's organizations in Latin America are already working to bring women's "human rights" issues into the political mainstream and to everyday life, with specific examples of their activities and the changes that these groups have helped to bring about or are striving to bring about in different countries. A third section will focus on four examples of Latin American NGOs concerned with the promotion, defense, or education on human rights that have begun to incorporate some aspects of women's rights into their programs. Because the particular organizations reviewed in the third section are all regional NGO networks, their actions have a potential impact on a continental level.

PERSPECTIVES ON "WOMEN AND HUMAN RIGHTS"

In feminist analysis, the explanation for the distinction between "human rights" and "women's rights" is rooted in the nature of our societies. Societies throughout the world are led for the most part by men, a situation that has existed for centuries. Male predominance in almost all spheres of public activity—politics, the formal economy, science, the arts—has meant that women have been "invisible" in the pages of modern history. This has largely been because of women's traditional restriction to the domestic or "private" sphere of life, a situation that is still prevalent in many countries.

The result is that human rights theories and criteria have largely been based on the male model of concerns and needs (Eisler, 1987, p. 297). The utilization of male life-experiences and of the public or political spheres of activity as the bases for most of the international human rights instruments explains why crucial issues such as genital mutilation, sexual slavery, rape, and domestic violence, which overwhelmingly or exclusively affect women, were not included in these instruments.

Although international instruments such as the UN Charter and the International Bill of Human Rights specifically mention gender equality, it is done in fairly general terms. The serious gaps in these instruments with regard to women's rights were eventually recognized by the United Nations and resulted in the adoption by the General Assembly of the Convention on the Elimination of All Forms of Discrimination Against Women in 1979.

In the Americas, as far back as 1923, the Organization of American States (OAS) became the first intergovernmental group that sought to take measures against sexual discrimination. During the OAS fifth International Conference, it was established that all programs discussed at future conferences would have to address the means of abolishing legal and constitutional barriers to women's rights. In the following Conference of 1928, the Inter-American Women's Commission was formed; in 1933, a convention on the nationality of married women was adopted; and in 1948, two additional conventions concerning women's political and civil rights were also adopted (Picado Sotela, 1986, p. 11). Despite this early evolution of women's rights in the region, specific legal and constitutional protection of women's rights has been inadequate in many countries.

In a study on "Women in the World" published in 1986 (Escalante, 1988, pp. 78–79), it was shown that while most Latin American and Caribbean countries (22 out of 30) had constitutional provisions relating to the overall principles of sexual equality, only 13 out of 30 had specific constitutional provisions for equality in the workplace, and only 10 out of 30 had provisions for equality in the realms of marriage and family. It must be added that even when there are laws in place that uphold women's rights, their application or effectiveness is often very limited.

Beyond the governmental sphere, there is also a lack of protection of women's rights by human rights NGOs, since specific issues related to women's human rights are not commonly listed among the concerns of these organizations. This is despite the fact that women have played a major role in human rights movements (this is notable in Latin America), often participating collectively as mothers, daughters, or widows of those whose rights have been violated.

Thus, while practices such as sexual slavery (which is rampant on several continents), rape, and wife-beating are forms of violence as deplorable as those acts routinely denounced by human rights entities, there has been a reluctance to react to these violations in the same way.

In the case of human rights NGOs, the failure to condemn such practices is partially rooted in society's reluctance to "interfere" in the private sphere of the family and the home, where many of these abuses occur. At the same time, few people would argue that human rights organizations are interfering when involved in the "private" or internal matter of a government's treatment of its citizens. In fact, the divine right of kings over their subjects did exist in a number of countries for a long period of history and now is universally rejected (Eisler, 1987, pp. 289–290). In the same way, the right of husbands to use violence against their wives must also be rejected, first explicitly in the conventions and laws and then, most importantly, in practice.

Human rights NGOs are also reluctant to address issues such as genital mutilation, forced marriage, or other issues of women's human rights because of their concerns about interfering with the cultural traditions of certain societies. It suffices, however, to think of other former practices of some ethnic cultures such as cannibalism or slavery to refute such an argument. The reality is also that many of the most fierce opponents of such practices today are women from those very societies (Eisler, 1987, p. 296).

The third, and most fundamental, problem is that of perception: both human rights NGOs and the general public do not appear to consider such violations as being as serious or significant as violations such as disappearances or illegal detentions (Eisler, 1987, p. 307). Yet the fact is that the discrimination suffered by women and the violations they experience have far-reaching and frequently fatal consequences. The lack of a broader perception of rights to include specific women's rights at the same level as more commonly accepted ones is due in part to the conditioning received in a male-oriented society on what is or is not important. A broader perception of human rights will require a new way of thinking about these issues.

For a human rights protection system to be truly valid, the laws, instruments, and practices must take into account both male and female needs and experiences. It must not assume that male requirements for protection are also appropriate for, adaptable to, or are priorities for women. The call is for a *gender* perspective on human rights, one that recognizes that women and men are "equal, but different" (Facio, 1989b, p. 33).

Although thus far this chapter has mentioned some of the more blatantly violent examples of the violation of women's rights, it is important to note that the concept of "women's human rights" as presented and pursued by numerous feminists and women's groups is very comprehensive in its scope. The definition goes beyond the protection of women against overt cases of violence to include such issues as the right to food and shelter, economic rights, rights within the family, educational rights, health and reproductive rights, and so on. Women's specific concerns go far beyond the civil and political rights that seem to be the major preoccupation of traditional human rights organizations (Hosken, 1981, p. 2).

It is also important to emphasize that the question of women and human rights is not only relevant to women. The fact is that the rights of all humankind are inextricably tied up with women's rights. As Fran Hosken (1981, p. 9) of Women's International Network explains, "men can never hope to achieve their own freedom or human rights unless women, on whom they depend for the creation of life, are free." And indeed, not only does the nonrespect of women's human rights undermine the whole principle of respect for all humans, but denying women basic rights—such as adequate education, food, or access to health services—can seriously undermine the chances of survival of future generations (Eisler, 1987, p. 302).

Many of the demands, hopes, and perspectives for women's human rights are embodied in the United Nations Convention on the Elimination of All Forms of Discrimination Against Women, which has been mentioned. It is considered by many Latin American feminists and by feminists around the world to be one of their most important working instruments. In the words of Hosken (1981, p. 6), "there is no doubt that in the international context, this Convention is the single most important document speaking for the human rights of women that has ever been devised."

The Convention embodies principles for the establishment of equality between men and women and the elimination of all discrimination against women based on sex or marital status. It is far-reaching in its measures, in that it addresses the political, social, legal, economic, and cultural spheres of women's lives (Tinker, 1981, p. 33). It also supersedes "all other documents, conventions and declarations" except for those agreements that would be even more effective to achieve equality.

One strength of the Convention is that its ratification by governments implies a legally binding obligation of those states to comply with its measures. One of those measures obliges states parties to amend their constitutions and national legislation to conform to the Convention's principles.

In the preamble, the Convention also identifies the establishment of a New International Order, the eradication of apartheid, racism, colonialism, neocolonialism, and foreign occupation and domination, and the strengthening of international peace and security, including nuclear disarmament, as essential elements for women's and men's equality. It is interesting to note that, while the Convention is explicitly based on the respect of specific rights for women, it also includes such global issues within its list of concerns.

LATIN AMERICAN WOMEN'S GROUPS AND WOMEN'S HUMAN RIGHTS

This chapter has reflected on theory, conventions, and national provisions in relation to the protection (or lack thereof) of women's human rights on a global level. What is more interesting, however, is to see how women's groups are putting theory into practice, challenging conventions and participating in changes to national constitutions and legislation, to uphold women's rights in their countries. This section will deal specifically with the struggles and advances of Latin American women's groups, many of which have a long tradition of working for the greater respect of women's rights in their societies.

Women's groups in Latin America are diverse in composition and orientation, and those focusing specifically on the promotion and defense of women's rights operate at a variety of different, albeit interrelated, levels. Some work as pressure groups to denounce violations and to press for action by their governments, while others work as support or assistance groups to victims. Many of the groups use a sociojudicial or legal framework in their work—for example, by defending individual rights cases or through the active promotion of legislative changes in their countries.

Education is an important aspect of the work of many of these organizations. There are groups participating in consciousness-raising activities that aim to sensitize other women, the authorities, and the general public as to the importance of women's human rights. Others conduct specific legal education sessions for women to inform them of their rights and how to use the law to protect themselves. Some groups provide paralegal training to women leaders within communities so that they in turn can help other women in the defense of their rights.

None of these activities are mutually exclusive, and many women's groups work in several of these areas. Given below are illustrative examples of but a few of the hundreds of Latin American women's organizations that have developed concrete activities in the promotion and defense of women's rights.

One of Peru's long-established women's organizations, Peru-Mujer, initiated a legal service project in 1984 that consisted of the training of women paralegal workers (*promotoras legales*) in urban and rural popular-sector communities. The trainees were chosen by their own community-based organizations and were provided with seven months of legal training and seven months of practical legal work, to become the principal promoters of women's rights in their neighborhoods. A second phase of the project established Women's Rights Defense Committees (CODEM) with trained paralegal workers of eight communities. The objectives of CODEM are to provide rights education for women, legal services, community services, and to actively promote the equal rights of women and men in their neighborhoods (Dasso, 1989, pp. 55–57).

In Costa Rica, the organization CEFEMINA has developed a program to deal with domestic violence against women and with the specific situation of battered women, which includes education, legal services, and psychology sessions. CEFEMINA's approach is to seek effective and appropriate ways to deal with such issues in the Costa Rican context, from the promotion of dialogue and debate between men and women on domestic violence to the proposal of new legislation within the Family Code to address the needs of victims of such violence (Caravaca, 1988, pp. 18–21).

One important regional initiative in Latin America has been the creation of CLADEM, the Latin American Committee for the Defense of Women's Rights, which was born of the recommendations of the Third World Forum on Women, Law and Development at the End of Women's Decade Conference in Nairobi in 1985. CLADEM is an expanding NGO network that links up women's rights groups from many parts of Latin America. It deals with specific women's issues (violence against women, domestic workers' rights, etc.) and with the issue of how the legal system affects women in different Latin American countries. One of CLADEM's major objectives is the elimination of discrimination against women through the use of alternative legal practices (*Mujer/Fempress*, August 1988, pp. 10–11).

On another level, one of the most interesting processes in which some women's groups have participated in recent years has been the reform of national constitutions. In the mid- to late 1980s, the elaboration of a new constitution by a Constituent Assembly in Brazil and the constitutional reform promoted in Colombia by broad political sectors were opportunities for women in those countries to bring forward proposals and amendments relating to women's rights.

In the area of specific national legislation, a comprehensive Project of Law for the Real Equality of Women was the object of intense, nationwide public debate in Costa Rica before it was formally presented to the country's Legislative Assembly in April 1988 by the governmental organ, National Center for the Development of Women and the Family. Although aspects of the project have met with significant opposition from some parts of the Costa Rican government (one of the most contested points is the establishment of minimum quotas for the participation of women in Costa Rican political institutions), it has thus far been strongly supported by national women's groups and has the support of the majority of Costa Ricans (*Mujer/Fempress*, October 1988, p. 24).

In 1989 the Law for Prevention and Intervention in Cases of Domestic Violence was approved in Puerto Rico. This law contains five basic articles concerning the prevention of domestic violence, the criminalization of various acts of violence perpetrated in the home and the fixing of penalties in relation to these crimes, the establishment of measures to issue rapid protection orders for victims of domestic violence, and the provision of resources to the government's Commission for Women's Affairs to reinforce its role in disseminating information, giving legal guidance on domestic violence, and providing professional training for those working in this area. It is a progressive law for the region as well as in international terms. The Commission for Women's Affairs proposed the law after holding various meetings with women of Puerto Rican feminist groups who had been trying to get such a law passed for over ten years (Valle, 1989, p. 1).

It is interesting to underscore the fact that women's groups in Latin America are increasingly using the law as a resource for achieving their own ends, whereas a decade ago few groups directly used the law and legal instruments to promote their rights. This was due in part to a traditional "mistrust" of formal law by these organizations (Acosta, 1988, p. 1).

A clear example of the importance and effectiveness of organized Latin American women's groups for the active defense of women's rights was a 1987 campaign led by CONG (Coordinating Body of Women's NGOs) in Venezuela (Rodriguez et al., 1987). CONG mounted an intense pressure and awareness campaign in defense of the 20-year-old single mother of a 2-year-old victim of rape and murder. The mother was pronounced guilty of "abandonment" of her child and sentenced to prison.

The awareness campaign of this group helped to put pressure on authorities and to shift public opinion away from implicating the mother in the crime because she had left her two children unattended for several hours on the evening of the attack. Not only had the original judgment not taken into account the role played by irresponsible paternity, but it ironically drew attention away from the culpability of the true perpetrators of the crime: two male adults from the woman's neighborhood. The eventual result of the campaign, which was instrumental in turning the tide of public and official opinion on this issue, was the release of the mother from prison.

As this last case illustrates, consciousness-raising and sensitizing the public on the issues is a crucial task for organizations promoting women's rights. It also demonstrates the kinds of challenges presented by ingrained sexual stereotypes and attitudes about women's roles and responsiblities. Although the above examples of women's organizations in Latin America are of those focusing on the issue of specific women's rights, many of them through a legal perspective, it must not be forgotten that many women's groups and women of other organizations are also focusing on specific issues related to housing, health, workers' rights, cultural rights, and others that are ultimately an indivisible part of the equation for fuller women's rights and, indeed, fuller rights for all of society.

Despite certain progress, it can be said that the challenges to women's rights in Latin America are still overwhelming from many points of view: political, economic, social, domestic, and so on. Given the currently severe economic crisis affecting most of the region, the socioeconomic conditions of many women are actually deteriorating, and there is a clear danger that they will deteriorate further. Women's continuing inequality in economic and social terms has given rise to a process known as the "feminization of poverty" in Latin America as well as in other parts of the world (Portugal, 1989, p. 3; Facio, 1989b, pp. 49–50). In the face of adversity, women's organizations have nonetheless risen to the challenge in Latin America. A number of them have now been operating for 10 to 15 years, and have gained experience, maturity, and respect in their countries. Informal and formal women's networks have emerged and exchanges and contacts have been made with other social organizations on the continent and beyond, through publications, international and regional fora, and other mechanisms. Despite—or perhaps because of—the current crisis, it seems to be a propitious time for some of the more consolidated women's organizations to consider greater collaboration on women's rights issues with organizations such as those defending human rights.

A positive aspect of the present situation is the attention now being devoted to specific women's concerns by some human rights organizations that did not traditionally focus on such matters, or did so only in passing. Given the apparent reluctance that human rights organizations have had vis-à-vis incorporating a woman-specific focus or concerns within their work, how can we account for this shift in attitude?

   In dealing with this question, I will look at four key Latin American institutions that work in the area of human rights and have an impact on a continental level. With varying approaches and levels of commitment, each of the four have begun to look at the issue of women's rights within the framework of their own programs. The four organizations are:

- the Education Program for Peace and Human Rights of CEAAL (Latin American Council for Adult Education)
- Commission for the Defense of Human Rights in Central America (CODEHUCA)
- Inter-American Institute of Human Rights (IIHR)
- Inter-American Legal Services Association (ILSA)

   There are a number of possible explanations as to why these institutions have begun to take the issue of women's rights into greater consideration. One factor might be the influence of the current leadership of these organizations. There are women occupying key positions in all four organizations at this time: the coordinator of CODEHUCA, the executive director of IIHR, and the director of ILSA are at present all women. Within CEAAL, of which the Education Program for Peace and Human Rights is a part, the vice-president of the overall network and coordinator of the Women's Network is also a woman.
   Donor influence might be another factor. One of the thrusts of Western donor agencies in the past several years has been the integration of women into all aspects of development. The current attention being paid to women in human rights programs could be a response to donors' preoccupations in this regard.
   One of the likely influences on these institutions is the pressure of organized women's groups throughout Latin America and the presence of feminists working at all levels of the organizations themselves. Through their work and diligence, such women have been able to bring the issue of women's rights to greater prominence in the field of human rights.
   The following section will examine the situation of each of the four organizations with respect to women's rights and human rights.

LATIN AMERICAN HUMAN RIGHTS ORGANIZATIONS

Education Program for Peace and Human Rights—CEAAL

The Education Program for Peace and Human Rights is but one of the many programmes or "subnetworks" of the Latin American Adult Education Council. Others, for example, deal with popular education and local development, popular theater for education, education for indigenous populations, and so on. Each subnetwork is essentially autonomous and thus works on its own within its particular mandate. This is why, until very recently, the CEAAL Women's Network and the Peace and Human Rights Program have not had much opportunity to collaborate.

In May 1989 the Women's Network held a Regional Workshop on Popular Education, Women and Democracy in Everyday Life. The workshop was attended by 20 women, including a representative from the Peace and Human Rights Program. This was the first time that the subject of collaboration between the two subnetworks had been raised. As an initial step, the two subnetworks will exchange information and identify groups of people that may be interested in helping them to organize a joint initiative on the theme of women and human rights (Rosero, 1989).

The overall objectives of the CEAAL Women's Network are to link women's groups and women popular educators of Latin America in a network of cooperation and to develop and bring into practice a "gender pedagogy"—that is, a type of popular education incorporating a gender perspective, that can be used to permeate all of society.

In terms of collaboration with the Peace and Human Rights Program, the head of the Women's Network, Rocio Rosero, sees potential in an initiative that would deal with the educational dimension of integrating the theme of "classic" human rights with women's rights. Like most feminists dealing with this theme, she bases her proposal on the inacceptability of continuing to keep women's rights segregated from the global concept of human rights. The task, as she sees it, is to raise the consciousness of society at large to the importance of women's rights and their "natural" place within the family of human rights. In addition, she feels that there must be awareness of the potential for reaching a new conceptualization of human rights and new human rights practices through the inclusion of rights concerning women (Rosero, 1989).

The current perspective of CEAAL's Peace and Human Rights Program in relation to women and human rights differs from that of the Women's Network. The Program does not stress a gender perspective, although it aims to create and utilize a broad definition of human rights. Program staff call their approach "universalist" (Escalona, 1989). Although it follows fairly traditional lines of thinking within the area of human rights, there appears to be some consciousness within the Program and its human rights affiliates that the future of human rights in Latin America will be strongly shaped by important social currents such as that of the women's movement.

During a Workshop for Training on Human Rights in Latin America held jointly by the Program, the Dutch Institute of Social Sciences, and the Peace and Justice Service (SERPAJ) of Chile in June 1989, one presentation brought out the following point:

On national levels as well as on a Latin American level, an important human rights movement has emerged with a spirit of newness in our continent. . . . The strategies for the defense and promotion of human rights are gaining specificity by being designed by social movements that originated on the continent and that are proposing new forms of addressing the struggle for human rights (Ramil, 1989, p. 31).

Commission for the Defense of Human Rights in Central America (CODEHUCA)

CODEHUCA is a network of human rights organizations that aims to promote the respect of human rights in Central America through education, legal and solidarity actions, and information dissemination. It was established in Costa Rica in 1978. Since its creation, the presence of women has been significant within its personnel and leadership, as well as within the ranks of its affiliate organizations. For example, the last two general coordinators of CODEHUCA have been women. This can be explained by the fact that women in Central America generally play a very crucial role in all human rights work of the region. Numerous victims of violations reported over the years have also been women. They were reported by CODEHUCA in the framework of their regular monitoring of disappearances, illegal detentions, and state torture in the region.

Despite the strong presence of women in their work, CODEHUCA's focus on the defense and promotion of women's rights has been limited. The organization has concentrated essentially on the global reporting of traditional human rights abuses.

Early in 1989, however, a significant event occurred. CODEHUCA made a presentation to the United Nations Commission on the Status of Women concerning the situation of women in Central America (*Brecha*, March/April 1989, p. 16). The presentation was essentially a petition for the support of a series of recommendations that would improve the conditions of women in the region and was unanimously approved by the Commission (*Brecha*, September 1989, pp. 12–13). An apparent result of a process of debate and analysis within CODEHUCA, this initiative sparked a great deal of interest among individuals and organizations who wished to know what CODEHUCA's program would now be in relation to women and human rights. In the September 1989 (pp. 12–13) issue of *Brecha*, its monthly publication, CODEHUCA finally introduced the elements of a "Women and Human Rights Project" that would permit the organization to work toward the goals presented before the UN Commission on the Status of Women.

CODEHUCA identified three basic project objectives: the strengthening of the work of women's organizations, the integration of the defense and promotion of women's rights into the overall struggle for the respect of human rights, and the promotion of involvement by regional women's groups in the defense and protection of specific violations directed against women.

In order to fulfill its objectives in this area, CODEHUCA has assigned specific tasks from the Women and Human Rights Project to each section of the organization. The Permanent Secretariat will be responsible for the organization of a regional forum on Women and Human Rights to discuss the current situation and propose policies and joint actions. The legal section will analyze the norms and laws of each country as they relate to the UN Convention on the Elimination of All Forms of Discrimination Against Women. It will then formulate proposals of legal defense against governments for the violation of the human rights of women, and for the act of omission in cases where these violations are not committed by the governments themselves.

The solidarity section of CODEHUCA will initiate a separate recording process for violations against women. It will then organize a system of channeling this information to international women's organizations as well as to the member organizations of its human rights network. In the research, training, documentation, and publication sections, similar emphasis will be placed on information regarding women and human rights, women's specific rights, and those organizations in the region dealing with these issues.

Inter-American Institute of Human Rights (IIHR)

The IIHR, based in San Jose, Costa Rica, is a Latin American institution working for the promotion of human rights through education, research, and training. Over the years, it has introduced the subject of sexual discrimination in a number of seminars and human rights courses. In 1988/89, this initiative was taken further when IIHR held two meetings to discuss the possibility of establishing a permanent program of Women and Human Rights. These preparatory meetings were attended by various members of women's organizations and specialists from Latin America who have reflected extensively on the theme of women and human rights. The meetings explored the "philosophical underpinnings" of a Women and Human Rights Program and also produced a proposal outlining a possible program structure and specific program objectives (Facio, 1989b:10).

IIHR proposed the establishment of either a separate women's program or a project to incorporate a gender perspective in all existing programs. The participants suggested that initially an autonomous program would be most effective, with the provision that it have some mechanism to eventually incorporate a gender perspective in all of the IIHR's work.

Three basic activities for the program were proposed by meeting participants. The first would be action-oriented research on the adequacy of international human rights instruments in the protection of women's human rights and on the prospects for the elaboration of new, broader concepts of human rights that would include a gender perspective. A second activity would consist of the training of women's groups in Latin America in the knowledge and use of international human rights instruments and in the development of strategies for the defense of human rights from a gender perspective. The third element would involve a permanent activity of consciousness-raising and sensitization of NGOs in Latin America on the issue of gender and the specific issue of human rights violations suffered by women because they are women.

IIHR has accepted most of the proposals resulting from the meetings and continues to prepare for the launching of its program. At its last Interdisciplinary Course on Human Rights held in San Jose in August 1989, IIHR circulated a questionnaire to all women participants (all of whom work in organizations dealing with human rights) on women and their role in human rights organizations (Cuellar, 1989). The results of the questionnaire are intended to help IIHR in the organization of the Women and Human Rights Program, which it initiated in 1990.

Inter-American Legal Services Association (ILSA)

ILSA is a nongovernmental network established in 1978 to promote more equal access to justice in Latin America and the Caribbean through the provision of community legal services and legal education to the poorer sectors of these societies. This work has invariably involved ILSA in the domain of human rights in the region.

Although ILSA had included the issue of women's rights and the law in some of its educational activities, it was in 1987 that it initiated a full Women's Program to be undertaken in two stages. The first stage took place between 1987 and 1988, and consisted of carrying out an inventory of institutions that were using law or a legal perspective for the promotion and defense of women's rights. Through the distribution of a questionnaire, ILSA was able to contact 250 organizations in the region that work in this area and gathered information on what types of organizations they were (NGO, governmental, etc.), what type of work they did, and who were the prime beneficiaries. The first phase culminated in a Regional Workshop held in July 1988, which brought together women representatives from close to 70 of the organizations that had been surveyed, with the objective of creating an informal network and working together on a project of common concern (Ramirez, 1988, pp. 7-8).

The proposal that emerged from the workshop was to conduct a critical analysis of the UN Convention on the Elimination of All Forms of Discrimination Against Women and to relate it to the work of Latin American women's organizations dealing with women's rights. The project has been initiated as a decentralized exercise where organizations in each country carry out their own research on the impact of the Convention on the work of local groups (Barney, 1989).

CONCLUSION

With the above examples, I have tried to describe some of the efforts being made by important regional organizations in Latin America to bring women's concerns more fully into their work with human rights. The efforts range from initiating relationships, to undertaking women's projects that are "a part of" but still somehow separate from the mainstream of activity, to proposals that would integrate a gender perspective into much of the work of an organization. Apart from the work of ILSA, the examples presented are essentially projects for the future. It is therefore impossible to know at this stage how they will really be implemented or what impact they will have. Even the ILSA project is relatively new and its impact in the area of women and human rights is yet to be fully analyzed. The greater presence of women's concerns in the human rights arena in Latin America—although it is barely visible at this point—is nonetheless an encouraging trend that must continue into the 1990s and beyond in order for the movement to rise to the immense challenge facing Latin America in the future.

The comprehensive nature of women's demands could finally bring the human rights movement full circle. As Riane Eisler (1987, p. 308) maintains,

the recognition that women's rights are the leading edge of human rights is both operationally and logically the prerequisite for the kinds of actions required to lay the foundations for a just social order. A unified theory of human rights encompassing both halves of humanity is essential if a basic respect for human rights is to become firmly rooted. Only then can the unfinished struggle for equal justice for ALL—the struggle for human rights—be completed.

REFERENCES

Acosta, Gladys (1988). "Los Derechos de las Mujeres en las Constituciones Politicas." Working paper presented at the ILSA Regional Workshop, July 29–31, 1988, Bogota.

Barney, Maria Jose (1989). Unpublished "Progress Report on Phase II of Project 'Defense of Women's Rights' ". September 5.

Caravaca, Alicia (1988). "Violencia Doméstica: Un Intimo Reto en Pro de los Derechos Humanos en la Familia." *Mujer,* no. 5 (CEFEMINA).

Cuellar, Roberto (1989). Unpublished IIHR document.

Dasso, Elizabeth (1989). "Constuindo um Novo Dia para a Mulher: Os Comitês de defesa dos direitos da mulher." *Crescer Juntas.* São Paulo: Rede Mulher (Portuguese edition of Vol. 8, December 1987, Isis International Women's Edition, no. 8).

Eisler, Riane (1987). "Human Rights: Toward an Integrated Theory for Action." *Human Rights Quarterly,* 9.

Escalante, Herrera (1988). "La Realidad Social de la Mujer en América Latina: Una Introducción Histórica y Sociológica." In Maria González Suárez (ed.), *Estudios de la Mujer: Conocimiento y Cambio.* Costa Rica.

Escalona, Lorena (1989). Conversation with Lorena Escalona, CEAAL Education Program for Peace and Human Rights, October 4, 1989.

Facio, Alda (1989a), "El Derecho Patriarchal Androcentrico." Working paper for IIDH Working Group "Mujer y Derechos Humanos," February 27–March 1, 1989. San Jose, Costa Rica.

Facio, Alda (1989b). "Un Programa de Derechos Humanos para la Mujer Latinoamericana." *Mujer/Fempress*, no. 93 (July).

Hosken, Fran P. (1981). "Toward a Definition of Women's Human Rights." *Human Rights Quarterly*, 3, no. 2.

Picado Sotela, Sonia (1986). *La Mujer y los Derechos Humanos, Decenio de Naciones Unidas: Igualidad, Desarrollo y Paz*. Costa Rica: Instituto Interamericano de Derechos Humanos.

Portugal, Ana Maria (1989). "Perú: Dar Vida, Recibir Muerte." *Mujer/Fempress*, no. 93 (July).

Ramil, Silvia Fernandez (1989). "Estrategias de Defensa y Promoción de los Derechos Humanos en Americalatina: Desde una Perspectiva Integradora." *El Canelo, Revista Chilena de Desarrollo Local*, 4, no. 13 (July).

Ramirez, Socorro (1989). "La Naturaleza Ambivalente y Dinamica del Derecho." *Mujer/Fempress*, no. 85 (October).

Rodriguez, Marta Yadira, Giaconda Espina, Diana Vegas, and Inocencia Orellana (1987). *La Mujer y la Lucha Solidaria: En el Caso de Ines Maria Marcano, Una en un Millon*. Caracas: CESAP.

Rosero, Rocio (1989). Unpublished CEAAL document.

Tinker, Catherine (1981). "Human Rights for Women: The U.N. Convention on the Elimination of All Forms of Discrimination Against Women." *Human Rights Quarterly*, 3, no. 2 (Spring).

Valle, Norma (1989). "Aprueban Innovadora Ley Sobre Violencia Domestica." *Mujer/Fempress*, no. 94 (August).

CHAPTER NINE

Changing Informal Settlements in Latin American Cities

YVONNE RIAÑO AND ROLF WESCHE

Informal urban settlements, which have long characterized the urbanization process in Latin America, expanded dramatically during the 1950s and 1960s. By the 1970s, large South American cities housed from 25 percent to over 50 percent of their inhabitants in informal settlements (Portes and Walton, 1981).

Simply defined, urban informal settlements are low-income residential areas that are built incrementally by their owner-occupants and are initially illegal due to either land invasion or private subdivision in contravention of official planning regulations. Unless eradicated, they tend to become accepted and legalized by government, evolve in appearance and land use, and, in many cases, are increasingly difficult to distinguish from other low-class residential areas. Given the eventual heterogeneity of (initially) informal settlements, distinction from other housing types for statistical purposes has been less common and less relevant during the 1980s.

Government attitudes toward informal settlements changed substantially over time. Until the 1960s, informal settlements were mainly regarded as a temporary aberration subject to eradication. By the early 1970s they were recognized as a permanent feature of the Latin American urban landscape and increasingly regarded as an appropriate contribution toward the resolution of the low-income housing crisis. "Self-help" housing was now seen as adaptable to the changing needs and means of low-income populations (Moser and Peake, 1987). Furthermore, it offered the prospect of political stabilization through broad-based home ownership, scope for cooptation by government, and reduced pressure on scarce public resources.

Consequently, government policy shifted from conventionally top-down, high-standard public housing schemes toward the upgrading of informal settlement and toward development of sites-and-services housing schemes. Self-help became the principal strategy to tackle the low-income housing problem.

This chapter reviews the changing character and role of urban informal settlements in Latin America during the 1980s. After briefly placing informal settlements within the context of the urbanization process, it focuses on two central issues: informal "self-help" housing and the political and social organization of informal settlement residents. A final section explores prospects and needs in the 1990s.

Generalizations for the whole of Latin America are necessarily precarious, as the urbanization process and the role of informal settlements have varied from country to country. Equally, the severity of the 1980s economic crisis varied as did government economic and housing policies to face it. Differences in political regime, sociocultural characteristics, and geographical conditions will also leave their imprint. Nevertheless, certain similarities emerge, which will be highlighted in this chapter.

Although Latin America was predominantly urban by 1980, urban population growth continued at a rapid pace in most countries. In the face of the economic crisis, open unemployment as well as informal employment increased, which resulted in the impoverishment of the urban working class. However, the impact of the crisis varied depending on national policies. Generally, public resources for social housing were constrained and self-help remained the principal housing solution for the poor.

Meanwhile, growth rates of intermediate cities increased and primacy generally decreased in the larger countries. This expansion of informal settlements in secondary cities is partly attributable to increased diseconomies faced by the poor in metropolitan areas.

Within larger cities, the location pattern of informal settlements dating from various periods has become increasingly complex, as has the spatial pattern of other land uses. This has led to the gradual erosion of strong spatial segregation of socioeconomic groups in some cities, such as Bogotá, Santiago, and Montevideo (Portes, 1989; Gilbert and Ward, 1988). Generally, the stereotype of informal settlements as "misery belts" constituting the urban periphery has lost some of its validity. Finally, the major expansion of informal activities in the secondary and tertiary economic sectors of Latin American cities during the 1980s has turned many informal settlements into key centers of informal employment.

Economic and housing pressure in informal settlements has promoted the recent resurgence of urban social movements. Traditional organizations such as trade unions have weakened, while "new social movements," church-sponsored grass roots communities, womens' residential associations, and the like have proliferated (Portes, 1989). Such organizations are now mainly based in the informal settlements of Latin American cities.

HOUSING IN INFORMAL SETTLEMENTS

The spread of house ownership among the urban poor, thanks to the proliferation of informal settlements, has been a striking feature of Latin American urbanization in recent decades. By the 1970s, government recognition of the advantages of broadly based house ownership led to increased tolerance, even facilitation, of the informal housing solution. In the 1980s, however, the informal housing solution has been subject to three major challenges: economic downturn, rising costs, and deteriorating relative location.

Though self-built housing is a response to poverty, it is no easy solution for the very poor. In fact, informal house ownership requires substantial initial capital, not only for construction, but in many cases also for the compensation of previous landowners, for community infrastructure, and for legalization. Such investment capital is mainly available to low-income populations during periods of relative national and regional prosperity.

Furthermore, the cost of self-built housing has increased in many cases, due to greater scarcity of suitable land in large metropolitan areas, inflation of the cost of construction materials in relation to wages, and the reduced ability of governments to provide material support. Finally, the increasingly remote, peripheral location of new settlements in large centers has reduced their attractiveness.

As a consequence, the spread of new informal settlements may have slowed and the trend toward increased home ownership among the urban poor, which characterized the preceding decades, may even have been reversed (Gilbert, 1989). In the case of countries under dictatorial regimes, the importance of informal housing has been reduced substantially as land invasions have been repressed and the construction of housing on unserviced land has not been permitted (Gilbert, 1989).

As the goal of house ownership encountered increasing obstacles, growing numbers of the urban poor reverted to renting. In many cases, informal settlements became the major source of rental accommodation (Gilbert, 1989). Gwynne (1988) estimates that by the latter 1980s, 50 percent of residents in informal settlements were renters.

Increased renting and reduced upward and spatial mobility of the urban poor have led to higher population densities in informal settlements with a corresponding deterioration of the living space. Often, second and third generations have been forced to remain in their parents' house (Gilbert, 1989; Volbeda, 1989; Riofrio and Driant, 1987). Informal settlement populations also were forced to lower plot and street size in order to accommodate higher densities (Volbeda, 1989).

Because the consolidation of informal housing, like its initial construction, is a function of the general economic environment, the process has been slowed during the 1980s. While the quality of the informal housing stock has improved (Perlman, 1987), completion of structures generally took more than 15 years and often engendered costs in excess of those for comparable formally built housing (Riofrio and Driant, 1987).

Settlements that reached a high level of consolidation generally took advantage of their central geographical location within the city, where easy access to markets and service areas provides opportunities for the development of informal economic activities. The worsening location of new peripheral settlements reduces these possibilities for informal economic activities and hence delays consolidation.

Due to reduced government ability to provide services for the urban poor, service supply has increasingly become the responsibility of the private sector, a reversion to conditions that prevailed in the 1950s and 1960s. Informal private enterprises not only provide building plots and rental housing but are often the main suppliers of water in informal settlements.

As the development potential and attractiveness of informal settlements, particularly of those located in remote peripheries of large cities, eroded during the 1980s, the comparative attraction of central slum tenements has increased and their resident populations have stabilized. The organization of informal economic activities is easier from these locations, as is access to the formal job market and public infrastructure and services. Time and money saved in transport and, in some cases, savings due to former rent control legislation have proved important assets. In fact, on the basis of Mexico City research, Eckstein (1990) suggests that the 1980s have reversed the relative advantage of inner-city slums and informal settlements, turning the former into areas of hope and the latter into areas of despair.

THE POLITICAL AND SOCIAL ORGANIZATION OF INFORMAL SETTLEMENT DWELLERS

While the housing achievements in informal settlements were disappointing during the 1980s, if compared with preceding decades, significant progress was made with regard to the scope and nature of popular organization. Residents of informal settlements have organized not only with the aim to improve their immediate physical surroundings but increasingly to protest against the general problems of poverty and to influence urban policy. By the end of the 1980s, popular organization has become more consolidated and larger organizations have emerged.

Protest activities have been carried out by associations representing several informal neighborhoods or major sectors of the city. Organizations of informal settlement residents have also established ties to other urban organizations such as professional groups, public transport users, and associations of tenants and trade unions. This is illustrated by Brazil, where such links were used to develop an urban reform proposal and to demand participation in urban planning decisions (Maricato, 1988). Protests have focused on the insufficiency and cost of public services, the lack of food supplies, the cost of living, and official urban development plans. Means of protest have consisted of civic strikes, occupation of public service offices, demonstrations, and blocking of roads and public transport.

This new nature and scope of urban low-income-sector organization seems to rest on the organizational experience accumulated by informal neighborhoods in the 1970s. It also is related to the return to democracy in many countries and the aggravation of the economic crisis (Portes, 1989). A further new characteristic is the explosive and violent nature of protests. Strikes, riots, looting of supermarkets, and violent clashes with the police have taken place in several cities of Brazil, Venezuela, and Argentina.

However, while the extent of protest activities against poverty has dramatically increased, resident involvement in local community activities such as self-help and petitioning seems to have declined in many cases (CEDER, 1989; Schuurman and van Naerssen, 1989; Eckstein, 1990). Local involvement requires constant expenditure of time and energy. Given the economic difficulties of the 1980s, informal settlement residents had to devote most of their time and energy to the numerous economic activities required for survival. Also, the increased proportion of renters appears to have had a negative effect on local community activities. By contrast, the role that women play in community affairs has become more central than ever. Beyond their domestic and income-earning activities, women have assumed tasks as community managers and played a critical role in local-level groups that aim at accessing health and infrastructure facilities.

In addition to political organization, the poor in informal settlements have developed complex survival strategies to cope with the economic constraints of the 1980s. These involve maximization of income generation and minimization of cost and levels of consumption. Income-generating activities include petty commodity production, small-scale trade, and subsistence activities such as urban farming. These informal economic activities are characterized by their illegality, small-scale operation, and heavy reliance on family labor, including children. They not only provide a service for the specialized needs of low-income sectors but increasingly produce goods and services for the formal modern sector. In order to lower production costs, many large-scale companies, including exporting firms, subcontract production to the informal sector in areas such as garment and shoe manufacture and construction (Safa, 1986).

As a consequence, houses in informal settlements are adapted also to serve production and trade functions. Informal settlements are thus increasingly serving the multiple functions of residence, production, and trade, and as a territorial base for the social and political organization of the poor.

Social self-help activities that minimize the cost of consumption have also become more prominent during the 1980s. Mutual help by members of informal social networks has included the pooling of incomes, exchange of information, goods and services, the sharing of facilities, mutual money loans, and credit facilities. Social services such as child care, provision of health and moral support, and help with house construction are also satisfied by informal social networks. Social networks are mostly built on the basis of kinship, common regional origin, and local vicinity. These practices of mutual help and reciprocity form part of a basic cultural characteristic of low-income populations that adapts to changing contexts (Altamirano, 1988).

Women in informal neighborhoods have assumed a key role in the survival of the urban poor (Chant, 1984; Volbeda, 1989). In the face of the economic crisis, women organized and participated in activities aimed at obtaining food for their families (Hardy, 1987). In Lima's informal settlements, the vital women's self-help movement that emerged during the 1980s includes 1,500 community kitchens (Durning, 1989). The informal-sector income of women has been shown to be of crucial importance for low-income households (Wood and McCracken, 1984).

PROSPECTS AND NEEDS OF THE 1990S

Economic and demographic indicators suggest that informal settlements will continue to play an important role and remain a central issue in the Latin America of the 1990s. Development prospects of informal settlements are tied to and will vary in function of the economic performance of individual countries, as well as government attitudes and policies toward land, housing, infrastructure, and urban resources in general.

Furthermore, local development prospects and opportunity structures for informal settlements will vary in relation to local circumstances. Informal settlements are now so heterogeneous that generalizations without reference to particular typologies are increasingly inappropriate. Local typologies of informal settlements are shaped by a combination of factors, such as a city's geographic location and economic activity; an informal settlement's location, age, size, and origin; local culture and history; and the residents' sociopolitical organization.

More research is needed to establish informal settlement typologies and the development opportunities and constraints they imply. Future policy must take account of the increasing diversity of informal settlements both within and among cities. Prospects for informal housing appear better in small and intermediate cities than in larger cities, since travel distances are smaller and more appropriate land is available.

Though the self-help housing concept still has an essentially positive connotation, it has increasingly come under question not only from an ideological standpoint (Burgess, 1982) but also because of the major constraints it faces during economic recession. By relying on the effort of the urban poor, governments were able to avoid their responsibilities in the provision of housing. The urgency of urban reforms was obscured by self-help policies. Given the difficulties of the poor to house themselves in times of recession and the increasing political organization of the low-income population, governments will be under increased pressure to carry out needed urban reforms. These will have to include facilitation of access to land by low-income groups as well as institutional reforms to debureaucratize and decentralize government agencies responsible for housing and infrastructure provision.

In addition to legislation and institutional reform, a precise definition and an adequate mix will have to be found for private and public roles in service provision. The relationships and division of tasks between the formal and informal sectors and between central and local governments also require clearer definition.

Other policy areas that need to be restudied and redefined are upgrading, housing subdivision, and renting in informal settlements. Government policies to legalize informal settlements and to include them into the formal housing and land market have often made them vulnerable to upward transfers in which original low-income residents are replaced by outside higher income groups. Tenants are the first victims of increased rents as a result of neighborhood appreciation. Although the majority of urban tenants in several Latin American cities live in areas that were urbanized by informal means, renting policies have been directed to formal-sector renting (Gilbert and Varley, 1990). Equally, credit programs stimulating housing subdivision have been directed to middle- and high-income residential groups. Other policy areas that need to be reassessed are access to construction materials for low-income groups and promotion of business ventures in informal neighborhoods.

Participation in urban management by low-income groups has also become a central issue. The expanded organization of the urban poor during the 1980s is not only to be interpreted as a reaction to the economic crisis but must be seen as a larger political claim. It involves a demand for enlarged participation in decisions at the urban level that affect the poor, an effort to establish a non-clientelistic relationship with the state, and, ultimately, a challenge to the state (Castells, 1983; Santana, 1989; Schuurman and van Naerssen, 1989).

Urban management decentralization designed to include the participation of low-income groups depends on a government's willingness to truly democratize urban management. It also requires the ability of urban low-income groups to organize themselves and exercise pressure. Prospects of increased pressure on governments will depend on the ability of low-income urban groups to maintain and extend their organizational activity, and to strengthen their linkage to broader city, regional, and national levels. The integration of existing local-level organizational experiences into a coherent global alternative remains one of the great challenges.

Nongovernmental organizations and radical political parties have played a key role in promoting the organization of the urban poor in the last two decades. It is not clear, however, to what extent urban populations at the grass roots level have gained true empowerment to organize themselves on their own terms, or whether continued external support is required for the survival and expansion of existing organizations.

A further challenge to the prospects of increased popular political involvement and broader participation in urban management relates to increased renting in informal settlements. Renters appear less politically involved than owners. Owners seem to be interested in changes at the city, as well as the community, level (e.g., changes in land taxes, regularization of land tenure). Renters are more concerned with personal problems (levels of rent, eviction problems, etc.). A falloff in communal activity and divisions is likely if renting continues to increase at the expense of home ownership.

Thus the informal settlement phenomenon needs to be reassessed in the function of the changing economic situation, its increasing heterogeneity, the greater interconnectedness between the formal and informal sectors, and the accumulated organizational experience regarding urban management that urban low-income groups have gained during the 1980s.

REFERENCES

Altamirano, T. (1988). *Cultura andina y pobreza urbana*. Lima: Pontífica Universidad Católica del Perú.

Burgess, R. (1982). "Self-help Housing Advocacy: A Curious Form of Radicalism. A Critique of the Work of J. C. Turner." In P. Ward (ed.), *Self-Help Housing: A Critique*. London: Mansell.

Castells, M. (1983). "The Social Basis of Urban Populism: Squatters and the State in Latin America." In M. Castells, *The City and the Grassroots: A Cross-Cultural Theory of Urban Social Movements*. London: Arnold.

Centro de Estudios para el Desarrollo Regional (CEDER) (1989). *Desarrollo urbano y vivienda popular en Arequipa*. Arequipa, Peru: Concytlc.

Chant, S. (1984). "Household Labour and Self-Help Housing in Querétaro, Mexico." *Boletin de Estudios Latinoamericanos y del Caribe*, 37.

Durning, A. B. (1989). "Mobilizing at the Grassroots." In L. R. Brown et al., *State of the World*. New York: Norton.

Eckstein, S. (1990). "Urbanization Revisited: Inner-City Slum of Hope and Squatter Settlement of Despair." *World Development*, 18, no. 2.

Gilbert, A. (1989). "Housing During Recession: Illustrations from Latin America." *Housing Studies*, 4, no. 3.

Gilbert, A. and A. Varley (1990). "The Mexican Landlord: Rental Housing in Guadalajara and Puebla." *Urban Studies*, 27, no. 1.

Gilbert, A. and P. Ward (1988). "Land for the Rich, Land for the Poor." in J. Gugler (ed.), *The Urbanization of the Third World*. Oxford: Oxford University Press.

Gwyne, R. N. (1988). "Contemporary Issues in Latin America." In M. Pacione (ed.), *Geography of the Third World: Progress and Prospects*. London: Routledge.

Hardy, C. (1987). *Organizarse para vivir: pobreza urbana y organización popular*. Santiago, Chile: Programa de Economía de Trabajo.

Maricato, E. (1988). "The Urban Reform Movement in Brazil." *International Journal of Urban and Regional Research*, 12, no. 1.

Moser, C. and L. Peake (eds.) (1987). *Women, Human Settlements and Housing.* London: Tavistock.

Perlman, J. (1987). "Misconceptions about the Urban Poor and the Dynamics of Housing Policy Evolution." *Journal of Planning Education and Research,* 7.

Portes, A. (1989). "Latin American Urbanization in the Years of the Crisis." *Latin American Research Review,* 24, no. 3.

Portes, A. and J. Walton (1981). *Labor, Class and the International System.* New York: Academic Press.

Riofrio, G. and J. C. Driant (1987). *Qué vivienda han construido? Nuevos problemas en viejas barriadas.* Lima: CIDAP, IFEA, TAREA.

Safa, H. (1986). "Urbanization, the Informal Economy and State Policy in Latin America." *Urban Anthropology,* 15.

Santana, P. (1989). "Movimientos Sociales, Gobiernos Locales y Democracia." *Revista Foro,* 8.

Schuurman, F. and T. van Naerssen (1989). *Urban Social Movements in the Third World.* New York: Routledge.

Volbeda, S. (1989). "Housing and Survival Strategies of Women in Metropolitan Areas in Brazil." *Habitat International,* 13, no. 3.

Wood, C. and S. McCracken (1984). "Underdevelopment, Urban Growth and Collective Social Action in São Paulo, Brazil." *Studies in Third World Societies,* 29.

PART III

THE SUSTAINABILITY
OF DEMOCRATIZATION

CHAPTER TEN

Back to Populism: Latin America's Alternative to Democracy

JULIAN CASTRO REA, GRACIELA DUCATENZEILER,
AND PHILIPPE FAUCHER

Democratic consolidation in Latin America has not yet been achieved. Although civilian legalism has replaced the authoritarian regime of exception throughout the continent, the creation of an open and accessible political system built within a stable legalized institutional framework and based on the recognition and exercise of citizenship as well as the respect for the principle of representation is so far incomplete.

Although the task of democracy building has been put on the agenda with the departure of the military, this process has been slowed down by the weight of political tradition. Faced with resistance and opposition that impede the introduction of profound and necessary institutional reforms, populism is seen as a way of overcoming the resistance of some while satisfying the demands of the rest. The attraction of populism is that of short-term consensus obtained through an ambivalent discourse of change and conciliation without the cumbersome responsibilities of representation.

The populist temptation presents itself as a powerful lever capable of breaking down barriers to change. It is above all the illusion of a political shortcut based on the belief that the simple voice of the people will suffice to shatter the traditional balance of power. For the opposition, the lure of populism is motivated by the proximity of power, by the obligatory show of conciliation that any candidate for office must demonstrate. For those in power, populism is a way of evading constraints to development and recovering legitimacy lost through institutional barriers.

The theory of modernization (Germani, 1962; Di Tella, 1965) views populism as both an ideology and a political movement associated with the transition toward a society of masses and in particular that of urban workers. The dependency theory approach (Weffort, 1968) links populism to the import substitution process of industrialization.

For a proper understanding of its nature, it is important to make a distinction between populism and economic development. Populism can be understood as a political arrangement characterized by the privileged link between charismatic political leadership of state and the masses, combined with ineffectiveness of social organization and political parties as intermediate channels of mediation. Interest groups have little autonomy and often through cooptation become little more than relaying mechanisms of control. Clientelism and corporatism are essential components of populism where the state becomes the exclusive and obligatory point of reference for social actors. Populism is therefore not a particular form of state or a social movement but a specific relationship between the state and civil society.

According to this approach, there is no necessary link between populism and any particular model of economic policy. Populism is not the compulsory political expression of industrialization through import substitution. In fact, populism has existed in Latin America for the past 60 years and has survived all phases of development. Born in critical times (as a response to the crisis of oligarchical domination in Argentina, Brazil, Mexico, and later in Peru), populism has reemerged today in a context of a weak civil society and a fragile political system characterized by the inability of groups to form autonomous representative organizations.

To a greater or lesser extent, at least four countries in the region, each in their own distinct context, form, and manifestations, are experiencing a resurgence in populism. In Peru, in order to bolster his failing popularity, Alan García has cultivated the legacy of Haya de la Torre and Velasco, two great populist leaders of the past. His successor, Alberto Fujimori, was careful to keep a distance from both the Right and the Left, appealing to the people, over existing political parties, for national unity and conciliation. In Mexico, a charismatic leader has managed to capitalize on the frustration of the masses better than more organized opposition parties had ever been able to before. In Argentina, the rejection of compromise with the corporations and the failure of the Austral Plan provided an opportunity for populism as a civil and progressive alternative. In Brazil, with the dismal failure of the Sarney administration, the presidential elections have intensified competition between political forces for popular support. Beyond these specific national cases, populism represents a common denominator of regimes characterized by ineffectual political representation compensated by latent corporatism and flourishing clientelism.

The weight of political tradition is reproduced by political actors as a survival tactic. The populist revival evident in Peru and Argentina and emerging in Mexico and Brazil is the manifestation of the failure of a democratic project.

It is the failure of governments unable to respond to the modernizing projects of civil society. It is their refusal to expose the system to true democratic competition and their inability to respond to reformist expectations to meet the challenges of the present. Populism is an escapist solution. Regardless of concessions, it is more a return to the traditional order than the expression of change toward the building of a democratic society.

THE CHALLENGE OF DEMOCRATIC CONSOLIDATION

The transition from a military regime to civilian rule assumes the building of a new constitutional order guaranteeing the respect of individual rights and liberties, the recognition of citizenship, and the agreement to play by the rules of the democratic game. The existence of a process of democratic consolidation signifies that following the departure of the military, restoration of the previous order is an insufficient guarantee for institutional development and the respect for democratic norms.

Consolidation does not necessarily coincide with the emergence of new actors articulating interests developed during the authoritarian period. This is too mechanical an interpretation for the description of systems historically characterized by highly deterministic politization of state domination over weak social organization. In this sense we are in agreement with Alain Touraine (1988, p. 308) and his belief that important political changes are likely to take place without structural transformation of society because, as he states, "political participation is quite independent of the defence of social interests."

The basic reason for the need of democratic consolidation is both obvious and fundamental: the institutional framework and political practice do not play by the rules of the democratic game. In this sense, consolidation should not be taken in terms of improvement or adjustment but the building of a new political system. One can therefore understand why the expression "consolidation" has prompted considerable resistance and can be subject to all possible types of diversions, as is evident through the numerous manifestations of populism.

Given the absence of military dictatorship, the Mexican political situation demonstrates a different dynamic from our other cases. Moreover, one can observe the tension between a complex society characterized by profound inequalities and a political system totally dominated by a hegemonic party monopolizing power based on a fabricated majority. This tension has increased with the democratic demands of social groups and the legal opposition, demands recognized by right and constantly subjugated in actual practice. The resulting impasse forces the opposition to rely on mobilization and in doing so recuperating the populist rhetoric so often manipulated by the governing elite.

The new civilian regimes are confronted with an exhausting struggle on three fronts: handling the transition, dealing with the economic crisis, and consolidating democracy. Faced with more pressing demands, democratic consolidation has been given a lower priority. The first task is that of managing the transition, reasserting civilian authority, and ridding the country of the most disgraceful elements of its authoritarian past.

In the first years of postauthoritarian democracy, the Argentine government was caught up in criminal procedures against military human rights violators and against those responsible for the Falklands War fiasco. Given the traditional role of arbitrator played by the armed forces in distributional conflicts, the dictatorial heritage left behind is certainly a heavier burden to carry than in any of the other cases presented. In Brazil, the government is regularly reminded of the military presence. In the middle of the constitutional debate, the armed forces decreed an unofficial veto to a proposition concerning the reintegration of military officers expelled in 1964 (Pécaut, 1987, p. 36) and imposed prerogatives on the government and the Constituent Assembly that, in their view, stem from their mission as guarantors of national security. In Peru, the strength of armed insurgency has made the army an indispensable protector of Peruvian political institutions. For the past several months, Peru has been living in a climate of uncertainty fed by rumors of extreme leftist armed insurrection and the constant threat of a military takeover.

The most serious economic crisis in postwar times has hit Latin America at a time when its political institutions are at their most unstable. It has paralyzed any possibility of economic reform and resulted in a long and painful series of stabilization plans. In all our cases it has become obvious that the economic crisis has taken over the governmental agenda. Peru, Brazil, and Argentina are on the verge of bankruptcy, and Mexico has been showing similar symptoms. Inflation has run out of control and public deficits have remained impervious to all attempts of budgetary restrictions. Since 1982, Brazil has been without a development program for the first time in 25 years and has finished 1989 with an annual inflation rate of 1,765 percent. In Peru, where the recession of the past few years has wiped out 20 years of growth, the situation has become desperate. In 1989 alone, the GDP fell by 12 percent and inflation went over the level of 2,500 percent (Hertoghe and Labrousse, 1989). Completely caught up in economic crisis management, the civilian regimes have had little time or energy to dedicate to the particularly delicate task of institutional and political reform.

Beyond economic and political uncertainties, structural barriers have retarded the process of democratic consolidation. The first stems from weaknesses in the representational system and the generalization of corporatist and clientelist practices deeply embedded in the political culture. Second, because of this absence of democratic culture, the political class and the partisan system have stagnated, reinforcing the deeply rooted hierarchical dominance of popular organizations such as labor unions. Played out in its authoritarian and populist framework, it is this political game that is contested by democratic interests.

RULES OF THE POLITICAL GAME

Democracy is much more than the mere exercise of electoral competition (Latin America has a long history of uncompetitive elections to prove it), no more than the simple existence of elected assemblies is a definitive sign of representation. The institutional approach to democratic consolidation therefore leaves much to be desired.

Populism is easily misinterpreted because its discourse, and to a less extent its practice, signifies the inclusion of the masses in debates previously reserved for political elites. Populism emerged with the transfer of power from the oligarchy to a system controlled by modernizing urban elites, intellectuals, and the developing state apparatus. This is why one often associates populist governments with progressive policies.

Since we do not want to disassociate populism from its national context, our definition remains decidedly broad. Although it is difficult to determine to what extent they are exclusive, three characteristics can be attributed to populism. In the first place, populism is associated with political mobilization based on symbolic rhetoric capable of inspiring the masses. Second, populism is a heterogeneous coalition primarily recruited from the working classes but also from the middle classes, the liberal bourgeoisie, and bureaucracy. In Mexico and Peru, populism coextensively mobilized the rural masses, an important ethnic and demographic factor in both countries. Finally, populism is associated with a series of measures destined to facilitate the transfer of agroexport production surplus toward the production of manufactured goods for the internal market.

Characteristically, populism is associated with a highly defined process of industrialization through import substitution. According to this logic—with all the trappings of the modernization theory's economic determinism—populism is merely a phase in the building of political linkages through industrial development, which eventually leads to the emergence of a modern society governed by the rules of democratic debate and liberal regulation. Therefore, in keeping with this line of thought, the authoritarian interludes, in destroying the institutional foundations of populism and accelerating the implantation and diffusion of market relations, contributed to social modernization. Having done away with the populist misadventure, and following the departure of the military, civil society would naturally evolve toward a fledgling democracy to be consolidated through the establishment of an appropriate institutional framework.

Paradoxically, the error of this approach is to have given too much importance to the social dynamic as an instigator of change and to have neglected the rigidity of organizational arrangements. Populism corresponds with the rise of the developmentalist state directly assuming entrepreneurial functions and actively participating in the emergence of national industry. More than creating the market, the state appropriates it and takes on the quasi-exclusive responsibility of resource allocation. In this sense, the social dynamic is totally absorbed by this new order, which not only defines but takes complete control of the mode of development. Such is the essence of developmentalism.

This passage toward industrial capitalism necessitated the transfer of resources to emerging industries. On a political level, this was inconceivable without the mobilization of the urban masses, previously excluded from the process, into a vast heterogeneous coalition held together by its opposition to the oligarchy and, to a lesser extent, by a goal of industrial development and social modernization. Strong linkages of mutual support developed between the state apparatus, the emerging bourgeoisie, and the various corporations while feeding the masses with rhetoric of better days ahead. A rapidly consolidated system of political arrangement took hold and a new elite emerged, taking full advantage of its privileged access to the state and its participation in a hierarchical and ramified network of patronage and resource distribution.

Clientelism and corporatism are fundamental elements of political reality in Latin America. Corporatism is the manifestation of a new alliance incorporating the middle classes and urban masses that has proved to be a major obstacle in the development of a pluralist system of representation. Clientelism must not be considered so much as deviant behavior comparable to corruption, but more as a form of political culture that evolved from a necessary survival instinct in a society characterized by extreme inequalities.

It is important to point out that clientelism has remained intact and has played a functional role in the corporatist structure to such an extent that the two systems coexist in a mutually supportive symbiotic relationship. Populism has been constructed on a corporatist base, incorporating the masses into the political system of state-approved organizations. The antipopulist military regimes in Argentina and Brazil, governing by decree against the people and the political class, never managed to modify the political culture. It follows today that the corporatist organizations have proved to be more durable elements of the political system than political parties and thus the structural elements at the base of the populist regimes have remained intact. Populist practices have survived while the developmentalist project is no longer relevant in the present economic context. We are therefore faced with a political situation that underlines the permanence of organizational arrangements independent of any particular economic project. The disconnection of the political game from social interests thus reaches an alarming level.

SITUATIONS OF POLITICAL IMPASSE

Political impasse is the product of ineffectual civilian governments. In Brazil, this weakness can be attributed to the absence of linkages between political organizations and existing interests in society. We are in fact confronted with a political market that restricts any policy initiative.

Politics then becomes more a system of consumption than of production and political elites are reduced to consolidating clientelist relationships rather than representing social interests and global objectives. Such a situation facilitates the leaders' role in changing strategies and alliances without embracing new ideologies or representing class interests (Touraine, 1988, p. 308).

This lack of representation is compensated by resorting to clientelist practices.

Clientelism has the effect of concentrating executive power. Demands tend to converge at the apex of this network, where the president, in the absence of any reform mission, facilitates the system's reproduction. Mexico, more than any other country, clearly demonstrates this dynamic in one presidential mandate after another. In Brazil, the initial success of the Plan Cruzado was accredited more to President Sarney and his inner circle than to the PMDB during the November 1986 elections (Pécaut, 1987, p. 34).

Clientelism also involves a game of personal influence and allocation of privilege for private gain. This network of patronage in search of collective advantage imposes a code of rules known as the "privatization of the state." In the context of economic crisis, the consequences of such practice can be catastrophic.

Given that the dynamic element in the system is that of the exchange of favors, ideological cleavages tend to blur in the heat of political bargaining. As Touraine (1988, p. 308) points out, the result is that of a very high degree of political availability, which translates into a surprising combination of alliances. In Brazil and Mexico, more so than anywhere else, we are in a position to clearly identify a political class dominated by families and clans whose primary objective is access to or control of positions of power. Ideological affiliation is secondary to criteria such as association with the opposition or with members of government.

Brazil

The military imposition of rules limiting party activities in Brazil has tended to distance the already remote political class even further from interests in society. These strict rules engendered the creation of political parties such as ARENA and MDB and later their atomization into a myriad of formations (PDS, PFL, PL, PDC, PMDB, PDT, PTB, etc.), which are more a collection of individuals, clans, and factions trying to position themselves on the political market than that of organizations defending interests or promoting a social project. For lack of any specific ideology, the primary objective of these political groups is to latch on to a successful coalition at all levels of government. The result is a complex and constantly fluctuating network of alliances.

Paradoxically, these commitments tend to immobilize. In the absence of any program, the government finds itself cornered into negotiating with all parties in a system where the primary interest of those participating is their strategic position on the political market. These never-ending negotiations result in a perpetual realigning of alliances, which render any policy initiative highly unpredictable and eventually paralyze government. This political impasse, accentuated by the November 1989 presidential elections, has existed in Brazil since the late 1980s. It is therefore not surprising that such fundamental projects as agrarian reform have totally aborted and that any attempt at reducing the budgetary deficit has come up against considerable resistance. Finally, in this perspective it is easier to understand the often-curious content of the new constitution.

Some political formations have nevertheless managed to resist the corporatist temptation. First of all, the two communist parties—PCB (the Moscow-affiliated Brazilian Communist Party) and the PC do B (Brazilian Communist Party, created after a split within the PCB)—remain faithful to their traditional class-oriented platform and distance themselves from the other formations. They nevertheless participate in the political alliance game. The PT (Worker's Party) was explicitly created in reaction to traditional political practices. Officially recognized in 1982, the PT has stayed away from any outside alliances, banking on the militancy of its members to escape marginalization. Having based their program on popular organization and initiatives, the PT's political action is seen as a radical and defiant critique of government and traditional political practices. The PT has for the most part been able to resist any clientelist co-optation or compromise.

Argentina

In Argentina, the democratic government of President Alfonsín was confronted with a political culture traditionally favoring mechanisms of extrapartisan and extraparliamentary participation. The country is characterized by a weak partisan system and by highly powerful pressure groups capable of blocking adverse policy but unable to impose their own hegemony. This impasse is the product of nine years of populist government between 1946 and 1955, a brief period of semidemocratic experiences, and finally military authoritarianism.

These three experiences resulted in the development of political practices far removed from the liberal democratic model. Populism, semidemocratic regimes, and authoritarianism together rendered mediations between citizens and government ineffective or nonexistent. Therefore, when the possibility of exerting pressure presents itself (which obviously excludes military regimes), it tends to directly target the state. The representational gap is then occupied by corporatist pressure compensating not only for inefficient political institutions but also rendering them inoperable by undermining their already feeble claim to legitimacy.

The two semidemocratic governments of 1958–62 and 1963–66 rendered the political system (political parties and parliament) ineffective insofar as both Radical Party victories were made possible only by the proscription of the dominant Peronist Party. Excluded from direct political participation and deprived of their partisan structure, the Peronists had no other choice but to channel their demands through unions, using them as a bona fide political pressure group. However, workers' associations had no monopoly over extrainstitutional participation. Capitalist interest groups adopted a similar conduct. The various bourgeois factions had difficulty expressing their concerns through established political channels and found it more convenient to act outside the political system in exploiting other political links through their associations.

Relations between business associations have always been confrontational, rejecting all representational interests from the opposition as illegitimate and forming opposing political and social alliances. Therefore, organized interests were generally led to defining their action outside of the traditional partisan framework with the resulting effect of rendering parliament and the parties only marginally representative of society and exerting constant corporatist pressure on the executive.

This lack of representation due to weak democratic institutions has impeded the emergence of social actors. In its place, highly structured corporatism resulted in institutional spillover and redundant political practices. Where institutions were unable to articulate collective interests, social actors tended to make exclusive use of parallel mechanisms of intervention for channeling their demands. This is why the commitment to democratic reform was at best marginal. Remaining on the periphery made it possible to question the regime's legitimacy when external demands could not be properly channeled.

Lacking a supportive political base, the only way for a government to remain in power is to administer public capital according to the force of the non-institutionalized pressures placed on it. Governmental function is thus reduced to the impossible mediation of distributive conflicts between various associations. Policy gives way to inflation as a mechanism of reaching compromise. The responsibility for failure inevitably falls on the government in power, which finds its support base gradually eroded with each initiative.

The third Peronist government of 1973–76 endeavored to break with corporatism by reenforcing the institutional political system and formalizing the rules of the corporatist game by way of a social contract. The government's attempt to break with corporatist behavior ended like other elected governments, with the channeling of social conflict outside institutionalized structures. The main difference with previous experiences was the tragic outbreak of violence that supplanted traditional demands. Following the 1976 military coup, the authoritarian government interrupted this dynamic and opened exclusive channels of mediation between business and the state.

The Alfonsín government had no better success in breaking with corporatist tradition. Given the lack of democratic culture due to the weakness of political institutions, the political setting is ripe for a return to populism.

Mexico

Of our four case studies, populism in Mexico is probably where the integration of popular classes was most notable. Mexican populism is the product of an all-powerful state in a country where the oligarchy was totally eradicated during the revolution of 1910–17. As a result, the populist discourse is deeply imbedded in the Mexican social structure and has remained a powerful political point of reference for over 50 years. Given the support of the masses who had participated in the destruction of the old order, the protagonists of Mexican populism have been able to remain highly autonomous to private interests (Zermeño, 1987, p. 61). This support came not only from the urban masses but especially, as was the case in Peru, from the rural proletariat. Mexican populism was therefore built on a base of already existing social action and organization and in comparison with the rest of Latin America was "much more radical, much more national, much more popular and much more statist" (Zermeño, 1987, p. 67).

Historical populism has its roots in the presidency of Lázaro Cárdenas (1934–40). As a military officer, Cárdenas was a radical and charismatic member of the winning faction of the civil war. In 1938 he consolidated his power, giving a corporatist structure to the state party PRM (Party of the Mexican Revolution), and integrating virtually all sectors of Mexican society with the sole exception of the clergy and business. Although this party has changed its name (to PRI, Institutional Revolutionary Party) and statute over the years, the corporatist organization of interests through collective and compulsory affiliation has remained unchanged in over five decades. It should nevertheless be pointed out that popular mobilization by Lázaro Cárdenas was an authentic instrument of political struggle. Today its use is restricted to that of electoral support similar to that of the Brazilian Estado Nôvo of 1937–43.

On the other hand, populist rhetoric had become an inalienable element of the administration of power quite independent of the actual content of the public policy adopted. All party declarations are invariably made in the name of the nation, the revolution, the people, and social justice. In this sense José Luis Reyna (1977, p. 161) considers the Mexican system as "populist corporatism" insofar as "populist ideology within a corporatist political regime has prevented the development in Mexico of real and representative political organization of the popular classes."

In a similar manner to our other case studies, two structural factors—clientelism and the nature of political organization—reenforce the need for a populist point of reference. Clientelism, as an instrument of domination, continues to flourish despite modernization initiatives undertaken by the three previous administrations. This is of no surprise given that without clientelism the system would no longer be able to function as it does. The corporatist heritage has reduced the perception of political authority to cynical and passive consensus. Clientelism is evident at all levels: in the corporatist structures of the state party, in public administration, and in relations between government and opposition.

Thus, despite major differences in form, the actual content of the daily political practice in Mexico has a high degree of similarity with Brazilian politics: the continuous shifting of alliances in order to be on the winning side, bartering for political favors, respecting the hierarchical status quo, and so on. Whether this haggling takes place between several small parties as in Brazil or within one single party as in Mexico, the end result is the same. The PRI is not an authentic political party in which government platforms are negotiated, but an interest party in which the struggle revolves around the access to positions of influence and power. The result is an analogous sociopolitical evolution that has transformed into a regional division of power between elites.

There are nevertheless two major distinguishing characteristics in the Mexican case: vertical stratification and centralization of clientelist networks. The creation of the state party, PRI, as a stabilizing and consensus-building mechanism between various leaders and their clientele (defined along corporatist and occupational criteria) resulted in a high concentration of power at the top. Previously, corporatist reform tended to weaken regional despots and substituted them for occupational and sectoral national bosses. The PRM (1934–46) thus deregionalized the power structure and provided for its concentration at the federal level with its pinnacle at the executive. The president decides on the order of these networks every six years, so that the heads of these networks can take advantage of the numerous alliances without upsetting the structure decided upon from the top (Monsiváis, 1987, p. 76). The disciplined respect of this hierarchy is fomented by the high interpenetration of clientelist networks and government administrative structures.

More so than in Brazil, the Mexican president is undeniably at the center of these clientelist networks, given his broad legal and informal powers. Those involved in political bargaining with the president on policy issues are not political parties but interest groups organized either from within the state-party machinery or from without. Because the president is restricted by the constitution to only one term of consecutive office, the issue of succession is of crucial importance in the recomposition of the models of intraclientelist distribution. Succession, not surprisingly, is determined by clientelist methods in which the incumbent president decides on his own replacement. Therefore one finds in Mexico a populism that, despite its point of reference, is geared to interest politics and reinforces clientelism. Populism helps avoid democratic power sharing and impedes the development of representative political institutions.

Peru

The Peruvian case is unique in that, of all the countries considered in this study, Peru is the country where populism made its appearance the latest and as a result took on mythical proportions as the vehicle of unrealized dreams.

For many years populism in Peru was nothing more than the project of the American Popular Revolutionary Alliance (APRA), founded in 1924 by the legendary Víctor Raúl Haya de la Torre during his exile in Mexico. The traditional alliance between the armed forces and the landowning oligarchy blocked the Aprista populists' access to power in spite of popular support.

Paradoxically, Peruvian populism did not take hold as a result of popular mobilization, but because of the 1968 military takeover led by Juan Velasco Alvarado. This is why it is more appropriate to refer to this case as "military populism." Even though the army was responsible for snuffing out previous attempts at establishing populism, populist themes and popular mobilization were recuperated by the military from 1968 on. Despite the Velasco government's ill-fated attempt to establish a corporatist structure in order to control popular mobilization, it must be granted that popular participation reached unprecedented levels in Peru during this period. As in the case of radical Mexican populism, Peruvian military populism opened the way for the mobilization of both peasants and urban workers to such an extent that even with the gradual retreat of the military, the corporations grew to occupy a front-line position in the Peruvian political spectrum.

Following the repeated failures of the elected government of Fernando Belaúnde Terry (1981–85) in resolving the political and economic crisis, populism returned in 1985 with a civilian face (Bourque and Warren, 1989, p. 9). Alan García, the first Aprista president ever elected in the country's history, restored populist style and policy to Peruvian political life. During his presidency, García made a point of reviving the most nationalistic and reformist aspects of the Haya de la Torre and Velasco heritage. In order to distance himself from both the discredited Right and the radical Left, García called for the creation of a national community, leaving aside ideological differences for the welfare of the country (*El Comercio*, July 29, 1985). When an electoral coalition, including major sectors of the armed forces and the Left, was formed in support of García's mandate obtained in the 1985 elections, everything seemed to fall into place for the implementation of populist reforms. The policy measures that followed confirm this change.

This situation begs the question of why Peru turned to the populist economic policy and style. Why did the new government not make use of its electoral support to reinforce democratic decision-making ? The pronounced social economic and regional inequalities present in Peruvian society provide a preliminary structural explanation. Given the absence of representational institutions or even—in contrast to Brazil and Mexico—of clientelist mediations, populism is an attempt to bridge the gap between the elite and marginalized sectors of society. Another structural factor is that which Susan Bourque and Kay Warren (1989: 10–11) call "political memory." According to this line of thinking, democracy is not to be invented but to be found in programs drawn up by great men who have been deemed right by history. Therefore there is no need of a new order but the refurbishing of past popular traditions to assure continuity.

The nature of popular organizations also tends to favor populism. Industrial and civil service unions, rural labor federations, entrepreneurial and street vendor associations, the military, and so on put forward sectoral demands without an overall common national objective. The resource grabbing typical of interest politics is played out on a more visible level in the absence of reliable clientelist networks. Finally, within the actual party in power there are those who prefer populism to the power sharing inherent in democracy. APRA's internal leadership structure, because of its long history, has a highly established and impenetrable hierarchy that tends to exclude those outside of the inner circle, and who do not toe the fanatical and intolerant party lines or accept its strict disciplinary code (Bourque and Warren, 1989, p. 11). It is therefore not surprising that Alan García made an attempt to distance himself from the militant Aprista tradition.

ELECTORAL DEADLINES

Populist resurgence or persistence (Mexico) can be found in the structural obstacles to the building of a system of political representation. These obstacles are at the same time reinforced by more circumstantial factors, such as the dramatic economic situation the whole of the region is experiencing at present and electoral timetables in which populist promises are valuable currency.

Given the extreme inequalities, Peruvian expectations are high and patience is short. The governments of Velasco, Morales-Bermúdez, Belaúnde, and García were all popular as long as their promises were perceived as having a chance of being kept. All were utterly rejected once it became evident that their actions were not up to the expectations they had originally created. These radical changes in opinion have heightened tensions in the country.

During the 1985 campaign, Alan García presented an electoral platform that ridiculed the liberal economic measures and austerity policies of his predecessor. His main objective was to take full advantage of the expanded electoral market following the 1985 law granting voting rights to illiterates (Bourque and Warren, 1989, p. 9). At the same time García tried to distance himself from the exclusionary and fanatical elements within the APRA Party in making overtures to sectors that had been previously outside of the party's sphere such as intellectuals, businessmen, and skilled labor (Bourque and Warren, 1989, pp. 11, 17). APRA ran a smooth and sophisticated campaign, complete with the open endorsement of the Socialist International and focused on the image of "Alan" and his personal rapport with society's most underprivileged.

García won the first round with 45.5 percent of the votes from a total electorate 87 percent larger than in the previous presidential elections. The United Left (IU), led by Alfonso Barrantes, came second with 21.3 percent; Luis Bedoya from the conservative Right (PCD) took 10.2 percent; and the designated successor to Fernando Belaúnde Terry, Javier Alva (AP), managed only 6.3 percent of all votes cast (Wilkie et al., 1988, p. 220). Recognizing García's insurmountable lead, Barrantes decided to throw his support behind the Aprista candidate and avoided a second round of elections. As a candidate of the people, it soon became evident that the new president had little more than his image to combat the institutional and economic crisis ruining the country.

Alberto Fujimori's unanticipated "Cambio 90" movement victory over Mario Vargas Llosa, the candidate of the right-wing electoral coalition FREDEMO, is a dramatic illustration of the tremendous influence of populist electoral strategies in Peruvian politics. The April 1990 presidential elections once again showed that last-minute unrealistic promises can have an effect on voter intentions, which in the latter part of 1989 had favored FREDEMO at 30 percent on a national level and 50 percent in Lima (*Latin American Weekly Report*, November 23, 1989; *Caretas*, January 8, 1990). The inevitable happened in the second round runoff, with Fujimori taking 56 percent of the votes over Vargas Llosa's 44 percent.

This victory underlines the fact that the election was not fought between parties or electoral platforms but between personalities, with victory going to the one who best managed to capture the imagination of the masses and in particular of the inhabitants of the *pueblos jóvenes* on the outskirts of the principal coastal cities. Fujimori's supporters celebrated his victory as a triumph over the *pitucos y blanquitos* (a derogatory nickname for the primarily white-skinned upper class in Peru) of which Vargas Llosa had become a symbol (*Latin American Weekly Report*, June 21, 1990). Promises of conciliation and soft treatment of all sectors of Peruvian society converted those not prepared for serious belt tightening. Unfortunately, such hopes have proved unfounded as Fujimori has carried out a severe liberal adjustment program (immediate devaluation, fiscal reform, privatization of around 250 state-owned enterprises) to appease international financial institutions (IMF, World Bank, IADB) so that Peru may be considered for future credit (*Latin American Weekly Report*, July 12, 1990). APRA in any case finds that the Fujimori program is barely distinguishable from that proposed by Vargas Llosa. Given the electoral promises, the support of the Left in the second round runoff, and the opposition to FREDEMO, little could be done in such a critical economic climate.

Fujimori's election appears to confirm two tendencies that have emerged in Brazil and Argentina, respectively: (1) the election of a candidate with little or no political background with his personal image as his primary advantage, and (2) a populist leader who once in power carries out liberal economic policies far removed from his redistributive electoral promises.

The most significant attempt of breaking with corporatist culture was that of the Radical government of Raúl Alfonsín in Argentina (1983–89). Soon after winning the 1983 presidential election, Alfonsín endeavored to lay the foundations of a democratic society in isolating the state apparatus from corporatist pressures. This involved taking power away from the corporations and reinforcing the political system. The government's intention was to create representative mediations with civil society that would put the government at a respectable distance from sectoral interests. In doing so, the higher offices of state would be able to deal with the crisis without granting concessions to those sectors most affected by government measures. Priority was given to legality and to the reinforcement of the institutions enshrined in the constitution. Little reference was made to social problems, as if debate within democratic institutions would suffice in resolving the dualist structure so deeply ingrained in Argentine reality following seven years of authoritarian regressive distributional policies.

The deteriorating economic situation, difficulties in redefining the role of corporations, and the establishment of a new type of state-corporate relations forced the government into announcing the Austral Plan in June 1985. The Austral Plan was more than simply a stabilization or an antiinflationary project, but constituted a political reform and a series of short-term measures that could be qualified as a development program. In terms of political reform, it excluded social actors in the global policymaking process. Corporations would be consulted only on limited sectoral aspects of economic policy—in other words, the government would deal directly with the people, bypassing the corporate network. In the wake of the Plan's failure, the blame of frustrated hopes and expectations fell squarely on the government.

The Alfonsín government had become isolated because the break with the corporatist tradition did not coincide with real and effective institutional reform. For lack of democratic culture, Argentine society had become locked in a vicious circle, turning once again to the populist alternative.

The major achievement of the Radical government can be summarized as the opening of an immense space of public liberties and the reactualization of democratic institutions in Argentina. Its major failure, and possibly that for which the government was judged, was its poor handling of the economic crisis. It was in this context that Radicals and Peronists once again confronted each other in the May 1989 presidential elections. The stagnant political culture and the economic crisis pushed the Argentine electorate to opt for the populist platform. The Peronist candidate, Carlos S. Menem, appealing to political memory, tradition, the people, and consensus, took 47.3 percent of all votes cast against 32.4 percent for the Radical Party.

During the 1988 Mexican presidential campaign, a dissident faction of the state party took the gamble of reviving the populist tradition. Through no coincidence its candidate was none other than the son of Lázaro Cárdenas. As with Alan García in Peru, Cuauhtémoc Cárdenas chose to appeal to political memory. In accusing the PRI of betraying the fundamental principles of the revolution, the dissident "democratic wing" presented itself as the legitimate inheritor of the Mexican revolutionary tradition. In keeping with populist tradition, Cuauhtémoc Cárdenas cultivated his image as a strong charismatic leader and as a savior of the people. His charisma was no doubt fueled by the weak tradition of autonomous organization in Mexican society.

The gamble paid off and the dissidents made an unprecedented showing in the history of the Mexican opposition, due in part to the backing of a strong political alliance among the left and several popular organizations into a broad electoral coalition, the Democratic National Front (FDN). The actual final results are still hotly debated and the opposition has denounced a massive electoral fraud. The official figures gave the PRI candidate, Carlos Salinas de Gortari, 50.7 percent of the vote against 31.0 percent for the populist coalition. The FDN has rejected these figures, claiming 41 percent for their candidate compared to 36 percent for the PRI. Whatever the final result, Cuauhtémoc Cárdenas lent credibility to the revival of the populist project forgotten by the government. Populism has inspired a large portion of the masses who had lost confidence in the elections as well as popular organizations struggling for their autonomy from the PRI.

The Cardenista opposition has tried to capitalize on the revival and continuity of popular interest in the electoral process. The Revolutionary Democratic Party (PRD) created in May 1989 is mainly controlled by PRI dissidents and more moderate elements of the defunct Mexican Socialist Party (PMS). As it consolidates its internal structure, the PRD has given clear indications that it is distancing itself from the populist style and evolving into a modern party. This transition is easier than in the past, given the absence of three other parties formerly aligned to the FDN. These parties, very much in the populist and clientelist tradition, are the Popular Socialist Party (PPS), the Authentic Mexican Revolutionary Party (PARM), and the Cardenista Front for National Reconstruction Party (PFCRN).

The unexpected presence and continuity of the Cardenista opposition has led to a paradoxical situation. The Salinas de Gortari government, while implementing a modernizing liberal economic program, still makes extensive use of traditional populist tactics within the party and the public service, as has been observed in recent state elections. Corporatist and clientelist structures to control the masses and maintain its grip on power are still very much in place. The opposition, on the other hand, demands a return to the nationalist and reformist economic policies typical of historic populism while rejecting the corporatist and clientelist populist style. This is particularly clear in two of the eleven propositions of political reform tabled by the Cardenistas in Congress in September 1989: banning political party corporate affiliation and equal governmental treatment of all political parties.

In contrast to Argentina, the Brazilian experience has shown no evidence of any political will to break with the past. Brazil today is characterized by political inertia in the absence of any social project and the determination of the political class in maintaining the status quo. With the failure of the Plan Cruzado, the participational gap between policymaking and the partisan system established by the authoritarian regime has shown a tendency to widen as the PMDB has gradually distanced itself from the Sarney administration.

Ever since the death of Tancredo Neves and the investiture of the vice-

presidential candidate, José Sarney, as his replacement, political life in Brazil
has been held in suspense. Within the PMDB there was a strong sentiment that
Sarney, because of his previous ties with the military, had usurped the rightful
place of those who had fought against the dictatorship. While the political class
eagerly awaited the end of the Sarney mandate, energies were channeled into
writing the new constitution. In stark contrast to the institutional framework
and the social norms it sustains, the new Constitution ratified in October 1988
is decidedly progressive. One can easily be cynical in reading the nationalistic
discourse in honor of democracy, respect for fundamental rights, and equality.
The text clearly demonstrates once again that whether or not the Left wins
the elections, the Right will hold fundamental power. But what is really at stake
is the much more profound reality of the enormous gap between the ruling
class and the Brazilian people. This social hiatus is constantly reproduced and
reinforces populist manipulation. The extreme alienation of the masses allows
for political leaders to act "in the name of the people" with the conviction that
the people, ignorant of their situation, will never stake claim to their constitutional rights.

Two years after the PMDB's November 1986 landslide victory, the political
formations geared up for municipal elections that had taken on national significance and allowed for the various parties to reassess their strategies and position themselves for the 1989 presidential elections. The results clearly
indicated the PMDB's drop in popularity along with the Right while the popular
parties (PT, PDT), strengthened their positions. Nevertheless, for lack of a
clear winner, the stage was set for an unprecedented battle of vote-grabbing
electoral promises.

The political landscape has been fundamentally transformed during the long
electoral campaign that brought Fernando Collor de Melo to the presidency
after two rounds of voting. The most salient feature of the elections was the
lack of success of the more established politicians despite the backing of highly
organized electoral machinery that had been so active on both the local and
national scene over the past decade. A similar trend could be observed in Peru,
where Ricardo Belmont's recent electoral victory as mayor of Lima, as well
as Alberto Fujimori's electoral victory, seem to suggest a shift in public opinion
toward political candidates with no political past: which at least frees them
from being associated with the disasters of previous administrations.

Ulysses Guimarães, the PMDB and congressional leader—probably the
most well-known political figure in the country—went down to personal defeat
as the head of a party demoralized and weakened by infighting among its numerous factions. During the darkest years of the military repression, Guimarães had resolutely although not without concessions directed the only
tolerated opposition in the country. Lionel Brizola, for his part, was unable to
consolidate support from the North-East and São Paulo and was relegated to
the third position behind the Worker's Party candidate, Lula. Lula's impressive
showing in the first round demonstrated that the PT had national support. His

loss in the second round to Collor de Melo was primarily due to the rural vote in the marginal areas of the country. Over the course of his campaign, Lula was forced to make overtures to the middle class and therefore back down on some aspects of his original platform.

The candidate on the Right adopted the same strategy with greater success. Collor de Melo managed to capture the public's imagination in using a reformist rhetoric designed to appease both the liberal Right (antistate) as well as the middle and working classes to denounce the government's poor administration of the crisis. Representing a party created for the circumstances, Collor de Melo won the presidency owing to the unconditional backing of the national mass media. His victory demonstrates the unmistakable weakness of political parties, the vulnerability of popular organizations, and the extreme volatility of the popular vote. Such factors perfectly illustrate the thesis of the populist revival.

So far nothing has been resolved. Be it in Mexico, Argentina, Brazil, or Peru, the economic crisis, instead of focusing debate on policy orientations, has opened the political game to an unprecedented number of actors with no concrete proposals to make in terms of change. Although such a debate did take place in Mexico, the agreement between the PRI and PAN in October 1989 has indefinitely upheld the status quo over any chance at democratic reform.

THE APPEAL OF POPULISM

In the same manner that corporatism takes on different national forms and evolves over time, the populist temptation tends to reemerge in forms that correspond to the type of perceived blockage and according to whether it originates in the government or in the opposition.

A recent study (Cothran and Cothran, 1988) demonstrates how the legendary Mexican populist of the 1930s, Lázaro Cárdenas, made use of the public budget. Although he was well known for generous social program spending, he also inaugurated the huge deficits that would become common practice in Mexico and would reach levels of 30 percent of the total budget. Given that the president held large discretionary spending powers, there is little doubt that deficit spending was intentional.

In the absence of any political base or program, government action is essentially reduced to the management of public capital allocation according to the influence of those interest groups with the most political capital to exchange in return. Clientelism accentuates the concentration of power while the objective of democratic consolidation is to open access to power through the respect for the principles of representation. The maintenance of a clientelist system is incompatible with the democratization of political life. Populism in the form of clientelism of the masses allows political leaders to avoid dealing with this problem.

The clientelist logic is also ingrained in the Mexican opposition. As such their policies do not correspond to the model of "authentic" ideology (Wanderley Reis, 1988, p. 9) but rather to the systematic and vague pragmatism articulated by "catch-all" parties. As is the case in Western democracies, interest groups, rather than complementing partisan and representative institutions, penetrate them. This explains the sudden arrival on the Mexican political scene of organizations defending the regional and specific rights of producers, vendors, parents, women, farmers, and so on, with no consideration for the institutional system as a whole. Political parties quickly assimilate these claims and integrate them into their electoral platforms. The opening of the political system therefore coincides with the increased influence of corporatist practices favoring a conservative bias for perpetuating the traditional authoritarian order. The influence of the popular sectors and their capacity for mobilization should nevertheless not be underestimated.

In a system characterized by patronage and where the power gap between state and society is both extremely broad and extremely narrow—broad due to centralization and narrow because of the personalization of power—the opposition eventually wins out. By opposition, we understand the leader who manages to present himself as the representative of change, as opposed to outsiders who have no influence in defending their positions.

In Argentina, populism promises in the same breath: growth, salary and profit increases, as well as a social and political pact without specifying where the resources for distribution will come from or how the new government will manage to succeed where others have failed in the past. Paradoxically, the economic platform, albeit vague, ambiguous, and contradictory, seems to have better success with electors than the political discourse. In telling the people what they want to hear, the Peronist candidate, Carlos Menem, created a magical climate of hope. The Peronist-organized *caravanas de la esperanza* (caravans of hope) emphasized Menem's "debt to the people" over the country's debt to foreign banks. Soon after Menem's victory, the financial realities of office quickly overtook the rhetoric of electoral campaigning.

In contrast to Mexican or Brazilian populism, Argentine democratic discourse is above all defensive, trying to reassure those for whom democratic values are of great importance. In Mexico, populism is presented as an alternative to the authoritarian PRI. In Brazil, the state-endorsed civil legalism remains trapped in the military tradition. In Argentina, *democracia* was the only slogan for which the Radical Party could claim any legitimacy. As a result the Peronists fell in line behind the rallying cry of *justicia social*, more compatible with their image, which, as with the APRA party in Peru, is subject to constant redistribution pressures.

In Brazil, the political market is subjected to strong pressures. The hunt for political clientele has resulted in a constant changing of alliances, which tends to blur ideological differences. Any attempt at change is engulfed in a conciliatory process that inevitably compromises the original intention. The system becomes paralyzed in a process of continuous faction splitting and short-lived alliances. For lack of a dominant party, any reform involving a shift in the balance of power away from the traditional political class or their organizations is doomed to failure.

The election of a head of state by universal suffrage is a crucial moment in the political life of a country. It is a delicate and unique exercise in which the system demonstrates its capacity for renewal in an orderly fashion in respecting individual and collective rights. In Brazil the 1989 presidential elections are particularly significant insofar as they have implied a redefinition of the political game. Although the entire political class has been mobilized, the constant clientelist-driven changing of alliances has deformed electoral consultation in limiting ideological differences (Marques-Pereira, 1986, p. 67). This game has been complicated by weak political organization on a national level and by the persistence of extreme regional disparities.

Now that the election of the "patron of patrons" is decided by universal suffrage, it is a new electoral game with new rules. Reaching the populace and capturing the indispensable popular vote have now become an essential element of political strategy.

In blurring regional and ideological differences, the populist discourse is a natural strategy for the prospective candidate. It consists of putting the leader above local and sectoral demands by way of a unifying discourse so as to capture the public mainstream (Touraine, 1988, p. 175). Populism speaks in the name of the nation and of the people against the oligarchy and foreign domination. Divisions between left and right become irrelevant. The main distinction is the demagogic opposition between the masses and the elite.

This discourse can be carried by political personalities of all shapes and sizes (Wanderley, 1988, p. 9). Brazil's most recent populist spokesperson, Brizola, proposes in his *socialismo moreno* to stop all debt payments to the institutions of Yankee imperialism as does Lula of the PT and Cuauhtémoc Cárdenas in Mexico. But above all Collor, the "knight in shining armor," while denouncing government inefficiency, has committed himself to a severe economic stabilization program and promises of greater social justice. Such is the opposition between the responsible administrator and the great reformer. Such was the position of García in Peru, and is still the case of Menem in Argentina, and concerning the ambiguous reformism of Salinas in Mexico.

CONCLUSION

The enormous power of populism resides in the ease with which it sidesteps obstacles confronting the building of a democratic order. The populist temptation increases in the context of weaknesses in the political system and the resistance to any fundamental change in the system of representation.

Where Touraine, with a sociologist's optimism, sees only the resistance of the old order, we observe the resurgence of a practice deeply ingrained in the power structure. If the present financial crisis does not bring back the authoritarian order, it will handicap any reformist initiative and increase the interest in populist solutions. It is the paradoxical case of authoritarianism with the consent of the poor.

While populism in both its style and institutional structure remain constant, economic policy tends to adapt to the environment. The long-outdated reformist nationalism of the 1930s has rapidly given way to a new generation of international liberal policies. In the name of modernization and progress, Salinas, Menem, and Fujimori, in spite of their undisputed populist heritage, are new converts to market-oriented economic policy. In the opposition, Brizola and Cárdenas are trapped in their archaic developmentalist platform, while Collor de Melo has developed his own political space for preaching the virtues of liberalism.

The situation in Argentina confirms our hypothesis. Menem has turned his back on the political system in his "government of the people." Immediately following his election he made overtures to the industrial elite, amnestied the military, and distanced himself from the Confederacíon General del Trabajo. In this case market-driven solutions to the economic crisis are incarnated in a populist structure. There is little doubt that this same orientation is being applied in Brazil. Economic stabilization will nevertheless be moderated by the regrouping of political alliances in preparation for the legislative and regional government elections slated for October 1990. As a result of the economic shock of March 1990, the economy plunged into a deep recession. The government failed to win its war against inflation and as a result it lost the gubernatorial races in the major states (São Paulo, Rio de Janeiro, Pernambuco) of the country.

The reconciliatory temptation is enormous. Promising that resistances and obstacles will disappear once the majority adopts the dogma of unity and solidarity is a convincing if not paradoxical political strategy in a context characterized by extreme economic and social inequalities.

REFERENCES

Bourque, S. C. and K. B. Warren (1989). "Democracy Without Peace: The Cultural Politics of Terror in Peru." *Latin American Research Review*, 24, no. 1, pp. 7–34.

Cárdenas, C. et al. (1988). *Radiografia del fraude: Análisis de los datos oficiales del 6 de julio.* Mexico City: Nuestro Tiempo.

Cothran, D. A. and Ch. C. Cothran (1988). "Mexican Presidents and Budgetary Secrecy." *International Journal of Public Administration*, 11, no. 3, pp. 311–340.

Di Tella, T. (1965). "Populismo y Reforma en América Latina," *Desarrollo Económico,*" 4, no. 16 (April–June), pp. 393–394.

Germani, G. (1962). *Política y sociedad en una época de Transición.* Buenos Aires: Paidés.

Hertoghe, A. and A. Labrousse (1989). "Le Pérou se décompose." *Le monde diplomatique,* No. 418 (January 13).

Marquez-Pereira, J. (1986). "Entre libéralisme et clientélisme." *Les Temps Modernes,* No. 491, (June), pp. 62–86.

Monsiváis, C. (1987). "Con usted hasta la crítica." In Abraham Nuncio (ed.), *La suce-sión presidencial en 1988.* Mexico City: Grijalbo, pp. 73–83.

Pécaut, D. (1987). "Des élections à la Constituante." *Problèmes d'Amérique Latine,* No. 80, 1st trimester, pp. 25–42.

Renya, J. L. (1977). "Redefining the Authoritarian Regime." In J. L. Reyna and R. S. Weinhart (eds.), *Authoritarianism in Mexico.* Philadelphia: Institute for the Study of Human Issues, 155–172.

Touraine, A. (1988). *La parole et le sang: Politique et société en Amérique latine.* Paris: Odile Jacob.

Wanderley Reis, F. (1988). "La construction démocratique au Brésil: Diagnostic et per-spectives." *Problèmes d'Amérique latine,* No. 90, 4th trimester, pp. 3–22.

Weffort, F. C. (1968). "El populismo en la política brasileña." In Celso Furtado et al., *Brasil hoy.* Mexico: Siglo XXI, 54–84.

Wilkie, J. W. et al. (eds.) (1988). *Statistical Abstract of Latin America, vol. 26.* Los Angeles: UCLA.

Zermeño, S. (1987). "Hacia una democracia como identidad restringida: sociedad y polí-tica en México." *Revista mexicana de sociologia,* 49, no. 2 (April–June), pp. 57–58.

CHAPTER ELEVEN

Public Trust and the Consolidation of Latin American Democracies

LUIS RONIGER

La démocratie sans le développement n'est q'une illusion, une façon de trahir les espoirs du peuple. (Democracy without development is but an illusion, a way of betraying the hopes of the people.)
—François Mitterrand in visit to Uruguay,
October 11, 1987

La excelencia de un gobierno no consiste en su teoría, ni en su mecánismo, sino en ser apropiado a la naturaleza y al carácter de la nación para quien se instituye. (The excellence of a government consists not in its philosophy nor in its structure, but instead in its appropriateness to the nature and character of the nation for which it is instituted.)
—Simón Bolívar in Congress of Angostura,
February 15, 1819

Few Latin American intellectuals would object to the visions expressed in these statements, yet their implications may be of great concern for those willing to consolidate democracy in Latin America. Conceding that development is not at the turn of the corner, is the fate of the new democracies to remain a mere illusion? Does procedural democracy conflict with the historically shaped "nature" or, to put it in a modern wording, the institutional trends and expectations in these countries?

The pace of change has been enormous in these respects. Only a decade and a half ago, most of the states of Latin America were under authoritarian rule. By the late 1980s, these nations—with the exception of Castro's Cuba and the partial exception of Haiti—had adopted some form of liberal democratic procedure as the basis of government. The massive and parallel occurrence of such processes of liberalization and democratization has been dramatic and impressive in its own. Their significance is further evident against the background of the post–World War II democratic transitions; in contrast with the latter, the new processes of liberalization and democratization in Latin America were mostly the product of internal contradictions, struggles, and disaggregation of commitments within the ruling authoritarian coalitions, rather than the mere product of external factors. Nonetheless, with the 1989/90 "avalanche" processes of liberalization in Eastern Europe, the return of Latin American nations to democratic rule becomes geared into a global trend that might increase the appeal of modern democracy in the area. As a result of this trend, what until recently seemed to be a century of revolution, liberation, and development turns to be reinterpreted from new perspectives as a century of renewed pluralism, of ethnic and national revival, and (in certain circles) of the presaged victory of capitalism over communism (Z, 1990; Touraine, 1990a, pp. 19–21; and compare Fuentes, 1985, pp. 69–71). These developments—as well as others, such as the constraints posed by the huge foreign debt of Latin America—heighten awareness to the tight interplay of global and domestic factors in the shaping of political processes. Factors such as the ambience of the international community or the impact of previous transitions on the reformulation of others are extremely important in analyzing the forms and pace of the move toward democracy in Latin America (Schmitter, 1986; Roniger, 1989). Here, however, I would like to focus analysis on the internal sociopolitical factors affecting the prospects of democratic consolidation in general and the extension and institutionalization of public trust in particular.

THE PROBLEMS AHEAD

The Latin American nations have changed their sociological and economic profiles significantly during the last decades. Economic transformations created possibilities of development but also gave rise to new inequalities, imbalances, and disparities. Economic growth, advancing per capita urban income, the growth of middle classes, and the development of the tertiary (service) sectors through public investment were accompanied by extensive rural-urban migration. Mass poverty became urbanized and hence more visible, and a new awareness arose of social injustice and unrest. Urban settlements continued to develop and metropolitan centers became huge and often highly polluted conurbations with considerable marginal sectors struggling for livelihood and greater access to public services. Finally, the strides of industrialism were followed in many of these countries by processes of deindustrialization, import-desubstitution, antiinflationary policies that handed over cost advantages to imports and injured local industries, and an external debt that was not used for further development of productive forces (save in authoritarian Brazil) and that further mortgaged economic development (Hirschman, 1987; Roniger, 1990a: Chaps. 1 and 3).

From a political perspective, many of the Latin American nations still seem to face, *mutatis mutandis,* the constitutional and political dynamics that they have faced during most of their history as independent nations—namely, some kind of Hobbesian situation and vision, whereby the state is expected but often unable to guarantee public order and personal security. Whether it is in Central America, Colómbia, or Peru, surveys indicate that the longing for personal security and public order still remains a major concern for millions of citizens in conflict-ridden polities (see, e.g., *El Tiempo* of Bogotá, October 4, 1987).

The other problems facing these polities are herculean as well. Issues of participation, of democratization in access to power, of the responsiveness of political elites to social demands, will continue to stand at the center of the political agenda in these polities, which are laden with social pressures. These problems are especially thorny since the move to democracy has occurred in most countries under severe economic situations (with some partial exceptions such as Chile and Brazil). Moreover, the transitions have not obliterated socioeconomic inequalities and social cleavages, clientelism and corporatism, and the inevitable confrontation between their own political dynamics and cultural expectations and the logic of a liberal democracy. [1]

At this stage, it is especially crucial to analyze first whether the political frameworks that are supposed to bring together social demands (e.g., parties and social movements) will manage both to forward dissent on the real issues at hand (social reforms, the foreign debt) and to reinforce the commitment to democracy as the system that allows for such open confrontation and provides an agreed-upon framework to deal with policy formulation and control over its implementation. The second analysis is whether the state will become more accountable and open to policy impacts generated in more autonomous forms of representation and participation. Hereafter I turn to analyze such prospects, taking as vantage points the insights of democratic theory in general and the study of social trust in particular.

DEMOCRATIC THEORY AND THE CONDITIONS FOR CONSOLIDATION OF THE NEW DEMOCRACIES IN LATIN AMERICA

In defining democracy, social scientists emphasize the institutional arrangements that allow competition for power and participation in the recurring election of authorities and the redefinition of policies. The empirical referents are usually the mass, liberal democracies characterized by relatively free, fair, and periodic competitive elections based on universal—or quasi-universal—adult suffrage, free of significant proscriptions. Following Robert Dahl's analysis of "polyarchy" (1971, pp. 1–20), scholars enumerate as major defining traits: competition for power, a highly inclusive level of political participation in the selection of leaders and policies, and a certain level of civil and political liberties—freedom of expression, freedom of the press, freedom to form and join organizations—sufficient to ensure political competition and participation (Diamond et al., 1987, p. 5; Morlino, 1987; and compare Macpherson, 1977, pp. 93–115 and Nohlen, 1988, pp. 41–42).

Historically, such freedoms—and modern democracies themselves—have developed in territorial kingdoms or former colonies through centuries-old processes of confrontation, negotiation, and contract, out of which modern states have been empowered and yet, at the same time, constricted by the language and the spirit of the law (Strayer, 1970; Rosen, 1990, pp. 2–3). Therefore, it is only natural to expect first, disagreements to be voiced and a debate to evolve on the goals carried out by such political systems; and second, differences in the conceptualization of the "moral purpose" of power in different societies and cultural areas. Confrontations at this level are essential and not merely accidental to democracy. Accordingly, on an ethical level, democracy has been conceptualized, especially (but not only) in Anglo-Saxon contexts—and following John Stuart Mill—as a political system envisioned to promote the advancement of society through the attainment of personal self-development while making the best use of moral, intellectual, and practical energies available "so as to operate with the greatest effect on public affairs" (Mill, 1977, pp. 392; Macpherson, 1977, pp. 44–76). " 'One citizen/one vote' is the functional equivalent, in the sphere of politics, of the rule against exclusion and degradation in the sphere of welfare, of the principle of equal consideration in the sphere of office, and of the guarantee of a school place in the sphere of education" (Walzer, 1983, pp. 305–306).

In the case of Latin America, such concern with higher issues and aims, with the moral purpose of power, has retained traditionally a more organic view, which holds that the political community and its center should stand above private interests. In the not-so-distant past, there were sectors that considered accordingly that the factional expression of private interests could be obviated, inasmuch as the rulers interpreted the popular will, worked toward the common good, and carried out the public mission in order and harmony, thus precluding anarchy and struggle (Stepan, 1980, pp. 51–84). Not only the military, but also political parties have sustained such elitist views on the polity. Such vision did not preclude partisanship, however, but could rather justify its exacerbation in the framework of pluralist societies and sectors being forced—and resenting—to comply with the awesome force of those willing to promote their own specific vision of the common good and the social order.

As we look to the future, this conception has other implications no less crucial for the prospects of consolidation of democracy. Inasmuch as eventually representative democracy can be considered as noninstrumental to the attainment of the common good—however this may be defined—democratic procedural institutions may be perceived as dispensable. Even when democracy has been respected—as in Peru in the early 1980s where, beyond the Southern Highlands, it was preferred to the alternative of the Sendero Luminoso (Shining Path), or at least was seen to be the lesser evil—representative democracy was publicly accorded a secondary value in comparison with social democracy. Again and again throughout the continent, procedural democracy is not considered—many would say, should not be—a value in itself. Putting Michael Walzer's characterization on its head, social democracy will be expected as an ultimate basis for human dignity and hence for procedural democratic legitimacy. Turning to a more immediate perspective, however, this raises the issue of the institutional conditions for its consolidation.

According to sociology and political science, such institutional supports include the multiple and criss-crossing organization of interests, the lack of monopoly over sources of information, and a degree of tempering both social inequalities and cumulative social cleavages that allows for accommodation and compromise among social and political actors on the methods and rules for peaceful conflict resolution. Politically, democracy requires acceptance of opposition, acceptance of the possibility that lower strata may mobilize, and acceptance of risks concerning the uncertain outcome of confrontations and the weighting of multiple interests (Eisenstadt, 1976; Morlino, 1987).

Beyond facilitating economic conditions, [2] sociopolitical developments are thus required for the consolidation of the new democratic regimes. One such development has to do with the changing nature of participation. Civil society should be able to develop autonomy and to participate independent of the political and administrative organs of the state, without undermining thereby the rule of the latter. In other words, sectors of civil society should be able to develop a public status that is not subordinate to state authority, while recognizing the latter's claims to rule. Voluntary associations, religious, linguistic, and ethnic organizations, professional and class unions, the mass media, gender and generational groups, as well as other civic groups should be able to attain public recognition and express themselves through various, mostly legitimate, channels of participation. This, in addition, implies a strong likelihood that the major political forces will agree to operate in forms that are sensitive to popular opinion and accountable to majorities.

SOCIAL MOVEMENTS, DISSENT, AND PROCEDURAL DEMOCRACY

Latin America has been witnessing a reappraisal of civil society and an incipient reformulation of the role of political actors and the state. The roots of such changes go back to the authoritarian statist regimes that tried to regulate civil society from the 1960s to the 1980s. Basically, these regimes did not develop a legitimacy of their own. Rather, the political discourse of the region remained liberal even during the authoritarian rule. A belief in this form of legitimacy was maintained by major sectors of the population and proclaimed even by the authoritarian rulers themselves and most of their early supporters. Many of the authoritarian leaders—for example, in the Southern Cone—portrayed their rule as an interregnum, a temporary state of affairs brought about by the urgent need to defuse the threat of communism, for example, or to avoid the danger of anarchy, or to root out administrative incompetence and corruption. They often promised a return to democracy as soon as circumstances allowed. And they retained a democratic discourse, while institutions typical of the previous democratic period (e.g., political parties) continued to function, although monitored by the state. Consequently, as the costs of maintaining authoritarian rule became more burdensome, liberalization and eventually democracy could be adopted as a viable option to authoritarianism.

A major development in this period was the progressive assertiveness of extraparliamentarian social movements. Thus, the process of liberalization and eventual democratization took place in some of these polities as a result not of demobilization (which was more typical, although far from universal, in Southern Europe) but rather of the spontaneous mobilization and reformulation of "open spaces" for autonomy. For instance, in post–1977 Argentina, as Elizabeth Jelin (1985) emphasized, there emerged social movements that claimed and sustained a public status independent of any delegation of power by the state. Movements such as the Mothers and Grandmothers of the Plaza de Mayo and other neighborhood and community-based associations emerged as relatively autonomous social actors. These movements raised ethical issues and recognized each other as sharing a nontotalistic, nonradical, but nonetheless highly moral and public mission. They demanded, for example, clarification concerning the fate of beloved kin who had "vanished" during the repression, and assumed de facto an autonomous presence that affected the public realm and helped to shape popular attitudes in the direction of preferring procedural containment of conflict over a repressive authoritarian one. They eventually contributed to a wide acceptance of representative democracy as the best possible regime for safeguarding individual rights. Similarly, in Brazil, resistance to authoritarianism was led by, among others, Catholic clerics, justice and peace commissions, professionals and journalists, and amnesty committees, who by raising ethical issues inhibited repression and thus opened the way for the expression of wide social demands (Moreira Alves, 1985).

Nonetheless, the current prevalence of civilian governments does not reflect a parallel institutionalization of procedural democracy. Indeed, the recognition of civic autonomy was largely due to the success of the popular movements in becoming connected with a public discussion about the moral purpose and boundaries of power during the authoritarian rule. But even in Argentina and more so in Brazil or Mexico, such recognition has remained largely conditional, for instance, upon their lack of impingement on the cherished attainment of political stability. Many of these movements have failed to find ways to institutionalize their input once the nations have moved to democracy (Diaz de Landa, 1990).

As in any democracy, the democratic "game" may be seen with opprobium in Latin America as soon as signs of regime ineffectiveness or erosion become prominent. Evidence of the former may take the form of inability to face the real national problems or to pass legislation because of "factionalism." The latter may be reflected in the opposition of sectors such as the church calling for a generalized "review of consciousness," student protests, electoral abstention, or public unrest following deterioration in the economy and the use of repressive means to contain discontent.

The very discussion of social issues is nonetheless extremely important in societies with acute social inequalities and intense pressure for social transformation—more so in societies like those of Latin America, where power is ideologically expected to be entrusted with a public mission. A social view of democracy—although posing a threat to the acceptance of procedural mechanisms as an end in themselves—may help bring discussion of social policy "out of the closet," that is, out of the exclusive control of the political elites. Thus, indirectly, it could increase the elites' accountability to wider sectors of the citizenship.

However, ruling coalitions face tremendous obstacles. In the current situation, they must build public trust while they are forced, willingly or not, to adopt harsh economic policies in order to dampen inflation and regain investments and growth, whereas expectations are high for redistribution "here and now," even in countries like Argentina where there has been a partial change of public opinion—especially among the upper classes—toward strategies of privatization, as reported by Fred Turner and Marita Carballo de Cilley (1990).

BUILDING PUBLIC TRUST IN LATIN AMERICAN DEMOCRACIES

To build public trust does not mean the encouragement of a total and unconditional confidence in the institutions of the state or in any other political and social institution. It rather implies that institutions (as people) may earn an unstated confidence in their viability, integrity, and credibility, as part of the commonsense knowledge of the constitutive order of events in everyday life and participation in the environment as a practical accomplishment, to use the terminology of phenomenology and ethnomethodology. [3]

Public trust concerns such varied aspects as the viability of monetary media of exchange, the legitimacy of authorities, the reliability of the political system, the efficacy of specialized institutions in spheres such as education and medicine, and the mode of trust in social actors with whom one interacts in both formal organizational frameworks and informal encounters. Public trust has been traditionally weak or, rather I would say focalized, in Latin America. Due to historical experiences, institutional trust has been granted mainly on particularistic bases, for instance, only as far as a certain party dominates the political scene, with the consequent factionalism, social and political violence, loss of public credit, and, consequently, inability to rule (as typically shown in the difficulties to implement taxation policies). [4] As a result, focal personal trust consequently has been reinforced. The focal character of trust has been reflected, for example, in the difficulties and apprehension exhibited by rural and urban sectors participating in wider interactions beyond the circles of kinship, immediate residence, and friendship. It has been also revealed in the entrenchment of clientelistic networks and factions (Miranda Ontaneda et al., 1980; Eisenstadt and Roniger, 1984, pp. 44–162; Roniger, 1990a). The potentiality of building societal trust through such hierarchical commitments has been realized in a focal mode. Accordingly, characteristic-based and process-based forms of trust have prevailed over trust in technical competence and role-oriented institutional commitments. Though clientelistic attachments have conferred social identity and credit upon "reliable" dependents of humble social origins, trust has remained narrowly oriented and unrelated to generalized criteria of role performance. Under conditions of focalization of institutional confidence, a high degree of energy, of emotional investment and instrumental involvement, seems to have been focused at the interpersonal level, albeit in focalized terms. This focal character has recreated anew the problems of its transference to unrelated social actors and of mastering uncertainty that could not be managed successfully through institutional means. Thus, while commitments have been manipulated across institutional frameworks and spheres of interaction, they remained unrelated to generalized principles of socially approved behavior, thereby reinforcing the vagueness of institutional rule enforcement and boundaries (e.g., between the political forces and the administration) and the fragility of institutional, role-oriented trust.

Under conditions of economic contraction, social unrest, and political turmoil, this pattern of focalized trust may evolve into one of generalized distrust, as that which characterized Colombia from the mid-1940s to the 1960s (at present compounded by the entrenchment of the narcotraffic power) and which threatens Nicaraguan and Peruvian societies during their current political transitions. The spread of trust focalization may be fostered under such circumstances even by the public institutions themselves, in their attempt to manage and contain generalized distrust.

The issue is how to generate reserve dynamics toward organizational autonomy, social compromise, and accountability of power holders, thereby enhancing regulation through delegation of trust by the state and role-oriented trust generalization.

A too-simple answer would be to attack the state deliberately, which some intellectuals see as the *bête noire* whose demise will lead to the entrenchment of democracy. I am not referring here to the privatization of markets and the autonomization of social movements, which may strengthen public trust under certain circumstances. In my view, the curtailment of the executive dominance may be advisable and feasible in some cases, such as in Argentina or the so called center-dominant polities of Mexico and Brazil, where both the state and the movements have been relatively strong, although here too the problem is not so unidimensional as it may appear at first glance. But in other cases, notably those facing narcotraffic interests and the threat of internal terror (e.g. Colombia, Peru), the generalization of institutional trust may be pursued only through the state in its broadest sense as an *estado de derecho*, which implies important loci of authority beyond the executive, and primarily the judiciary, system as a central component of the state. That is, only by making the state both stronger and constrained legally and administratively, as well as attempting to increase its accountability to social movements and public opinion, some generalization of institutional trust may be effected.

In the growing complexity of modern institutional life, there are structural forces working toward the formalization of trust, as discussed by Niklas Luhmann (1979) among others. That is, the importance grows of technical, role-related competence as a basis for trust bestowal (see, e.g., Barber, 1983); markets for trust production and verification develop; and institutional rational-bureaucratic ancillary supports for the containment and regulation of trust flourish (Shapiro, 1987). However, in the context of Latin American situations, to build extensive public trust implies more than the mere formalization of trust. Indeed, the above means do not eliminate vulnerability but rather can recreate it in a system of proceduralism, litigation, and an ever-growing reliance on markets for trust production, such as those producing ancillary certifications, computerized verifications, and formal guarantees of trustworthiness that cannot serve as massive substitutes for trust and that in the Latin American societies may even exacerbate the disenchantment with procedural democracy.

To build public trust in this context means to generate new institutional processes that, dynamically, will contribute to its generalization, so that eventually trust may become a public good—that is, following the definition by Albert Hirschman (1970, p. 101), a benefit that can be consumed by all members of a given society in such a manner that consumption by one member does not detract from consumption by another. Specifically in the case of trust, such consumption in fact enhances the prospects of others enjoying such good. Here several moves may be instrumental in generating institutional trust.

First, we should consider several consequences of the new regimes' inefficacy in dealing with the economic and financial crises of the 1980s. As the new governments, faced with huge foreign debts (especially in Argentina, Brazil, Chile, Ecuador, Mexico, Peru, and Uruguay) as well as inflationary and hyperinflationary pressures, failed to ease the social impact of the crisis in that decade, a growing skepticism took hold among wide sectors of the population toward competitive politics in general and democracy in particular (Weffort, 1988). But as the crisis continued, it became increasingly apparent that the popular sectors were resorting for survival both to formal and informal networks and to economic systems of self-reliance, the so-called informal sector of the economy (De Soto, 1987; Lomnitz, 1988). Lower classes protested in ways that had serious repercussions on the awareness level of major political actors and on the relations between political parties and the state (Girado et al., 1986; Cardoso, 1987); and, at higher echelons of the social ladder, more demands were voiced concerning the decentralization of decision-making and privatization of the economy.

These developments reflect both a civic disillusionment with and skepticism of current politics, which may reorient the polity toward new redefinitions. Sometimes they imply a search for separation from center-oriented politics and controls, which may actually contribute to the consolidation of public trust in Latin American democracies. Also, this very policy failure and disastrous economic situation (with some exceptions, such as Brazil and Chile—[Hirschman, 1987 and CEPAL, 1988]) may reduce the appeal of sectors such as those represented by the Argentine Colonel Seineldin envisaging a future governmental takeover. In addition, although the situation may be seen as standing at the edge of Durkheimian "anomie" or a Hobbesian "state of nature," this development can in turn generate an as yet unknown move toward a postideological stance in these societies, whereby wide sectors of the population in general and social movements in particular may come to value democracy's relevance for allowing public discussion on the uses of national resources and public control of official policies and state management, thus contributing to the legal and social bounding of power.

Second, in some of these societies there has been debate and move of positions within the political spectrum. Sometimes this shift has taken place within the traditional political parties that have retained saliency, as in the case of Uruguay and Honduras. Still in others, there have been moves away from the traditional format of the political scene and specifically of dominant political parties. For example, in Colombia, a traditional stronghold of bipartisanism, the introduction of electoral politics and parliamentarism at the municipal level in 1989 has introduced a pragmatic dimension in politics, allowing the emergence of new cadres in touch with the local population and attentive to their demands. The adoption by a guerrilla movement of a political nonviolent participation in politics (the FARC under Betancur) is a further indication of this trend. Working in the same direction, although destabilizing the polity, is the role played by the narcotraffic industry (Uricoechea, 1989; Klare, 1990). In Peru, a similar phenomenon has been under way recently, with the 1990 second-turn presidential candidates—the presaged Mario Vargas Llosa and the eventually elected Alberto Fujimori—coming from the arts and academia, respectively, and lacking former political affiliation. Moreover, there is probably no better indication of the changing winds of Latin American politics than the election in June 1990 of Fujimori—an Evangelist, of Japanese descent, without significant organizational support and even without a clear program of government—as president of Peru.

Third, connected with the above is the willingness of some of the more recent political leaders to try to elaborate policies beyond partisan consider-

ations, even risking their traditional bases of support and leading to the reformulation of political alliances in the short term in order to promote long-term
economic development. This may constitute an important trigger to institutionalize wider public trust, provided it could result in enhancement of state
efficiency and involve the reaping of early policy results. In the case of Argentina, this has been a crucial factor accounting for Menem's success so far in
maintaining the level of political support necessary to sustain his economic policies of reform, privatization, and wage control (Turner and Carballo de Cilley,
1990, p. 7).

Finally, for its consolidation and enhancement of public trust, a democracy
requires the institutionalization of conflict management and regulated competition for access to power and allocation of public goods. This means compromises: on the part of major power holders in handing over positions of power,
and on the part of opposition sectors in refraining from using or inciting to use
force to impose favorable policy outcomes. A problematic institutional area
that must be worked out concerns the relations between the major political
forces of presidentialism and parliamentarianism. In the past, parliamentary
forces initiated or supported destabilization of the polity; and parliamentary te-
nets were viewed often with scorn or contempt, as the corrupted locus of politicians led by instrumental considerations and partisan gains. While political
parties played a major role in negotiating some of the recent democratic transitions with the former authoritarian rulers, they have yet to elaborate a workable trade-off between pursuing their view of correct policy and refraining
from delegitimating the system. There are cases, such as Uruguay beginning
with Sanguinetti and Argentina during Alfonsín, in which political parties have
retained a high public profile while cooperating (in tacit and overt forms, respectively) toward the institutionalization of democracy. Argentina managed
in 1989 to hand over the reins of civilian presidential power to a once-
ostracized opposition through a contested election. Still, the extreme Left is
beyond the pale in most Latin American polities; guerrillas continue to be a
tangible threat to the foundation of democratic states as varied in their internal
policies as Colombia, Peru, and Nicaragua; and most political opposition still
threatens to destabilize the democratic polities.

CONCLUSION

The development of a broad commitment to democratic procedures of conflict management is essential for the consolidation of democracy in contemporary times, where the gap between the rulers and the ruled has narrowed in
comparison with traditional societies. Processes as varied as the impact of the
mass media, intellectual diffusion, and socioeconomic and technological transformations bring about wider impingement of state organs upon social forces
but also the greater impact of conflict expression by traditional and new social
actors on the center of society and on governmental policies and output. For

a commitment to procedural containment of conflict to exist, a trade-off must be reached between a wide public acceptance of routine exposure to the overt expression of conflicts and trust among opposing political and social groups in their mutual commitment to the system and, hence, their acceptance of limits in the political use and profit to be made out of those conflicts.

It is as yet uncertain whether formal civil freedoms will be matched by social participatory democracy—that is, by responsiveness to demands for increasing egalitarianism and redistribution of national resources, and whether the authoritarian traits still present in these polities will be contained within representative democracy. Given that the strength or weakness of any procedural democratic regime becomes evident when crises explode around policy dilemmas, leaving the government unable "to solve problems for which disloyal opposition offer themselves as a solution" (Linz, 1978, p. 56), the sustainability of the new democracies requires a strong political will. Taking a static projection of actual trends, it seems premature to discount in Latin America the possible future recurrence of the already familiar pattern of social and political pressures and subsequent democratic breakdown. I have suggested above that to the extent that these societies may move to a sort of pragmatic (still political but somehow "postideological") stance, while being still committed to the attainment of public good, institutional public trust could be widened and political forces may find it easier to withstand uncertainty and confront the dynamics of a democratic system without delegitimating it and generating a recurrent breakdown of democracy.

NOTES

1. The new democratic regimes allow for political competition and greater participation and freedoms than are customarily recognized by authoritarian systems. Many of them nevertheless fall short of the defining standards of democracy (Baloyra, 1987; Diamond et al., 1987; O'Donnell et al., 1986; Selcher, 1986). Thus they have been characterized as limited democracies, protected democracies, and institutional hybrids (Morlino, 1987, pp. 54–55), and as semidemocracies and "hegemonic" party systems (Diamond et al., 1987, pp. 5–6).

2. To create such conditions seems an extremely difficult task. Basically the issue here concerns the trade-off to be reached between the interest of Latin American nations to be integrated to the world market and their need to cut down the payments on the foreign debt. The attitudes of the financial international decision-makers toward most of the region's nations as a "basket case," where policies are to be dictated without consideration for the human costs, further hampers the attainment of such conditions. (I am indebted to Elizabeth Petras for her insightful observations on this point.)

3. For a general theoretical discussion see Roniger, 1990b.

4. Probably one of the most extreme but not unique cases of such focalization of public trust is Colombia, from the nineteenth century and well beyond the Violencia years and their no-less-violent aftermath into the 1960s.

REFERENCES

Baloyra, E. A. (ed.) (1987). *Comparing New Democracies.* Boulder, Colo.: Westview.

Barber, B. (1983). *The Logic and Limits of Trust.* New Brunswick, N.J.: Rutgers University Press.

Cardoso, F. H. (1987). "Democracy in Latin America." *Politics and Society,* 1, pp. 23–41.

CEPAL (1988). "Panorama economico de America Latina." Comision Economica para America Latina y el Caribe, informe de 1988.

Dahl, R. (1971). *Polyarchy, Participation and Opposition.* New Haven, Conn.: Yale University Press.

De Soto, H. (1987). *El otro sendero.* Bogota: La Oveja Negra.

Diamond, L., S. M. Lipset, and J. Linz (1987). "Building and Sustaining Democratic Government in Developing Countries: Some Tentative Findings." *World Affairs,* 150, no. 1, pp. 5–17.

Diaz de Landa, M. (1990). "Movimientos sociales, poder comunitario e innovación urbana." Session RC03 at the XII Congress of Sociology, Madrid, July 12.

Eisenstadt, S. N. (1976). "Basic Characteristics of the Modern State." In S. N. Eisenstadt, E. Gutmann, and Y. Azmon (eds.), *State and Society.* Tel Aviv: Am Oved (in Hebrew), pp. 87–97.

Eisenstadt, S. N. and L. Roniger (1984). *Patrons, Clients and Friends.* Cambridge: Cambridge University Press.

Fuentes, C. (1985). *Latin America at War with the Past.* Toronto: CBC Enterprises.

Girado, J. et al. (1986). *Movimientos sociales ante la crisis en Sudamerica.* Bogotá: CINEP.

Hirschman, A. O. (1970). *Exit, Voice and Loyalty.* Cambridge, Mass.: Harvard University Press.

———. (1987). "The Political Economy of Latin American Development: Seven Exercises in Retrospection." *Latin American Research Review,* 22, no. 3, pp. 7–35.

Jelin, E. (1985). "Otros silencios, otras voces: el tiempo de la democratizacion en la Argentina." Buenos Aires: CEDES.

Klare, M. (1990). "De la guerre contre la drogue à la guerre tout court?" *Le Monde Diplomatique,* March, pp. 4–5.

Linz, J. L. (1978). "Crisis, Breakdown, and Reequilibration." In J. L. Linz and A. Stepan (eds.), *The Breakdown of Democratic Regimes.* Baltimore: John Hopkins University Press, Part I, pp. 1–24.

Lomnitz, L. (1988). "Informal Exchange Networks in Formal Systems: A Theoretical Model." *American Anthropologist,* 90, no. 1, pp. 42–55.

Luhmann, N. (1979). *Trust and Power.* New York: John Wiley.

Macpherson, C. B. (1977). *The Life and Times of Liberal Democracy.* Oxford: Oxford University Press.

Mill, J. S. (1977). *Collected Works.* Toronto: University of Toronto Press, Vol. XIX.

Miranda Ontaneda, N. et al. (1980). "Clientelismo." *Enfoques Colombianos,* No. 14.

Moreira Alves, M. H. (1985). *State and Opposition in Military Brazil.* Austin: University of Texas Press.

Morlino, L. (1987). "Democratic Establishments: A Dimensional Analysis." In Baloyra, *Comparing New Democracies,* pp. 53–78.

Nohlen, D. (1988). "Mas democracia en America Latina?" *Sintesis,* 6, pp. 37–63.

O'Donnell, G., O. C. Schmitter, and L. Whitehead (eds.) (1986). *Transitions from Authoritarian Rule: Prospects for Democracy.* Baltimore: Johns Hopkins University Press.

Roniger, L. (1989). "Democratic Transitions and Consolidation in Contemporary Southern Europe and Latin America." *International Journal of Comparative Sociology*, 30, no. 3–4, pp. 216–230.

————. (1990a). *Hierarchy and Trust in Modern Mexico and Brazil.* New York: Praeger.

————. (1990b). "Towards a Comparative Sociology of Trust in Modern Societies." Paper presented at the XII World Congress of Sociology, Madrid, July 13.

Rosen, P. L. (1990). "The Constitutional Dialectic and the Conundrum of Hate Legislation." Carleton University, Department of Political Science.

Schmitter, C. (1986). "An Introduction to the Southern European Transitions from Authoritarian Rule." In O'Donnell et al., *Transitions from Authoritarian Rule*, pp. 3–10.

Selcher, W. A. (1986). *Political Liberalization in Brazil.* Boulder, Colo.: Westview.

Shapiro, S. P. (1987). "The Social Control of Impersonal Trust." *American Journal of Sociology*, 93, pp. 623–658.

Stepan, A. (1980). *Estado, corporatismo, e autoritarismo.* Rio de Janeiro: Paz e Terra.

Strayer, J. R. (1970). *On the Medieval Origins of the Modern State.* Princeton N.J.: Princeton University Press.

Touraine, A. (1990a). "The Long Road to Democracy." *The Unesco Courier*, June, pp. 19–25.

Turner, F. and M. Carballo de Cilley (1990). "Changing Values in Argentina." Paper presented at the XII World Congress of Sociology, Madrid, July 13.

Uricoechea, F. (1989). "Colombia y America Latina Siglo XXI: Escenarios de Cambio." Paper presented at the XIII Annual Meetings of the Associação Nacional de Posgraduação e Pesquisa em Ciências Sociais, Caxambu, Minas Gerais, Brazil, October 23–27.

Walzer, M. (1983). *Spheres of Justice.* New York: Basic Books.

Weffort, F. (1988). "Los dilemas de la legitimidad politica." *Sintesis*, 6, pp. 15–36.

Z (1990). "To the Stalin Mausoleum." *Daedalus*, 119, no. 1, (Winter), pp. 295–343.

CHAPTER TWELVE

"Governability" and the Receiver State in Latin America: Analysis and Prospects

JORGE NEF AND REMONDA BENSABAT

THE RECYCLING OF AN OLD CRISIS

A strategic realignment of political forces has begun to take shape in Latin America in the 1990s. It involves not only the emergence of new development ideologies but, more importantly, it represents the formation of concrete sociopolitical alliances and political projects both within Latin America as well as on a larger continental and global scale. The fundamental contradiction between national security and revolutionary alternatives of the previous decade has given way to new coexisting but equally antithetical modalities of conflict management. On the one hand, there is the attempt to enhance the "governability" of a catastrophic socioeconomic order through IMF-inspired packages of "structural adjustment." Its political correlate is a formula of "transition" with recivilianization to prevent the crisis of domination brought about by the decomposition of military regimes. On the other hand, and largely as a consequence of the inability of present policies to grapple with the real socioeconomic problems in the region, new forms of resistance have emerged. These "alternative" projects are an attempt to articulate the interests of those sectors of the civil society either victimized or left out by the authoritarian experiments of the 1970s and the restricted democratizations that followed. Unlike "transition," these are highly fragmented and heterogeneous strategies. They run from passive survivalist options to maximalist—and generally armed—confrontation.

Parallel to the aforementioned tendencies, new forms of official and "semiofficial" violence have become intertwined with endemic conflicts, creating an extremely volatile, polarized, and fragmented political environment. Violence, however, is not limited to the political and the criminal. The generalized economic recessions, combined with structural adjustments, have increased income concentration, unemployment, poverty, and marginalization. In most countries, the state has become the executor and debt collector of a bankrupt economy on behalf of transnational creditors. In fact, its central role has manifestly changed from that of promoting development and—at least in theory—protecting political and economic sovereignty, to that of facilitating surplus extraction and international subordination.

This chapter will offer a general interpretation of these trends. [1] Our central thesis is that the "politics of repression" of the national security regimes and subsequently the "politics of exclusion," which characterize today's Latin America, cannot be seen either as conjunctural phenomena nor as aberrations. They should be understood as one continuous social project that maintains the existing socioeconomic order and its related forms of political control, both domestically and internationally. Despite political turmoil and persistent violence, the underlying social, economic, and international forces that have enjoyed "metapower" in most of the region still prevail. In this context, the Latin American state is intrinsically weak and unstable; it lacks both a broad base of legitimation and effectiveness to implement policies and programs.

LEGITIMATION CRISIS AND THE TRANSNATIONALIZATION OF THE STATE

Conventional treatments of the problem of legitimation (Lipset, 1963; Habermas, 1975), following the state-centric model of political analysis, have assumed that constituencies and coalitions are national. This assumption is unrealistic for most of the dependent, peripheral, or neocolonial societies of the Third World. Indeed, one central characteristic of the Latin American countries is their penetrability and internationalization. Support for specific policies, and even for a whole regime, depends upon an often-contradictory interplay between domestic and foreign constituencies.

This pattern of "complex dependency" constrains the degree of choice in policy formulation and implementation. The effectiveness—and at times the very existence—of a regime depends more on external than on internal constituencies. Conversely, broad domestic legitimation is generally limited unless a government is able to continuously raise the level of goods and services it can provide. Such growth is rare in economies characterized by chronic underdevelopment. A normal consequence of weak and unstable growth is increased social marginalization of vast sectors of the population. Accumulation of wealth in the hands of a small elite at home and its transnational associates can raise the intensity of support among a very limited social base, but it reduces the popular legitimacy of the regime.

Such intense but narrow support may not be "adequate" to offset a growing alienation resulting from the poverty and powerlessness of most of the populace. Alienation, in the long run, often leads to mobilization through existing or emerging power brokers. The legitimacy of the political structure is brought into question as the discrepancy between the rhetoric of legitimation (or ideology) and the actual implementation of the elite's program emerges. Confronted with a devaluation of its own political myth and faced with opposition from below, the ruling elite normally resorts to naked enforcement of the status quo through cyclical repression. The tensions within the peripheral state are a reflection of these contradictions. Political and socioeconomic democratization cannot be easily reconciled with the existing mode of dependent development, which dominates the entire region. Nor can it be reconciled with the current trend toward the transnationalization of the state.

THE GENESIS OF THE RECEIVER STATE: A LONG-RANGE VIEW

The structures and patterns of production in the Latin American region are the outgrowth of a center-periphery mode of international division of labor. Economic "modernization" by colonial and neocolonial powers has often been antidevelopmental, as genuine national initiatives have been undermined by decapitalization and marginalization. Nearly two centuries after formal independence, structural underdevelopment continues. Politically, this underdevelopment expresses itself in a system of domestic and international governance—or regional regime (Keohane and Nye, 1977, pp. ix–x)—with its corresponding networks of interests. However, the influence of international economic and political relations can be understood only through their reflection in the domestic political economy and its related social conflicts. Latin America's dependent development has to be seen as being linked to the complex dynamics of mass-elite relations that occur in the domestic setting. Far from being the single cause of underdevelopment, dependency is a structurally persistent intervening variable that reinforces domestic inequality.

The social structures resting upon these complex political and economic patterns have also tended to endure. The ranch, the hacienda, the mining town, and the Central American plantation created conditions for the emergence and perpetuation of a comprador (as opposed to "national") elite, outward-looking in orientation and parasitic in function. This "weak" bourgeoisie is neither genuine nor independent from foreign capital and, most important, it has not been able to wield political hegemony over other fractions of the dominant classes. The comprador functions as the linkage or intermediary between the national society and the dominant foreign power for the implantation and reproduction of foreign capital, setting the conditions for a type of rentier economy and state.[2]

The Export Economy

Formal political independence did not significantly alter the function of the elite or the peripheral role of the Latin American economies in the international division of labor. Neocolonialism, first under British and subsequently American control, was entrenched and modernized, thus perpetuating structural underdevelopment and vulnerability.

Internally, the expansion of the export economy in the late nineteenth century laid the foundations for the emergence of a "modern" labor sector. The transformation of peasants into a wage-earning class was accelerated by war (as in Chile), "liberal" reforms in the countryside (as in Mexico, Guatemala, and El Salvador), or export-oriented commercialization (as in Argentina, Brazil, and Uruguay). The poor lost either their communal lands or their clientelistic ties to the latifundio system, or both. Peons, tenant farmers, and tillers of communal lands who moved to the mines, plantations, or docks became instantly proletarianized. As a consequence, relations between the relatively cohesive elites and the fragmented masses rapidly changed from the quiescence of latent class conflict to a manifest and specifically political confrontation between classes.

In the Southern Cone countries, in Costa Rica, and in post-revolutionary Mexico, the emergence of middle-class, white-collar reformism rerouted working-class frustrations through institutional and electoral channels. Political democratization, at the expense of social and economic democratization, gave vent to an institutionalized form of class struggle. This suprastructural adjustment was neither automatic nor smooth. Its effect was preempting, if not defusing, a possible social revolution. It also brought about an earlier bureaucratization, giving the state greater relative autonomy. Political changes, however, did not mean a fundamental alteration in the elite-controlled socioeconomic order. The middle classes, in fact, tended to act as both "buffers" and guardians of the status quo.

Conditions in the lesser developed countries (especially in most of Central America and the Caribbean) were very different. The middle classes were much smaller and weaker—mere appendages of the landed elites—and enjoyed little autonomy. Also, foreign intervention was more pervasive. The role of the largely patrimonial state vis-à-vis the majority of the population was simply one of enforcement. With the spread of popular mobilization resulting from the commercialization of agriculture, a pattern of repression and resistance was established. Rural rebellions, while frequently bloody and certainly persistent, were also intermittent, localized, and disorganized.

The Impact of the 1930s Depression

With the Great Depression, the "old" order came to a grinding halt. The elitist sociopolitical arrangements built upon export expansion became untenable. The ultimate impact of the crisis upon the political formula, however, largely depended upon the relative level of historical development of domestic capitalism as well as upon the degree of internal social differentiation. Two general patterns emerged. In the relatively more developed countries, after an initial period of chaos and confusion, the elite's response was one of economic expansion with selective social cooptation, under the political management of the middle sectors. In Central America (with the exception of Costa Rica) and the Caribbean, however, this alternative was blocked. Economic retrenchment and social exclusion by military dictatorships (the "dictator of the 1930s") became the standard elite response.

In most of South America and Mexico, a mixture of import-substitution industrialization (ISI) and political populism became the dominant mold. Where populism prevailed, the role of the state was greatly expanded, thus securing employment for the middle strata whose status had been threatened by the drastic decline of the export economy. This expanded role permitted the maintenance of mechanisms for cooptation of potentially resentful members of the educated classes.

Until the beginning of World War II, import substitution constituted an attempt at state intervention to prevent a social and political catastrophe. With exports precipitously falling and without an import capacity, governments undertook the role of activators of the national economy. With the outbreak of the war and the relative recovery of Western economies, demand for Latin American raw materials increased dramatically. This gave impetus to a new policy of economic planning and management: import substitution with export expansion.

ISI made it possible to strengthen and expand the populist programs of the prerecession years. By now, a large state machinery under firm middle-class control was already in place. International conditions, such as World War II, also facilitated alliances between blue-collar unions and the bureaucratic middle strata. Since lower-class mobilization had been limited, an alliance of the middle sectors with the unionized working classes (with the exception of Argentina in the 1950s), did not pose any real threat to the economic and social positions of the traditional rural and commercial elites. On the contrary, it served to isolate the rural poor by drawing a wedge between the latter and their urban counterparts while broadening the basis of legitimation of the existing political structure.

This legitimation rested upon improvements in working conditions, wages, and union rights for urban workers. The expansion of middle-class welfare programs, which had existed since the 1920s, extended the sources of employment to the middle classes charged with their administration. Moreover, state involvement in planning, financing, and implementing industrial recovery policies brought about qualitative changes in the role of the state in the economy (Glade, 1969). The state bureaucracy constituted an important means of integrating emerging strata into the preexisting elite-controlled social structure.

Thus, despite its populist appearance, the overall system remained elitist in structure and corporatist in style of decision-making. While the middle class had penetrated the state bureaucracies and become an integral part of the new populist coalition, the socioeconomic structure could not be similarly transformed without antagonizing the dominant classes. Government power was formally relinquished by the traditional ruling elite, on the implicit condition that the socioeconomic structure would remain relatively untouched.

Import substitution had severe built-in constraints. During this period, no serious emphasis was placed on traditional export substitution diversification, developing the peasant economy, or on self-sufficiency. True, the economies grew; but despite the myth held by Latin American economic nationalists, it is doubtful that the economies would have "taken off" on their own even if sustained growth had continued into the 1960s. The continuity of structural underdevelopment and the parasitic nature of the elites placed insurmountable constraints on any incrementalist economic strategy.

External financing for development schemes declined once demand for raw materials stabilized and subsequently fell in the 1950s. Furthermore, import substitution did not alter the rentier nature of the export economy; it only responded pragmatically to a crisis of imports for the conspicuous consumption of the elites. These sectors would not accept the financial burden of the state's development schemes. Government social security and development programs were thus chronically underfinanced and depended for the most part on increases in the money supply, on unpredictable export earnings, and ultimately on newly created sources of foreign aid.

The most severe limitations on import-substitution industrialization, however, were social and political in nature. A full extension of the logic of import substitution into the realm of self-sustained national development required a dramatic expansion of an otherwise extremely limited market. In economic terms, such expansion meant transforming the bulk of the population subsisting outside the "official" economy into a mass consumer market with the capacity to buy nationally produced goods. To create such broad national markets would have required a drastic modification of the social structure, especially the lowering of class barriers and, in particular, a true revolution in the agrarian order. However, the elite-dominated socioeconomic structure perpetuated just the opposite: the continuity of a narrow market oriented toward conspicuous consumption. By the mid-1950s, import-substitution strategies had outlived their original purpose—system maintenance—under the tutelage of a loose de facto coalition between the blue-collar, middle, and elite sectors.

Once import-substitution strategies were exhausted, inflationary politics replaced the uneasy "social contract" between otherwise antagonistic social groups. Wage and price spirals soon became a protracted form of civil strife. The state mechanisms produced and accelerated "the pushup effect" of the institutionalized class conflict. In this context, the political issues of "democracy," stability, and legitimation became inextricably linked to economic questions of growth and distribution. As labor militancy increased, particularly in the Southern Cone countries of Brazil, Argentina, Chile, and Uruguay, the middle strata sought to reconstitute the ruling coalitions by shifting their political stance further to the right. To sustain the status quo, the governments attempted to revitalize the industrialization process through harsh stabilization policies. Rather than revitalizing ISI, such policies had the effect of forcing Latin American economies back to the traditional mold of export and outward-oriented development. Unlike the predepression era, however, the international political economy was clearly unfavorable to Latin America.

By the late 1950s, a crisis of accumulation in the midst of accelerated mass mobilization affected the entire region. The cumulative effect was a breakdown of the state. The timing and velocity of political crises varied from country to country, though it manifested itself throughout the 1960s. In Central America and most of the Caribbean (with the exception of post-1948 Costa Rica) the state as an entity based on a constitutional order never really emerged; nor could anticyclical ISI policies be implemented. For them the crisis was more crudely one of domination: the inability of the existing repressive states and their foreign constituencies to control through military force. The Cuban Revolution (1959) was the first of a wave of national revolutionary movements backed by a political coalition very different from those of the past. Indeed, that revolution highlighted the growing internationalization of domestic conflicts in Latin America, a tendency that continued with the Nicaraguan revolution and with the protracted insurrections in Guatemala and El Salvador.

In the countries that were more developed politically and institutionally, the crisis of the state manifested itself mainly as a legitimacy crisis. Both the elitist socioeconomic order and Pax Americana were maintained by resorting to repression, and by creating a new, but not necessarily legitimate, political coalition. Such a coalition entailed an alliance between the comprador bourgeoisie (in this case the externally linked corporate and technocratic elite, which gave content to government programs) and the equally transnationalized military establishment. The latter, representing a unique U.S.-trained, -indoctrinated and -financed fraction of the middle class, provided the force required to keep the population at bay (O'Donnell, 1986, pp. 247–250).

Authoritarian Capitalism

The bureaucratic-authoritarian "states of exception" that emerged in South America—a forerunner of which was the Brazilian "liberating revolution" of 1964—were in fact attempts at capitalist modernizations from the top (as well as from the outside). The benefits of this new authoritarian capitalist order accrued to a small elite of domestic entrepreneurs and speculators supported by a technocratic-military middle class and their respective business and military constituencies in the United States. The social cost for the majorities was always high, as overall living conditions declined and the gap between elites and masses widened dramatically. Rather than unleashing thorough counterrevolutions, however, these regimes acted as repressive brakes against social mobilization, economic nationalism, and incipient socialism. Economic growth was emphasized as a consequence of a forceful reinsertion of the countries' economies into the international division of labor, both as exporters of raw materials and, to some extent, nontraditional goods. The project also envisioned the "backward" integration and expansion of industry into the production of intermediate and capital goods. Export-manufacture would enable the carving out of a new niche in the international economy. With the exception of Brazil in the late 1960s and the 1970s, economic modernization, far from "deepening industrialization," meant increased reliance upon the resource sector. It also involved the creation of favorable conditions through deregulation, denationalization, and a dismantling of labor organizations, so that transnational corporations could invest and increase profits: Latin America had been made "safe" for foreign investment. The large amount of international financing required was facilitated by the massive deposits of petrodollars borrowed from Western private banks.

The illusion of "economic miracles" led to staggering indebtedness. As both the governments and the private sector in the region increased their financial obligations, the failure of production and exports to keep pace with borrowing and, most importantly, with swelling interest rates, finally resulted in economic crises. The combined impact of economic crises, the exacerbated and manifest contradictions within the state, and the latter's growing ungovernability created the internal conditions for military withdrawal. These circumstances were compounded by a new international factor: a "trilateralist" hegemonic coalition in Washington seeking to reverse the close identification between capitalism and authoritarianism. "Transition" became the functional requisite for maintaining the status quo.

Restricted Democracy and Indebtedness

Transition, in this context, had strict limits. Although the experiments with authoritarian capitalism (perhaps with the sole and fortuitous exception of Chile) proved to be dismal failures as far as development was concerned, the radical restructuring of the economies along neoliberal lines was profound enough to prevent a return to economic nationalism. Likewise, the revamping and transnationalization of the security establishment made the pursuit of nationalist foreign policies utterly impossible. In this sense, the political arrangements to emerge in Latin America as a result of "redemocratization," while possessing the formal trappings of sovereignty and democracy, are neither truly democratic nor sovereign. These are weak civilian regimes, with limited political agendas, narrow support, significant exclusion of popular sectors from the political arenas, and where external constituencies, both economic and military, enjoy de facto veto power and hold the key to regime support. The central role of the state has changed from promoting development and delivering public services to facilitating the service of the debt and implementing structural adjustments. The ultimate effect of this type of state on society is a perpetuation of dependence, underdevelopment, and chronic vulnerability, requiring ever-increasing doses of external supports. This vulnerability can be dramatically illustrated by the debt trap.

A STRUCTURAL PERSPECTIVE: THE CRISIS OF THE LATIN AMERICAN STATE

The breakdown of the populist formula, with its neo-Keynesian economics, its import-substitution industrialization, and its emphasis upon state intervention in the economy, was an almost inevitable consequence of its inherent contradictions. Increased participation could coexist with dependent capitalism only under conditions of economic expansion. The loss of internal legitimacy was compensated for by broadening the class alliance to the international level and by forcefully demobilizing the bulk of the population. The "invisible hand" required a long arm: economic liberalization and sociopolitical repression became "both sides of the coin" (Letelier, 1976, pp. 138, 142).

Ironically, the end of the cycle of the National Security regime in the 1980s was also a consequence of the latter's inner inconsistencies. On the one hand, there was the long-run impossibility of reconciling the management of national security with economic management; on the other, there was the additional difficulty emerging from the extreme vulnerability of authoritarian capitalism to external economic and political forces.

National Security and Trilateralism

The National Security model performed essentially the same containment function, and maintained the same socioeconomic forces, that the developmental reformism of the Alliance for Progress was supposed to maintain. National Security, with its antidemocratic biases, however, emphasized stability at the expense of development, the satisfaction of social needs and democracy itself. Paradoxically, while the "depth" of social control increased, the scope of government activity in the economy and social welfare usually shrank. Economic and political "rationality" translated into the creation of favorable conditions for private foreign investment, a reduction of the state's role in the economy, and transnationalization through the repression of civil society. The state itself reflected the preponderance of the military-technocratic alliance and an exacerbated tension between the state and the politically excluded populace. The peripheral capitalist state, which in the more advanced countries had become the "entrepreneurial" state (Nef, 1990, pp. 355–356), experienced a complete turnabout: from protectionism to free-trade; from industry to primary exports. In the least developed countries, national security involved a further and more "modernized" militarization of the repressive socioeconomic and political order.

The development of both authoritarian capitalism and "normalization" in Latin America have been greatly influenced by two parallel trends in the United States. One is "Pentagonism" (Bosch, 1968), particularly the ideology of "national security," counterinsurgency, "civic action," and Low Intensity Operations. The other is the global business ideology espoused first by the Council of Foreign Relations (and its regional counterpart, the Council of the Americas) and at present manifested in the "trilateralism" of transnational corporations. These two projects, with their respective wide-ranging sociopolitical alliances (and contradictions), constitute the leading forces behind the logic of "transitions" to and from "bureaucratic-authoritarian regimes."

The policy orientation of Pentagonism is neo-Keynesian (demand-side economics), ultranationalist (U.S. Manifest Destiny), and rabidly anticommunist. The objective of the state is highly specialized: the provision of "security" through the administration of violence. Since military structures, doctrines, and techniques—not to mention hardware—are among the most easily transferred technologies in the contemporary world, continental military professionalism has become the most homogenizing bureaucratic trait. In this sense, military modernization, especially along counterinsurgency lines and the concept of the "internal enemy," has meant the transnationalization and denationalization of the officer class. This in itself is a fundamental structural limitation on the sovereignty of the Latin American nation-state.

Likewise, the spread of transnational corporations and a transnational economic and business ideology have meant a substantial transfer of organizational technology as well as a free-trading, antiprotectionist, supply-side, and monetarist view. It has also provided a vehicle for the transnationalization of a corporate, managerial, and intellectual elite (Sunkel, 1971). Pentagonism and trilateralism are often symbiotically related. Their impact upon traditional conceptions of the state and the role of the public sector in Latin America are quite significant. The technocratic-corporate state of the 1970s (i.e., authoritarian capitalism) was in part an uneasy alliance between the highly specialized and efficient exercise of violence by the public sector and the management of the economy by the private sector.

A similar power play occurs within the supporting coalitions in most Latin American states. There is a transnationalized "hard-line," "conservative" Pentagonist officer corps (referred to as duros) and an equally transnationalized "soft-line," "liberal," trilateralist commercial and financial elite (referred to as blandos). Domestic manufacturers, traditional landowners, and the various fractions of the petite bourgeoisie generally take a backseat, often shifting alliances either as minor partners within the power bloc or more often as allied factions.

The Illusion of Democratization

The antecedents of the present policy of normalization (or civilianization) are to be found in the Linowitz Report of 1975. "From positively favoring military governments and subverting democratic ones under Nixon and Kissinger, the U.S. government came out demonstratively in favor of the transition from authoritarian to democratic rule" (Latin America Update, 1980). Fundamentally, however, despite emphasis on military withdrawal and a return to democracy, the approach advocated a type of restricted or limited democracy, restricted in terms of both the provision of government services and popular participation. At close scrutiny the formula is not only conservative in socioeconomic terms, it is also antidemocratic, even by comparison to the kind of populist reformism that existed in the 1930s in Latin America and the Western world. It is this restrictive project that has unfolded throughout Latin America under the guise of "redemocratization."

Contemporary Latin America is not undergoing a change toward increased democratization, at least not in the conventional sense. The concepts of "military withdrawal" and "limited democracy" as presented by the Carter administration, Reagan's "responsible right" and "friendly authoritarian regimes," or Bush's new open policies mask the consequences of a continuous pattern of dependence. The search for a new hegemony has resulted in an equally limited, though superficially attractive, formula: the splicing of limited "democracy" with neoconservative economics. While this imagery is quite appealing to North Americans and to Latin America's consumption-intensive middle classes, it also rests on flimsy and largely ideological assumptions, such as the continuous expansion of world trade and the mutuality of interests between the center and the periphery. Moreover, this restricted democracy relies upon the continuous use of selective mechanisms, including tactical repression, as an effective deterrent against the organization of labor and mass mobilization. Finally, the very same economic, social, and political forces that perpetrated the antidemocratic outrages of the past, are ever more firmly entrenched under a legal facade.

THE RECEIVER STATE

The generic political formula to emerge throughout Latin America in the late 1980s is what we have called the receiver state. This modality of conflict management involves a liberalization rather than a genuine democratization of the political and socioeconomic order consolidated during the period of authoritarian capitalism. Its main features involve:

1. Transnationalization: The main supports of the state depend on alliances between internal and external constituencies, especially those in both the transnationalized defense and security apparatus and in the business community.

2. Corporatism: Both the transition from authoritarian rule and the fundamental "pacts" and "social contracts" that regulate the functioning of the political regime are semiconsociational agreements among elites. These elites encompass the same socioeconomic, political, and institutional forces that controlled the repressive state. In addition the pacts include other "moderate" and "permissible" brokers (e.g., Christian Democrats or Social Democrats) who were excluded in the past. The dominant economic and military sectors maintain an enduring relational control over the transition process.

3. Depoliticization: Significant areas of state activity are corporately outside effective political (i.e., democratic) control and accountability. This is particularly the case with security and financial matters, which are in the hands of National Security Councils and "apolitical" central banking institutions.

4. Demobilization: Unions, popular political parties, and grass roots organizations are severely curtailed in their structure and activities. They are kept fragmented, with little access to channels of influence.

5. Privatization: Most economic activity moves away from planning and regulation into market forces and deregulation. This also applies to areas of state activity in "social services"—health, welfare, housing, transportation, education, and so on. In fact, it means the dismantling of the welfare state.

6. Debt management and structural adjustment become central tasks of the state: The implementation of austerity packages and mechanisms for debt servicing (such as debt-equity swaps) supersede the conventional "developmental" role of the state. The state's central function is to facilitate debt collection and to maintain the confidence of both the creditors and the international financial institutions (i.e., the country's "creditworthiness").

7. Deindustrialization: The state facilitates the fading out of import-substitution industrialization policies. Instead, orthodox approaches based upon "comparative advantages" are encouraged. While in general this means a reinsertion of the country into the world economy as "conventional" export-producer, "export-substitution" from traditional to "nontraditional exports" is also encouraged. The central role of trade here is to produce hard currencies primarily to serve the debt, and secondarily to import manufactures from industrial countries.

8. Limited or restricted democracy: The political system contains safeguards to prevent and proscribe popular and radical social forces from acquiring political prominence. Likewise, foundational issues (such as property relations) and various policy agendas are left outside normal political debate (e.g., banking, defense, security, international alignments). Perpetrators of human rights violations during the national security regime are given immunity from prosecution. The security forces remain largely autonomous from civilian control, civilian courts, and fiscal responsibility; their "extraterritorial" privileges are left untouched.

9. Conditional franchise: Although elections are the cornerstone of formal democracy, they are "controlled." That is, they must be honest but "keeping

the proper balance[:] . . . parties of the Right-Centre and Right must be helped
. . . and parties of the Left-Centre and Left should not win by an overwhelming
majority" (O'Donnell et al., 1986, p. 62).

10. The entrenchment of the status quo: The overriding commands (or limits) of the model described here involve two fundamental premises. One is that
"the property rights of the bourgeoisie are inviolable."

11. Military guardianship: The second premise is that "the armed forces
serve as the prime protectors of the rights and privileges covered by the first
restriction . . . their institutional existence, assets and hierarchy cannot be
eliminated or even seriously threatened" (O'Donnell et al., 1986, p. 69). These
limitations are usually enshrined in military-designed "constitutional" documents or amendments produced during the years of emergency and rationalized on grounds of national security. In addition, sweeping "antiterrorist"
legislation, in conjunction with the above-mentioned constitutional provisions,
gives the officers the ultimate power to intervene—this time "legally"—to uproot any perceived threat.

The receiver state is not a transitional phase in elite domination leading to
a new genuine democracy: the return to "free" and participatory politics.
Rather, the terrorist state of the 1970s and the receiver state of today are two
different manifestations of the same set of interests. Both represent the consensus of a largely transnationalized reactionary coalition. This consensus involves the prevention of: national self-determination or a nonaligned Latin
America, challenges to both the regional and national "order" and its internal
and external constituencies, and real economic, social, and even political
democracy.

The present mode of conflict management, while reducing the most blatant
abuses of human rights, has left Latin America's most persistent, pressing, and
fundamental socioeconomic and political issues largely untouched. Limiting political participation under conditions of constant social mobilization (e.g., migration, urbanization, and literacy) only adds to the severity of these problems.
The combination of transnational integration of the Latin American elites (economic, military, and bureaucratic) into a U.S.-centered strategy of "governability" and the growing marginalization of internal Latin American
constituencies has perpetuated a multisided crisis of both the state and the civil
society. In the absence of legitimacy, violence has become the most common
political currency. Under the thin veneer of "normality," violence itself—
including banditry, terrorism, repression, official abuse by security forces, and
generalized lawlessness—has evolved into a distinct style of conflict management. The shrinkage of political spaces reduces the uncertainties and complexities of governance into a simple first-degree military equation: power equals
force. When national consensus fails and inflationary politics exhausts its limited possibilities, repression and revolution remain the ultimate options.

In the course of Latin American history, mass resistance has expressed itself
through various forms of social struggle. In recent years, however, the appeals

for radical changes in the existing social, economic, and political orders appear to be stymied by counterinsurgency, pseudodemocratization, and the debt burden. From a long-range structural and historical (as opposed to conjunctural) perspective, revolutionary struggles and situations have not withered altogether, though their tactics and manifestations have changed. What is noticeable in the last decade is that the focus of popular movements has shifted from the "triumphalist" centerstage of guerrilla warfare, leftist political parties, organized labor, and militant intellectuals, to the "chorus": shantytowns, grass roots organizations, and everyday life. In this sense, new forms of exploitation and control have generated new forms of popular struggle and new manifestations of consciousness.

THE CHALLENGE OF REAL DEMOCRACY

An analysis of contemporary Latin America since the early 1980s suggests that, despite formal redemocratization, the reduction of political spaces and alternative solutions for compromise continues. Consensus-building has become ever more tenuous as the debt-ridden economies do not have the economic capabilities for stable governance. The authoritarian capitalism of the 1970s and early 1980s was characterized by extreme political repression, yet there was also rapid, though inequitable, economic growth. The period between the mid-1980s to the early 1990s has been one of consolidation of basically the same exclusionary socioeconomic model in the midst of economic catastrophe. This makes real democratic institutionalization nearly impossible.

Although many would attempt to equate the openings in Eastern Europe with those of Latin America, there are two striking differences. One is that popular actors in Latin America have played a less significant role in the political and economic agenda of transition than in the East. The other, and probably the most important, difference is that the dominant regional superpower has not experienced the kind of dramatic political transformation that preceded the changes in Eastern Europe. A glasnost and perestroika of the Western Hemisphere seems to be a long way off. Instead, the call by the Bush administration to expand the Mexico-U.S. free trade zone on a continental basis contains all the asymmetries, trappings, and unipolarities of a neoimperial design: a virtual "puertoricanization" of Latin America. In addition, the "War on Drugs" provides a fresher rationale for continuous military intervention. As the current *fórmulas de recambio* run their course and the present crisis deepens, it is likely that the weak and limited civilian regimes of today will be replaced, once again, by equally weak, yet violently repressive, military regimes.

Democratization and "development" in Latin America, if they are to occur, would remain largely meaningless unless their effects cease to be confined to the upper and middle classes. Profound social conflicts rooted in extreme and persistent inequities cannot be circumvented by the illusion of democratization. In addition, Washington's proclivity for seeing North-South issues and internal dynamics through East-West lenses—despite the new coexistence between the United States and the USSR—has the potential for both the radicalization and the regionalization (and even continentalization) of conflict. As we saw in the early 1970s, detente between the superpowers does not preclude U.S. intervention in Latin America. In fact, the opposite has been the case. A lingering tendency to transform indigenous and complex political and social problems into the equation of military force and "communist aggression" (and, today, "narcotraffickers" and "terrorists") is dangerously simplistic and carries the seeds of self-fulfilling prophecies and greater entanglements. Above all, it undermines internal stability, development, and democracy.

The preceding analysis of "redemocratization" challenges four widely held yet fallacious assumptions of transition and, for that matter, pluralistic theories of politics. One is that profound social conflicts can be arbitrated by the mechanisms of liberal, participatory democracy in the context of a dependent and penetrated society. The second is that the liberal-democratic state is a "neutral" mechanism in which conflicting demands can be accommodated and equity-producing policies can be formulated and implemented. The third belief is that the socioeconomic status quo can be changed "from within" without violently altering the role of the state as an enforcer of the status quo. Last is the belief that the peripheral state is indeed a national state, rather than a structure that maintains precisely the dependent and underdeveloped nature of the society.

The receiver state is not a truly stable and democratic project for and by Latin Americans. As the decade of the 1990s unfolds, the question of the redemocratization of Latin America will have to be readdressed. The issue of democracy cannot be an abstract question concerning the governability of the status quo. It is about creating an enduring and just socioeconomic and political order for people engaged in the concrete practice of freedom.

NOTES

1. This chapter synthesizes—as well as expands upon—our thoughts on the subject of democratization in Latin America contained in a series of articles written since 1980 (see, for instance, Nef, 1986, 1988).

2. For a definition of the rentier state see Graf (1988, pp. 218–247): "The essential feature of the rentier state in the world market is that it severs the link between production and distribution. State revenues accrue from taxes or 'rents' on production, rather than from productivity activity" (p. 219).

REFERENCES

Bosch, J. (1968). *Pentagonism: A Substitute for Imperialism*. New York: Grove Press.
Glade, W. P. (1969). *The Latin American Economies: A Study of Their Institutional Evolution*. New York: Van Nostrand.

Graf, William D. (1988). *The Nigerian State: Political Economy, Class, and Political System in the Post-Colonial Era.* London: J. Currie.

Habermas, J. (1975). *Legitimation Crisis.* Boston: Beacon Press. Latin America Update, September–October 1980.

Letelier, Orlando (1976). "The Chicago Boys' in Chile: Economic 'Freedom's' Awful Toll." *The Nation,* August 28.

Lipset, S. M. (1963). *Political Man: The Social Basis of Politics.* New York: Anchor Books.

Keohane, R. and J. Nye (1977). *Power and Interdependence: World Politics in Transition.* Boston: Little, Brown.

Nef, J. (1986). "Redemocratization in Latin America or the Modernization of the Status Quo?" *Canadian Journal of Latin American and Caribbean Studies,* 11, no. 21.

———. (1988). "The Trend Towards Democratization and Redemocratization in Latin America: Shadow and Substance." *Latin American Research Review,* 23, no. 3.

———. (1990). "Latin America: The Southern Cone." In V. Subramaniam (ed.), *Public Administration in the Third World: An International Handbook.* Westport, Conn.: Greenwood Press.

O'Donnell, G. (1986). "Toward an Alternative Conceptualization of South American Politics." In Peter F. Klaren and Thomas G. Bossert (eds.), *Promise of Development: Theories of Change in Latin America.* Boulder, Colo.: Westview Press.

O'Donnell, G., P. Schmitter, and L. Whitehead (eds.) (1986). *Transitions from Authoritarian Rule: Prospects for Democracy.* Baltimore: Johns Hopkins University Press.

Sunkel, O. (1971). "Capitalismo Transnacional y Desintegración Nacional en América Latina." *Estudios Internacionales,* 4, no. 16.

CHAPTER THIRTEEN

Chile: Redemocratization or the Entrenchment of Counterrevolution?

NIBALDO GALLEGUILLOS AND JORGE NEF

Many observers of the Latin American political scene have characterized the present trend as a transition from the "bureaucratic authoritarianism" of the 1970s to a new phase of redemocratization. In this context, it appears paradoxical that Chile, once hailed as the most democratic of the Latin American republics, has been one of the very last of these countries to head in the direction of a political opening. These same observers note that, despite a late start, the repressive forces that dominated the state since the mid-1970s are retreating in defeat as the civil society recovers the various political spaces usurped by military rule. This common wisdom deserves careful probing and in-depth analysis.

We will begin by clarifying a number of key terms for studying transition in general: rebellion, revolution, repression, and counterrevolution. For the purposes of our study, we will define these terms with regard to two variables: the social actors involved (i.e., the "elites" or the "nonelites") and the degree of institutionalization of the process.

We understand *rebellion* as the violent mobilization of nonelite sectors against a given system of socioeconomic and political inequalities. *Revolution* is the consolidation of a rebellion that has succeeded in drastically and irreversibly altering the socioeconomic and political order. *Repression* entails the application of force by the elite and its agents to prevent an alteration of the status quo—that is, the existing structure of wealth, power, and privilege. *Counter-revolution* is the utilization of symbolic—that is, legal and constitutional—or physical means of coercion to undertake a fundamental strengthening, modernization, and consolidation of an elitist socioeconomic order. A distinction must be drawn here between the creation of a counterrevolutionary "social order" and the modalities for its management, that is, government. The unleashing of counterrevolution requires heavy doses of physical repression; this is not necessarily the case for its management once a counterrevolution has been institutionalized. Both revolution and counterrevolution share one characteristic: they are both profound or foundational socioeconomic upheavals—one oriented toward turning society upside down, the other geared toward modernizing and entrenching the establishment (Greene, 1984, pp. 9–20; Black, 1984).

Full-fledged social revolutions, as opposed to revolutionary situations, have been rare in Latin America, and the same holds true for counterrevolutions. Analyzing the ongoing "democratizations" from the perspective of the previous paragraph provides for a more potent heuristic device than the prevailing linear vogue of "transition theory." Our thesis is that Chile is not undergoing a transition to "true democracy." Instead, it is going through a process of normalization of a profound counterrevolutionary social transformation unleashed by the 1973 coup and consolidated in the 16 years of military dictatorship. This chapter will examine this subject from a largely systemic and historical perspective. To do so, one needs to be able to comprehend, as well as compare, the circumstances and dynamics that brought about both the bureaucratic authoritarian regime in 1973 and the present opening.

THE EMERGENCE OF THE BUREAUCRATIC AUTHORITARIAN REGIME

The nature and intensity of the 1973 coup were unprecedented in Chilean politics and discontinuous with indigenous political practices. Not only was it the most violent event in Chile's twentieth-century history, but it was also the bloodiest of such coups, even when compared with the violent politics of the region.

The Context of the 1973 Crisis

The military coup took place during a period of acute social mobilization in which popular forces posed a serious challenge to the existing socioeconomic order. Elite brokerage structures had, as a consequence of internal fragmentation and popular mobilization, been weakened. The middle/upper-class social pact with its populist overtones (the "state of compromise") that had held the Chilean republican edifice since the Great Depression had lost its legitimacy. Import-substitution industrialization, upon which this pact had been structured, had become exhausted toward the early 1950s.

Successive but weak centrist political coalitions, built upon middle-class fulcrums, came and went between 1952 and 1970. The common denominator of all these various and shifting alliances was an ever-increasing inability to deal with Chile's socioeconomic crisis by means of neo-Keynesian policies (Stallings, 1978). Popular participation and expectations—reflected in indexes of urbanization, literacy, union membership, voter registration, and electoral turnout—increased dramatically, yet productivity remained stagnant. Thus, the capacity of the state to handle social conflict through distributive policies became severely restricted: stagflation was the structural manifestation of a profound sociopolitical stalemate (Hirschman, 1964, p. 84).

Paradoxically, dynamic immobilism through the 1950s and the 1960s allowed the popular forces, despite persistent inflation and policy deadlock, to increase their bargaining capacity by means of the existing political and parliamentary mechanisms. Popular political power far outweighed the level of economic participation in the productive surplus. Conversely, the traditional socioeconomic forces found themselves losing the once-undisputed monopoly of the political stage and increasingly at odds with the constitutional arrangements set up in 1925 to protect their interests. The peculiarity of Chile's "crisis of hegemony" was not that the popular sectors suddenly realized the irrelevance of bourgeois democratic practices. In fact, it was the elites—and their middle-class allies—who found themselves caught in an unyielding legal-rational framework of their own making. After the Popular Unity victory at the polls on September 4, 1970, a liberal democracy faced, for the first time in history, the theoretical possibility of a peaceful and legal road to socialism.

More conjuncturally, the emergence of the Christian Democrats, which in the short term (e.g., the presidential election of 1964), offered a moderate alternative to radical social change, had the long-term effect of destabilizing the pattern of centrist dominance in Chilean politics. In fact, the ambiguous policies of the "Revolution in Liberty" ended up alienating their right- and left-wing supporters, producing instead a revolution of rising frustrations. The 1970 election, in which the Christian Democratic Center and the Right ran separate candidates, in fact made a victory of the leftist Popular Unity coalition (with slightly over 36 percent of the votes) possible.

Allende's election sent shock waves throughout the Chilean business community; its protoaristocratic middle-class associates in the upper echelons of the administrative, professional, and military sectors; and, most certainly, among its business, political, and military constituencies abroad. The combination of structural crisis with conjunctural panic (O'Donnell's [1979] "imminent fear"), as perceived by Chile's elites and their U.S. allies, created simultaneously the objective and subjective conditions to strike out in order to restore the balance. Allende's program may not have been a revolution, but it presented a number of seemingly irreversible challenges to the old order. It appeared impossible for the elites to hope for a simple electoral return to the past.

Cultural Polarization and Ideological Confrontation, 1970–73

Chilean politics have always reflected sharp class distinctions. However, exclusionary tendencies became ever-more pronounced during the Popular Unity period. Ideological polarization was facilitated by the disintegration of instrumentalist, centrist political alternatives such as those of the Radicals and Christian Democrats.

The Left's moves at enhancing an alternative "popular" culture and to democratize Chilean society were increasingly perceived by the establishment as a threat to its own survival. Virtually every term in daily discourse became politicized. Stereotypical and Manichaean labeling led to a situation where tendencies toward compromise and moderation rapidly disappeared. Contributing to this "zero-sum" game was the ideological mutation of the Right, which from the 1960s had begun to lose faith in electoral politics.

Extreme ideological polarization was facilitated by a number of other factors. One was the emergence of ultraconservative and antidemocratic movements such as Fatherland and Freedom in 1970. Another was the emergence of a militant new Left looking at Cuban-style insurgency (the Leftist Revolutionary Movement—MIR) as a methodology for political change. A third factor was the corrosive effect of the culture of the Cold War, especially within the armed forces, as expressed in counterinsurgency and the National Security doctrines espoused by the U.S. military and police training. Following Allende's election, this Cold War mentality would crystallize in the conscious attempt by the Nixon regime at disinformation about, and destabilization of, Chilean politics.

Catastrophic Stalemate and the Correlation of Forces

By 1972 the entire political spectrum had moved from polarized pluralism to a clearly and rigidly bipolar situation. At one side stood the Right, allied with the Christian Democrats, representing a myriad of business and white-collar interest groups intent on toppling Allende at any cost. They were ideologically and logistically supported in their offensive by both the official and clandestine actions of the U.S. government. The whole of the Chilean upper strata had joined with a majority of the professional and white-collar classes to stop, dismantle, and roll back "Chile's Road to Socialism." On the other side, and in a defensive position, stood the relatively fragmented and weaker Popular Unity coalition, representing the interests of organized labor, numerous shantytown and peasant organizations, and even sectors of the middle classes. Despite its "Third-Worldist" appeal, the government received little material international support.

Allende increasingly empowered the military in a vain attempt to maintain the political balance. Yet the officers remained more loyal to their class and ideological allegiances than to any abstract notion of the "national interest." Admittedly, Allende never had "power." At best, his Popular Unity had control over the executive. But even there, the administration could not count on the numerous autonomous agencies, or the majority of the tenured levels of the technobureaucracy, or the repressive apparatus of the state. By the imposed legal entanglement contained in the Estatuto de Garantías, [1] signed by Allende and his congressional opposition in 1970, the executive relinquished its constitutional right to appoint and promote the heads of the armed forces and the national police. With regard to these, the traditional balance between the police (the Carabineros), and the armed forces, which provided a deterrence against military adventurism, had been steadily eroded. Instead, Special Forces, trained by U.S. advisors in counterinsurgency against would-be internal enemies, gave the Army a tactical superiority. Police training in similar doctrines also helped to blur the fundamental distinctions between these forces.

Political Processes: The Escalation of Violence

The extreme polarization described here affected the country's entire social structure and culture. It expressed itself through a system of interest groups and political parties' brokerage, with incompatible ideologies ultimately affecting the very core of the state. By 1973, the balance of forces was clearly turning against Allende. Despite slight gains in that year's parliamentary elections, the Right had been able to outmobilize the Left and was also engaged in a strategy of insurrection. Increasingly, a rightist-induced climate of chaos forced the government into relying to a greater extent on the repressive mechanisms of the state. As middle-class strikes and the sabotage of business increased, the government unwillingly became ever more dependent on the mythology of military professionalism—that is, on the politicians' long-held idea that the armed forces were a nondeliberative, apolitical organization.

A new law that controlled weapons and firearms was used by the right-wing-controlled judiciary and the armed forces to launch an offensive against the hastily organized workers' self-defense committees, the latter created to counterbalance extreme rightist militancy. By September 1973 the officer class was prepared to launch the coup it had been rehearsing for years. In this regard, the Navy and the Air Force had, since early 1972, been establishing close contacts with Chile's major business organizations, right-wing think tanks, and, with their American advisors, in a joint effort to remove Allende from the presidency.

Effects: Demobilization, State Terrorism, and Restructuring

The extreme violence unleashed by the coup and the military regime that followed was bloody but far from purposeless. It was oriented, first, to disman-

tle the leftist government and the various political parties that made up the
Popular Unity. But the military regime aimed even beyond these obvious tar-
gets. During 1973 and 1974, "low-intensity operations" bore into the very social base of the Left, destroying labor unions, neighborhood groups, and
popular organizations. The strategy of demobilization of Chile's working
classes involved the imposition of an unabashedly terrorist state aimed at destroying the vanquished. Contrary to what centrist supporters of the military
regime expected, the new coalition in power did not end its anticommunist cru-
sade at the boundaries of left-of-center organizations. The military moved
quickly to declare illegal all leftist political parties, to close down Congress, and
to suspend all political activities. Furthermore, the military went a long way
toward eliminating all forms of democratic practices by declaring the country
to be under various states of war or emergency for extended periods of time.
National security became state policy; dissidents of all kinds were exiled, tor-
tured, or murdered.

It soon became apparent that the civilian-military coalition was neither a
caretaker regime to open the way to "politics as usual," nor just a fascist
anachronism. The earlier, defensive phase had essentially been one of "demoli-
tion" of opponents, policies, and institutions, but increasingly, from 1976 on,
a neoconservative political and economic offensive, in the form of a relatively
cohesive project, began to take shape (Galleguillos, 1987). The latter involved
an "authoritarian state" geared to producing a consolidation and amalgamation
of Chile's capitalist classes. This model entailed a drastic reduction of the
power of labor, a fragmentation of the middle classes, and a transnationalization of the state, all wrapped in anticommunist and pseudonationalistic
rhetoric.

Since mid-1975, when an alliance between the Army (by then firmly under
General Pinochet's control) and civilian technocrats (the Chicago Boys and the
procorporatist Opus Dei supporters) became hegemonic within the regime,
public policies consciously pursued the materialization of authoritarian capitalism. Radical reductions of state expenditures—matched by massive increases
in military personnel and budgets—were combined with monetarist policies
of free trade, deregulation, denationalization, and deindustrialization. Inroads
made in land reform during previous governments were reversed, favoring
agribusiness and the creation of medium-sized, high-tech farmers. Social security, banking, and health care were privatized. In this, the military built an
alliance with finance capital, transnationals, and exporters, counting on the
support of a managerial technocracy that would give an ideological base to the
project. Moreover, since 1976, Chile's "new sociopolitical order" became increasingly proceduralized and formalized in legal and constitutional mechanisms. The culmination of this process was the promulgation (after an
ostensibly rigged plebiscite) of the 1980 constitution. This "legality" reflected
the real power configuration of the de facto political system—one in which pluralism and effective democracy had no place (Nef, 1983a, 1983b).

THE TRANSITION FROM THE BUREAUCRATIC AUTHORITARIAN REGIME

With the opposition divided and neutralized by the politics of fear, with the firm backing of a revamped elite coalition where finance capital was predominant, and with the hegemonic support of the military bureaucracy, Pinochet's dictatorship remained firmly in control. Although over the years civilian opposition grew in scope and intensity, the correlation of forces always favored the regime. This was the case even during the economic catastrophe of 1982–84. Despite diplomatic condemnations, there was also continuous support from U.S. military and business interests. When an economic boom started in 1986, the regime appeared at last to be sufficiently confident to implement its new sociopolitical order along the lines of that contemplated in the 1980 constitution.

The Context of Transition

The dictatorship was able to maintain the upper hand by imposing its own agenda, ground rules, and timetable on the opposition. Despite much acrimony, the Christian Democrats finally conceded that they had no alternative but to play according to the dictatorship's rules. The Left reluctantly followed suit, and by 1988 the process of normalization was set in motion. A plebiscite was scheduled for October 5, 1988, which would either confirm or reject an extension of Pinochet's rule for eight more years. In the unlikely event of his defeat, there was to be a simultaneous presidential and parliamentary election, in December 1989.

Electoral registration was at first resisted by the anti-Pinochet forces as a trick to give his regime an aura of legitimacy. However, by mid-1988 registration was actively promoted by all kinds of civic and political movements. More than 61 percent of the total population (or over 95 percent) of all eligible voters registered, a much greater proportion than in any election in the country's democratic history. After a brief campaign, nearly 7.5 million voters went to the polls. The political and psychological circumstances of this new "consultation," however, were quite different from those of the previous two occasions (1976 and 1980). So was the outcome: the regime lost with a margin of 55 to 43 percent and had to concede defeat.

Voter turnout was over 90 percent, with few spoiled ballots; in 10 out of the 12 regions into which the country is divided, the "yes" vote lost. [2] At the level of the 44 provincial jurisdictions, 32 (or 73 percent) went for the "no" side, with only 12 (27 percent) going to Pinochet. The major urban and industrial centers overwhelmingly voted "no." [3] In metropolitan Santiago, where nearly 40 percent of the voters live, Pinochet lost. His supporters were concentrated in three upper-class neighborhoods, in the overwhelmingly fruit-producing rural communities, and in the districts with a large concentration of military personnel. The "no" vote was strongest in the working-class districts and in the marginal shantytowns but was also significant in the mostly middle class neighborhoods. Once again, class reemerged as a determinant in Chilean politics.

The Changing Correlation of Forces

Interpreting the Results of the 1988 Plebiscite. There is, however, a different and far less optimistic reading of the electoral results: 43 percent of the voters chose Pinochet. Even discounting control, vote-buying, intimidation, or misinformation, there remains a sizable proportion of the population that supported a clearly antidemocratic alternative. This is quantitatively and qualitatively a more important constituency—one that is much larger than those sectors that in the past supported alienated "antipolitical" solutions of a more conservative, populist, and fascist bent. Moreover, unlike the "no" vote, which represented a conglomerate of 16 dissimilar parties, with limited cohesion and stability, the antidemocratic vote constituted at least a strong one-third of the electorate. Its significance cannot be underestimated, especially during these early stages of the transition.

The December 1989 Presidential and Congressional Elections. Pinochet's defeat at his own game sent the regime scrambling for ways to retain, if not to reinforce, its control of the political process. The military-civilian coalition's survival instinct turned into a legislative and bureaucratic frenzy. A new administrative statute granted job tenure to civil servants,[4] something they had not enjoyed during the previous 16 years. A new organic law authorized the auctioning of university-owned television stations to private bidders, who could be nationals or foreigners. Another gave the Central Bank complete autonomy from the government. A further law stipulated that windfalls from copper exports should be deposited in the Central Bank to pay the state's debt to that institution. A new organic law for the armed forces exempted them from government intrusion into such matters as the organization, promotion, and acquisition of equipment, weaponry, and so on.

Hurriedly but assuredly, the regime made scores of appointments to the judiciary, especially the Supreme Court, as well as to the Central Bank, the Constitutional Tribunal, the Comptroller General's Office, the State Bank, the Radio and Telecommunications Corporation, and the National Television Network. More significantly, the dictatorship appointed nine of its supporters, including four former generals, to the Senate. In addition, a very rapid process of promotion occurred within the armed forces. Last but not least, the dictatorship drafted an electoral law in order to ensure the success of the minority right-wing sectors. Implicitly acknowledging that his supporters could not win an open and fair election, Pinochet resorted to this law in order to get them into Congress through the back door. Thereby, the regime assured a parliamentary representation for itself that their numbers did not warrant.

Despite all this maneuvering, the shocking defeat suffered by the dictator in the 1988 referendum created much dissension among his own supporters. Eventually, two right-wing candidates decided to run for the presidency with predictable results: both, former Minister of the Economy Hernán Büchi and businessman Francisco Errázuruz, were soundly defeated. [5]

The winner, Christian Democrat Patricio Aylwin, ran a safe campaign under the auspices of the Concertation for Democracy, a broad coalition made up of 16 political parties, including Christian Democrats, Social Democrats, and reformed Socialists. In addition, Communists, some socialist sectors, and fringe leftist groups joined Aylwin's candidature, although they were not allowed to be members of Concertation for Democracy or run candidates for Congress under its umbrella. They created an ad-hoc, instrumental party with the name of PAIS (Party of the Broad Socialist Left). The exclusion of these groups was symbolically reflected in Aylwin's campaign slogan: *Gana la Gente* or The Gentle People Win (*gente* in Spanish refers to those middle and upper strata who do not consider themselves to be part of the popular or lower sectors. For the latter, the derogatory expression *pueblo*, or people, is reserved).

Adding to the constitutional and legal constraints that prevented leftist parties and popular sectors from competing on equal terms with the rightist and centrist coalitions was the highly antidemocratic process of nomination inside of political parties. Because fewer seats were available, [6] the nominating process was characterized by manipulation, pressure tactics, and outright authoritarianism. Aylwin's own nomination was marred by bitter infighting within the Christian Democratic Party.

Once the results were known, the opposition's euphoria at having Aylwin elected as the new president, with an absolute majority of the electorate, was tempered by the failure of the system to provide him with a majority in Congress. In fact, the Right had clearly benefited by the electoral rules. With a strong representation in Congress, the Right ended up in a position to deny the new administration the legal instruments needed to dismantle the most authoritarian and antidemocratic features of the Pinochet regime.

Given the present configuration of Congress, it appears almost impossible for the new administration to deliver on its promises. With only 22 senators, Aylwin's administration lacks the numbers needed to amend, much less abrogate, the legislation dealing with the armed forces, elections, the municipal governments, the Central Bank, the constitutional tribunal, the electoral courts, the National Security Council, the 1978 amnesty law for military personnel involved in human rights violations, and, reforming Pinochet's constitution. To amend or abrogate these laws, majority votes of four-sevenths, three-fifths, and two-thirds would be needed.

The Role of the Military in the Transition. The process of transition toward some sort of democracy appears to be greatly influenced by the nature (organization, institutions, ideology, politics, economic policies) of the outgoing military regime. In retrospect, it can be affirmed that the military regime attempted to redefine the content of politics: to transform the previous democratic institutions and replace them with new, controlling, and restrictive mechanisms of limited political participation.

This has created a situation in which the new civilian administration is confronted with the complex and unavoidable issue of the reform of the military institutions. After General Pinochet left the presidency in March 1990, Chile faced the same question that Argentina, Brazil, Peru, and Uruguay had faced earlier: how to incorporate the armed forces into the process of democratic transition while at the same time acknowledging that the armed forces continue to control the repressive apparatus of the state.

This issue of the transformation of military institutions is multifaceted. From a juridical point of view, it involves the constitutional role of the military in the new democratic regime. From a military professional point of view, it involves the reorganization and redeployment of the armed forces so as to reduce their opportunities for political intervention. This also includes the notions of war in which officers are trained to counteract the pervasive authoritarian doctrines of national security prevalent in the 1960s and 1970s. In addition, the democratization of the military implies the redefinition of the structures, hierarchy, and command so that senior officers could be made subject to regulation by civilian authorities. From an ideological point of view, the reform of curricula currently being taught in military academies—as well as the mechanisms for enfranchising officers and soldiers in the political process as citizens—must be considered. Finally, from a political standpoint, the tasks assigned to the armed forces and their degree of obedience to constituted civilian authority require careful consideration. In this latter respect, two questions are paramount: What should be done concerning an officer's responsibility in the violation of human rights, sedition, and insubordination? And which state organization should be in charge of exercising direct hierarchical control upon the armed forces? The urgency to find answers to these dilemmas goes beyond their academic significance. They highlight the fragility of the entire process of transition toward effective democracy.

Once the context of a transition toward democracy is set, there are at least two major issues that need to be addressed immediately: One is how to make the military become a loyal partner in the process of redemocratization. The other is how civilian sectors plan to define the military's new role in the transitional period. Concerning the first issue, the likelihood of the ongoing transition becoming a successful democratic experience is limited. It cannot be expected that the military will voluntarily relinquish all the social, economic, political, and corporate privileges that it has obtained since assuming power in 1973. This is especially true after having demonstrated so clearly and persistently its contempt for democracy.

What the military and its civilian allies call "democratic transition" does not resemble Western liberal democracy, nor the elitist democracy Chileans had known since the early 1830s, nor the "lukewarm" attempt at popular democracy under Allende. Rather, the present transition is one leading to the consolidation of the military's "vision" of the type of political regime the country needs. Its "vision" is the "only vision." The military has not been "forced" to accommodate the demands that the anti-Pinochet opposition made in the last five years. It has been the former (and now ruling) opposition that has had to adapt to new conditions.

Concerning the second issue, the political "hybrid" that is emerging during the Aylwin interregnum is that of a democratic government presiding over—and straight-jacketed by—an authoritarian state and a consolidated elitist socioeconomic order, which is both restrictive and exclusionary. The maintenance of this order is guaranteed by the "guardian" role that the military bestowed upon itself. In fact, article 90 of the 1980 constitution consecrates the constitutional obligation of the armed forces to uphold the essential foundations of the very political regime it and its civilian supporters "founded" in 1980. This clause ensures the military's continuing domination of the political process unless this disposition is itself eventually abrogated, which appears extremely unlikely at present. There are various other mechanisms in the constitution that, when taken in their totality, make the military's guardianship role an even more crucial one. The armed forces' control of the National Security Council (CSN) allows them to influence the makeup of the Senate, since the CSN appoints four members to this body. Legally speaking, General Pinochet may become an additional fifth member when he retires. Moreover, the military can exert its custodial role through the Constitutional Tribunal, since two of its seven members are also appointed by the CSN. These interlocking and self-reinforcing mechanisms for the defense of a counterrevolutionary order are compounded by the rules regulating the nonremovability of the current commanders in chief and director-general of the police.

More ominous is the fact that national security doctrines continue to influence the ways in which the armed forces perceive their relations to civil society. These doctrines are constantly reformulated in order to address and rationalize new and changing sociopolitical conditions. The strongly anticommunist stance of the 1960s and 1970s is now being enhanced by an even broader definition of "internal enemy." In 1987 the region's armed forces indicated that the threat to the preservation of the so-called Western Christian civilization comes not only from subversive or communist forces but also from legal, middle-of-the-road political parties, groups, or movements who, in military eyes, play into the hands of communism. In fact, Social Democratic and Christian Democratic parties are also enemies of their "order." General Pinochet defined the "new enemy" as none other than Antonio Gramsci, the late Italian ideologue (*El Mercurio*, February 9–15, 1989, p. 2). By expanding on the old definition of "the enemy," Pinochet and the military have shown once again that they are far ahead of the politicians when it comes to the demarcation of what is or is not acceptable in the new political, institutional order. While the new alliance in government tries to present itself as a moderate political actor and condemns as anathema any strategy based upon revolutionary violence—thus expecting to neutralize the military by not giving them the excuse to intervene again—it dangerously ignores this redefinition of the enemy that is now taking root within the officer corps. In fact, the military has already singled out Gramsci's ideas, supporters, and actions as its next target. Clearly, this time-lag in the leftist and centrist strategy vis-à-vis the armed forces is far too important to have politicians ignore its possible consequences.

In its first three months in office, Aylwin's administration attempted a divide-and-rule strategy by trying to isolate the army and its commander in chief, General Pinochet, from the other branches. In fact, Aylwin confirmed both the commander in chief of the air force and the director-general of the Carabineros in their posts, while asking for Pinochet's resignation. The general refused. Moreover, Pinochet created the first of a series of clashes with Aylwin by purposely ignoring the new civilian minister of defense as his hierarchical superior. Aylwin retaliated by creating a commission to investigate human rights violations during the dictatorship. Pinochet and the Army, for their part, publicly condemned the commission and its members. The president, showing remarkable strength, summoned Pinochet and Army officers to tell them they were interfering in the government's affairs, which was unacceptable under the constitution. This behavior suggests that the new government is acting under the naive belief that the armed forces are professional institutions and, as such, cannot play a political role. Allende, as stated previously, paid dearly for such naivete.

The government's ambiguity should come as no surprise to the informed observer of the Chilean process. The governing coalition is neither sufficiently solid nor politically strong enough to engage in the radical transformation of the military, at least not during these early stages of the present administration. However, it can be anticipated that the "military question" will continue to be avoided—if for no other reason than to prevent a breakdown of the coalition at a time when its corresponding forces are too weak to stand alone. The Left is aware that it cannot push the Christian Democrat president to do things that he is not willing to do. It remembers that it was Patricio Aylwin who called for the military to overthrow the Allende government, which a Christian Democratic Party (CDP) newspaper said had been taken over by a "Jewish-Communist cell." The Christian Democrats, for their part, know that their alliance with the Left is a precarious one. This is a historical opportunity for the CDP to recover from a lackluster performance in other parts of Latin America. Its only chance to succeed rests on its not alienating the military. The furthest this party appears willing to go is to continue its mild attempt to distance General Pinochet from his forces; it has tried this, to no avail, since 1983.

In short, we do not anticipate the drastic reform of the military, which is essential if the country is to truly move in the direction of democracy. Postponing such reform will more than likely encourage the armed forces to continue in their pervasive and perverse role of custodian of whatever limited democracy they are currently permitting Chileans to have.

CONCLUSIONS: THE EFFECTS OF DICTATORIAL RULE AND THE NATURE OF COUNTERREVOLUTION

The implications of Pinochet's counterrevolution on any future transition toward democracy remain far-reaching. The 1988 plebiscite and the 1989 elections show that the alternatives to the status quo are limited. Many of those who have benefited under the regime would prefer the trappings of liberal democracy: a civilian government, an election every four or six years, less reliance on a coercive apparatus. But they hesitate to support a restoration of the system that preceded the coup—that is, one that gave rise to a socialist president. The new electoral system thus could not resemble the one that had traditionally provided a forum for the institutionalized class conflict. In other words, it could not be representative.

The electoral system thus "enshrined" in legislation has been fine tuned to minimize the risks in the future of there being any "legal" representative working-class political parties, given their potential to form a united front against the status quo. This approach immediately dispenses with any bona fide socialist, communist, or Marxist party, and limits the platform of party coalitions that include substantial left-wing factions. [7] Furthermore, besides requiring at least a grade twelve education, political party leadership positions cannot overlap with union leadership, thereby severing crucial links with actual representation at the grass roots level. The so-called new democracy or, at best, its transitional phase, will continue to exclude the majority of civil society.

The nature of social conflict has changed under the military. The working class is much smaller, and is represented by more atomized and weaker labor movements; there exists a great pool of the unemployed, which includes not only skilled workers, but also professionals and white-collar *empleados*. The peasantry, to a large extent, has become displaced and forced to relocate in urban centers, rural settlements, or urban *poblaciones*, joining ranks with the marginalized sectors and the squatters. Simple survival has replaced political conviction within those sectors that have stood to lose the most under the regime's socioeconomic and political policies. However, it is precisely these sectors that—justifiably—constitute a potentially volatile revolutionary force (Galleguillos and Nef, 1988).

In its efforts to restructure the economy, the military dismantled import substitution industrialization and economic nationalism and sought to provide a new basis for capital accumulation (O'Brien and Roddick, 1983). The reorganization that ensued led to significant changes within the social structure itself. Moreover, as the state reduced its role in the economy, even social welfare became tied to market forces. This meant the end of Chile's welfare-state tradition.

Given the severity of the debt crisis in the region and the continentalization of national security doctrines, the state itself has become—as is the case in most Latin American countries—more internationalized, transnational, and increasingly penetrated by foreign capital and military alignments. By substantially reducing its role in the economy and relying more on international forces, the Chilean state has had to institute more policies of the type espoused by the International Monetary Fund and international lending institutions. So far the Chilean model has been hailed by these institutions and neoliberal economists as a "success" story (Edwards, 1985). Under the present pacts of elites, these economic policies are bound to remain in effect.

On the military-strategic front, national self-determination has been increasingly replaced by penetration based on the most extreme notions of U.S. continental security. Thus, vis-à-vis external pressures, the Chilean state, like most peripheral states, has become both repressive and weaker.

The military regime retains "metapower"—that is, close and enduring control over the process of transition and beyond. This means that the current transition may not fundamentally alter the structure of authority or the foundations of society. This has little to do with a tacit agreement made within the regime, or to pressures from civil society. The nature of the regime's restructuring of Chilean politics and society over the past 15 years sets limits on the kind of political order that can emerge in the post-Pinochet era. The correlation between social and political forces—that is, the interplay between support and opposition within the Chilean state—has been dramatically altered. The pluralistic stalemate of the past has given way to a modified stalemate where the military retains a permanent veto power over society. This is not to say that decisions from above, regarding the moment and nature of transition, take place exclusively and permanently in isolated quarters (i.e., a pact of elites) as contemporary transition theory seems to imply. Rather, they are influenced by factors from below (i.e., popular movements) as well as by multiple and often contradictory international pressures. The generalized perception within Chile regarding the severity of the crisis that preceded the 1973 coup undoubtedly contributed to the regime's longevity and the intensity of its support. Pinochet and his civilian allies have taken every opportunity to stage public reminders of the fate that would have befallen a Chilean society under Allende's "Marxist-Leninist" program.

The new governing coalition—despite its two electoral victories and current tactical alliance—continues to be divided into a multiplicity of political organizations. In this context, all evidence points to a political scenario where the best the democratic forces can hope for is a limited and meaningless democratic facade. One model could be the lengthy and convoluted process following the defeat of the military-inspired constitutional referendum in Uruguay in 1980, which culminated with a limited democratization in the 1985 elections. Fundamentally, however, it should not be forgotten that the Chilean authoritarian regime goes well beyond Pinochet. It is an institutional arrangement tied by bureaucracy, class interests, complicity, ideology, and external constituencies. The aging and discredited general has been replaced by a democratic government of fine credentials without fundamentally altering the counterrevolutionary status quo.

For those who remember 1973, the healthy attitude toward the present opening is one of cautious cynicism. It is unlikely that the Right, the Center, or the Left are as different today from what they were in the past (as they claim). It is ironic to witness those who destroyed Chile's most precious traditions now presenting themselves as the new saviors. For the time being, Chile remains far away from entering a true process of transition to democracy. The relevant and unavoidable question to ask is: where is it headed instead?

NOTES

1. The Chilean Congress, vested with the capacity contained in the 1925 constitution to choose between the two presidential candidates with the largest pluralities, but short of an absolute majority, always followed the practice of endorsing the popular decision. However, parties usually pinned their support on political concessions. The CDP conditioned theirs in 1970 to certain demands exacted from Allende. Because he needed their votes, after a week of negotiations, on October 9, his Popular Unity and the Christian Democrats agreed on a list of provisions to secure guarantees on "civil liberties"—an Estatuto de Garantías. The latter, in fact, curtailed enormously the executive functions contained in the constitution and put Allende in a weak position vis-à-vis the armed forces (see *NACLA Newsletter,* March 1971, p. 3).

2. Women, for the first time in a Chilean electoral contest, outnumbered male registered voters. They had been a preferred target group of the regime's propaganda effort; however, they also rejected the official proposition in a similar proportion to the men. This in itself was an interesting development, since in the past, the female electorate tended to reject the Left by an overwhelming majority. For instance, the gross percentage differentials in 1952, 1958, 1964, and 1970 of male over female preferences for the Left were, respectively, 0.9, 10.1, 12.5, and 11.1; while those of female over male votes going to the Right, Center and minor parties were, respectively, 6.3, 10.1, 12.9, and 10.9.

3. Even in those rural districts where close control, public spending, and a fruit-export-based economic bonanza made the likelihood of a resounding victory for the "yes" side possible, the results were close. Only in those very small settlements, where the majority of the electorate were military personnel, did the regime win hands down (with a 10 to 13 percent support for "no").

4. An insurmountable obstacle to be encountered by the new administration is the one represented by the civilian bureaucracy that has remained in their posts after Pinochet's exit. After 16 years of arbitrary rule, most public organizations (the universities, the Comptroller's General Office, state enterprises, municipalities, public corporations, and the like) are heavily staffed with prodictatorship supporters. One needs to remember how frequently anti-Popular Unity bureaucrats sabotaged the implementation of important programs for purely partisan reasons.

5. The results were:

	Votes	Percentage
Hernán Büchi	2,046,580	29.4
Francisco Errázuriz	1,074,210	15.4
Patricio Aylwin	3,842,887	55.2

(*El Mercurio*, Friday, December 15, 1989, p. 1.)

6. There were only 38 seats to be filled in the Senate and 120 in the Chamber of Deputies, against 50 and 150, respectively, in the pre-coup era. In addition, up to ten individuals can be appointed to the Senate by the president, the National Security Council, and the Supreme Court.

7. The Left could not hide its disappointment with the congressional results. Most affected by the legal and constitutional limitations was the Communist Party, which for the first time in its history was completely shut out of Congress. Moreover, the communists are faced with a widespread rejection by most of the population, including sectors of the reformed Left. The socialists, for their part, moved quickly after the results became known to reunify their various, and ideologically different, factions. The PAIS was dissolved after it failed to capture enough support from the electorate.

REFERENCES

Black, J. (1984). "Participation and the Political Process: The Collapsible Pyramid." In J. Black (ed.), *Latin America: Its Problems and Its Promise*. Boulder, Colo.: Westview Press.

Edwards, S. (1985). "Stabilization and Liberalization: An Evaluation of Ten Years of Chile's Experiment with Free-Market Policies, 1973–1983." *Economic Development and Cultural Change*, No. 33.

Galleguillos, N. (1987). "The Making of the Chilean Authoritarian State: A Case Study of a Defensive Coup d'Etat." Ph.D. Dissertation, University of Toronto.

Galleguillos, N. and J. Nef. (1988). "The Trend Towards Democratization and Redemocratization in Latin America: Shadow and Substance." *Latin American Research Review*, 23, no. 3 (Fall), pp. 131–153.

Greene, T. H. (1984). *Comparative Revolutionary Movements: Search for Theory and Justice*, 2nd ed., Englewood Cliffs, N.J.: Prentice-Hall.

Hirschman, A. (1964). "Alternatives to Revolution." In Laura Randall (ed.), *Economic Development: Evolution or Revolution?* Boston: D.C. Heath.

Nef, J. (1983a). "The Revolution That Never Was: Perspectives on Democracy, Socialism and Repression in Chile." *Latin American Research Review*, 18, no. 1.

———. (1983b). "Economic Liberalism and Political Repression in Chile." In Archibald R.M. Ritter and David H. Pollock, *Latin American Prospects for the 1980's: Equity, Democratization and Development*. New York: Praeger.

Nef, J. (1988). "Alternatives to Development in Contemporary Latin America: An Interpretative Essay on Politics, Ideology and Social Change." *Cahiers GRAL*. Montréal: Université de Montréal.

O'Brien, P. and J. Roddick (1983). *The Pinochet Decade*. London: Latin American Bureau.

O'Donnell, G. (1979). "Tensions in the Bureaucratic-Authoritarian State." In David

Collier (ed.), *The New Authoritarianism in Latin America*. Princeton, N.J.: Princeton University Press.

Stallings, B. (1978). *Class Conflict and Economic Development in Chile 1958–1973*. Stanford, Calif.: Stanford University Press.

CHAPTER FOURTEEN

Argentina: An Underdeveloping Country?

ALBERTO CIRIA

Argentina's saga from being a colonial backwater of the Spanish Empire to a success story of sorts (at least for its socioeconomic elites) between 1880 and 1930, and then again to a contemporary declining nation, is one of the puzzling national developments of our time (Corradi, 1985). Abundance of natural resources, export staples (meat and grains, which also fed the domestic population), the absence of a demographic boom, early urbanization, a fundamental "British connection" in trade and investments, large-scale immigration from Southern Europe, and the consolidation in the nineteenth century of an economically dominant and politically hegemonic class, the agrarian bourgeoisie, or *oligarquía*, represented key elements of the Argentine progress.

The domestic agrarian bourgeoisie developed a model of accumulation based on the comparative advantages of the fertile Pampas, good transportation facilities, and Great Britain's presence as the major economic partner: meat and cereals were exchanged for manufactured goods, coal, financial services, and portfolio investments. The myth of an exceptional Argentina remained entrenched, and it was also shared by other social classes than the agrarian bourgeoisie with its cultural dominance.

The 1930s (a Depression; a military coup that overthrew a moderate civilian regime and had the support of crucial agrarian interests) paved the way for a Conservative restoration that practiced political fraud and implemented private accumulation without social redistribution. From then on, the rigidity of the economic model and its extreme vulnerability to external influences became manifest. Two patterns consolidated: a deterioration of the terms of trade, with some relative exceptions like after World War II or the early 1970s; and the search for new markets to ship Argentina's export staples, once Britain's preferential position vanished after the late 1940s.

Also, the 1930s were a period in which Argentina's Conservative governments, faced with a decline in world trade, introduced a defensive state interventionism in important economic sectors and fostered import-substitution industrialization to partially cope with the drop in imports (Dorfman, 1983). Earlier than in other Latin American countries, Argentina experienced an industrialization process stemming from the light, consumer goods sector, but without a corresponding "industrial revolution": the new industrialists (many of them foreign-born) were more concerned with subsidies, high tariffs for foreign imports, and preferential treatment as official suppliers, and in time they would become willing members of the populist coalition headed by Juan Perón (1895-1974) in the 1940s.

However, the structural weaknesses of Argentine ISI remained its concentration on the internal market and its general noncompetitiveness in the international arena, together with a heavy dependence on the foreign exchange generated by agropecuarian staples. Dependence also was present in the pattern of consumer or semidurable goods that were "produced with imported machinery and intermediate inputs" (Waisman, 1987, p. 65).

During the last decades, the pattern of Argentina's trade has remained significantly consistent: the highest proportion of exports still belongs to grains and beef, usually over 75 percent of total exports (in recent times, major additions to these staples have been sorghum and soybeans). With the exception of the USSR since the 1970s, Argentina has generally lacked established, reliable markets for its exports (*nontraditional exports*—namely, everything that is not meat, grains, hides, or wool—have historically maintained a very low level).

Leading authors have suggested that a *proyecto industrialista* (industrialist project) developed between 1930 and the mid-1970s by leaps and bounds, in spite of periodical crises in the political realm, especially visible in the alternation of civilian governments and military dictatorships (Ferrer, 1989). But by 1976 the cleavages in Argentine society included daily violence, state-sponsored or -tolerated terror, guerrilla actions, economic mismanagement bordering on chaos and hyperinflation, and the political exhaustion of a Peronist regime that had been freely elected to office three years before. The March 1976 military coup introduced a crash program of free market economics and clandestine repression, whose effects are still at play in today's Argentina.

The economy remains a relevant structural factor for an explanation of the Argentine conundrum. But there is a combined legacy in the sociocultural field, and also in the political one, that should be integrated fully in any kind of assessment. Our general hypothesis suggests that Argentina experiences the combined effects of a double tradition: the legacy of authoritarian/corporatist ideas and institutions *and* of democratizing ones, the argument here being the pervasiveness of the pattern rather than its originality (Ciria, 1990).

In the late nineteenth century the Conservative elites practiced an efficient authoritarianism that acquired durable features. The patriarchal structure of the family, *machista*, and sexist characteristics that cut across classes were reinforced by the educational system and the Catholic Church. Reforms in the political system (1912) allowed for minority representation, manhood suffrage, and the extension of the franchise to the middle classes, but they did not democratize the country's political culture. Owing to the lack of a mass-based, electorally viable Conservative Party, the agrarian bourgeoisie and its allies were unable to mount coalitions to lead them to victory in a free balloting. So the stage was set for extraconstitutional alliances with sectors of the armed forces (the Conservatives' adversaries, in turn, would change from Radicales to Peronists).

Hipólito Yrigoyen's government (1926–22 and 1928–30) mixed national *caudillismo* with formal democracy in the political sphere. By 1930 a coup paved the way for a regime that disguised its authoritarian penchant with a democratic facade, not an uncommon occurrence in later Argentine history.

The political success of Peronism in the 1940s and 1950s underlined the ideological strength of authoritarian/corporatist currents in the movement's makeup (Perón's military thought, his version of Social Catholicism). Peronism had an organized labor component and a pyramidal-bureaucratic structure: a majority of voters kept on selecting Perón and his candidates for office, but the Perónist state became increasingly more repressive and intolerant of the political opposition, which participated in military conspiracies to overthrow a formally democratic regime (Ciria, 1983).

After 1955 the "democracy of the democratic ones" continued debilitating the liberal-democratic tradition. The argument states that if Peronism would be returned to power by a majority of votes in a free election, its leader would again display yesterday's dictatorial élan. Consequently, a series of legal mechanisms politically and electorally banned the Peronist movement during the 1955–73 period. These years saw not only the consolidation of authoritarian/corporatist ideas among military officers and right-wing civilian and religious groups, but also the strengthening of a mixed political system that regularly combined "classical" institutions of liberal democracy with direct "corporatist" negotiations between the state/executive power and economic-financial groups, the Confederación General del Trabajo (General Confederation of Workers, CGT), the Catholic Church, and, most obviously, the armed forces themselves.

This model closely applied to the unfinished terms of civilian presidents (1958–62 and 1963–66) and Congresses; on occasions, a more traditional neo-corporatist project showed its familiar face (General Juan Carlos Onganía, 1966–70), but it was soon replaced by other officers' preferences for the previously alluded mixed political system.

The 1973 elections symbolized a coming to terms of norms and reality underlined by Peronism's return to office. In a parallel way, another development was also influencing the substance and style of Argentine politics: the then growing process of politicization of the military together with the militarization of many politicians—for example, youth organizations both inside and outside Perónism, such as the armed guerrilla Montoneros or the Ejército Revolucionario del Pueblo (Gillespie, 1982).

The 1976–83 military dictatorship introduced deep changes in Argentina's economy and society; paradoxically enough, the military rulers reinforced economic and diplomatic relations with the Soviet Union, proclaimed their "Western, Christian" preferences, went to war in 1982 with Great Britain over the Malvinas/Falklands Islands (in spite of a well-documented U.S. opposition to the tragic adventure), and engaged in a dirty war against thousands of internal enemies, the *desaparecidos* (disappeared ones) (Vacs, 1984; Cardoso, 1983; CONADEP, 1984).

A significant tertiarization of the economy went hand in hand with the deterioration of public enterprises and public services. Starting in 1976, the military regime and its economic advisors, such as José A. Martínez de Hoz, began a dismantling of the productive structure built since the 1930s. Some features of these policies were the predominance of speculative/financial investment over productive investment (the *plata dulce*, or easy money syndrome), paralleled by a hefty increase in the country's foreign debt, which allowed for the overvaluation of the local currency and widespread wheeling and dealing; an open-door attitude toward foreign goods, trying to decrease the state's overprotection to local industries servicing the domestic market; and a net decrease in the number of industrial jobs, and therefore a potential decrease in the strength of Peronist workers' organizations.

Deindustrialization's social consequences were far-reaching, and transcended the end of the dictatorship. By 1987 the industrial product was equivalent to that of 1972, and from 1975 to 1987 industrial employment fell 35 percent (some 400,000 workers). However, some sources point out that there was a complementary process of centralization and concentration at play in certain industrial areas: pressure groups like the so-called *capitanes de la industria* (captains of industry) became major national players, in their search for state subsidies and purchases. Foreign banks and local representatives of multinational corporations were other powerful actors (Nun and Portantiero, 1986).

The agrarian sector was modernized since the 1970s, especially in the Pampas region: technologically modern agricultural concerns took the lead in the production of grains, which contrasted with a severe crisis in the cattle industry during the 1980s. Side by side with this "reagrarianization" of Argentina's exports, a detrimental trend coalesced: a true culture of speculation. Surviving, even prospering, against high inflation and inordinately high interest rates became a popular game. Small investors, pensioners as well as industrialists, found that liberalization of the financial system, and the many speculative options available, could be an easy way to make a living, or to increase profits: entrepreneurs played the U.S. dollar or the state's guaranteed bonds to keep their own corporations in the black, to amass superprofits, or to circumvent crippling regulations to productive activities. Everybody became an investor, as fired workers used their severance packages to beat inflation at its own game (Ikonicoff, 1989).

Rather than for productive or social projects, a large part of the foreign debt incurred by official and private sectors (the latter's obligations were guaranteed by the dictatorship in 1981) was devoted to fan financial speculation and parasitism, shady deals, and capital flight to safe havens in Europe or the United States (Golubboff and Hopenhayn, 1989). In due course, the debt's weight required a series of structural adjustments—with IMF acquiescence to each individual program—which became increasingly harsher under the civilian administrations since 1983. A well-known economist has suggested that the military-neoconservative reaction against the industrialist project predates in Argentina the Latin American external debt crisis of the early 1980s, and it has to be understood in the context of a weak social consensus favorable to industrialization, the opposite of what happens in Brazil (Lewis, 1990).

In connection with the social consequences of the economic model launched by the military and, with some degree of latitude, continued by democratically elected presidents, the statistical evidence confirms the trend toward tertiarization of salaried employment (by 1980, three out of five economically active individuals), and a parallel growth of a (mainly urban) census aggregate known as *cuentapropistas* (self-employed). There has been some shrinking of middle entrepreneurial strata and a significant redefinition of the popular sectors. These are less synonymous with the industrial proletariat category (the social backbone of historical Perónism), they have more internal heterogeneity, while the public-sector employees have grown in importance and militancy (Palomino, 1987).

TRANSITION TO DEMOCRACY: THE PRESENT AND THE PAST

The free election of Raúl Alfonsín in 1983 brought back the Unión Cívica Radical (Radical Civic Union, UCR) to power with a liberal democratic program, hopes of social and economic reforms, and a promise of modern leadership. For over a year, Alfonsín's government attempted to implement a neopopulist economic program (ultimately frustrated) aimed at beating inflation at its own game, which was replaced in June 1985 by the first of a series of orthodox adjustments, the Plan Austral, following IMF guidelines. In spite of a temporary improvement in the economic picture, the administration was unable or unwilling to deal with the culture of speculation. The new technocratic team in charge presided over a repeat performance of financial adventures introduced during the military dictatorship: "millions of small-scale speculators as well as private sector enterprises" participated "in this casino-like economy" (Gabetta, 1989). The *Patria Financiera* remained a reality. The Financial Fatherland was made up of "the big corporations and banks which speculate ultimately on interest rates and the dollar exchange rate, thereby keeping the money-spinning Argentine 'bicycle' working at top speed" (Coron, 1990).

From June 1985 to mid-1989 a new currency that replaced the peso, now called the austral, was devalued 4,500 percent; monthly interest rates peaked at 200 percent in July 1989; workers' participation in the GDP (with historical figures of 45 percent under Peronist governments) declined to 28 percent; unemployment reached 15 percent; and so on. Pent-up sectoral demands of a very "corporatized" society accumulated, from economic groups to labor unions, while the majority of Argentine provinces remained mired in poverty and deprived of basic services (tax evasion was the second most popular sport after soccer).

Relationships between the Radical administration and the armed forces (1983–89) showed a mixture of tradition and quite mild reforms. There were civilian attempts to exercise control over the military-industrial complex; budgetary restraints aggravated tensions between generals and politicians; Congress passed legislation prohibiting the direct involvement of the armed forces in cases of internal conflict. But the crucial issues of human rights violations and the trials and punishment of military officers linked to the post–1976 repression were paramount during Alfonsín's tenure.

Selective punishment of some top-ranking military leaders was followed by two laws approved by Congress that extended a blanket amnesty, in practice, to hundreds of actual or potential defendants: society, in fact, was unable to close a dramatic chapter of its recent past that weighed heavily over its present. On top of that, in 1987 and 1988 there were three mutinies headed by right-wing, fundamentalist Catholic junior officers. The defeated uprisings, though, posed an eventual threat to political stability, as had been the case of many other frustrated coups in Argentine contemporary history.

Another key social and political corporation, the CGT, called 13 "general strikes" between 1985 and 1988 to challenge Alfonsín's IMF-compatible adjustment policies, as expressions of symbolic opposition: strikes did not exclude (at times they even presupposed) negotiations and pragmatic in-camera deals between labor and government. This shows that the CGT as well as other major corporations in Argentine society tend to bypass the formal political process and "to enter into deals outside and around representative institutions" (Corradi, 1985, p. 152).

After the May 1989 elections that Peronist Carlos Menem won handily over the UCR candidate, the Alfonsín administration was forced to move up the inauguration date five months ahead of schedule (July instead of December), because of its inability to control key variables of the economy like monetary and fiscal policies: hyperinflation returned with a vengeance, while food riots—and their sequel of dead and wounded—underscored the dramatic dimensions of the times. Crisis management was at its lowest, and persuasive evidence later indicated that part of the economic and financial establishment had initiated a kind of corporatist aggression against President Alfonsín, thus helping to precipitate his early retirement from the political scene (Majul, 1990).

In contrast, with a vaguely populist electoral platform (a "productive revolution"), Menem introduced another structural adjustment shock treatment. Reversing a historical trend that surprised old-line Peronists but pleased former ideological rivals, this program was the result of secret negotiations between Menem's economic advisors and top executives from Bunge and Born, "a holding company that produces food and consumer goods for the internal market and exports grain" (Christian, 1989).

This strategic alliance, as Menem used to describe it, gathered owners and managers of one of Argentina's biggest multinationals with free-market technocrats and neoconservative politicians, namely Alvaro Alsogaray and his small Unión del Centro Democrático. Some priorities were: restructuring of Argentina's economy by an increase in the exports of beef, grains, and oil; reorganization of the state through privatizations or shared management for a variety of public enterprises, including the particularly troublesome phone company, the railways, and the national airline; a series of deregulations to eliminate state monopolies; the reduction in protectionist measures—subsidies, high tariffs, tax breaks—to weed out noncompetitive, cost-inefficient domestic industries; the struggle against inflation (in 1989 the cost of living rose 4,923 percent); a temporary freeze of prices, after allowing hefty markups to wholesale and retail business; and a very moderate rise in salaries. The government promised control over its printing of currency, a decrease in the state's deficit, periodic revisions of public utilities' rates, and a real tax reform. The moratorium preached by Menem during his electoral campaign was replaced by negotiations with the IMF and foreign banks on how to continue servicing the huge accumulated foreign debt (by mid-1990 interest payments that had been suspended in 1988 were again disbursed, in nominal sums).

The program of Menem and Bunge and Born had a considerable social impact, especially among organized workers, the poor, and the marginalized. Mostly for tactical and personalist reasons, the CGT split into two factions, which competed in their opposition to a deindustrializing policy and a state that is becoming leaner and meaner in matters of social security and welfare. This division within organized labor was especially important because it happened in relation to a Peronist government in its third political incarnation after 1946 and 1973. Industrialists and contractors traditionally having a cozy arrangement with an overprotective state also voiced their discontent with the official alliance. The interests of the banking community, both local and foreign, were important, too, in determining the government's strategy, which included a spectacular public rapprochement with the United States, in the hopes that

President George Bush's administration could help Argentina's case vis-à-vis the IMF during the protracted negotiations.

By December 1989/January 1990, however, history repeated itself, as if to indicate the intractability of the Argentine economy. Inflation again accelerated to 79.2 percent in January 1990, after the prices-salaries truce broke down before its anticipated deadline. The austral reached new, abysmal lows in relation to the U.S. dollar, and utilities' rates were increased once more. The alliance with Bunge and Born disintegrated, while the state attempted to diminish the weight of the financial sectors by forcing short-term depositors to accept long-term U.S. dollar-denominated bonds. New realignments of economic groups and political organizations took place during the first six months of 1990: the great majority of factions within the officialist Partido Justicialista (Justicialist Party, PJ) closed ranks around Menem and his neoconservative project; an anti-Alfonsín sector of the UCR coincided generally with the president's plan.

The Sociedad Rural (Rural Society, SR), a powerful lobby that includes the upper reaches of the agrarian bourgeoisie, together with representatives of agribusiness enterprises, have become crucial allies in this stage of Menem's policies that prolong many features of the Bunge and Born months. Hyperinflation was brought down in a few months but at the cost of a profound recession that has affected industrial production and general consumption. For the time being, the structural adjustment appears to be directed to generate a surplus to partially pay the external debt's services, while agroindustry (and eventual foreign investments) try to reproduce the economic growth of pre-Depression Argentina (Abalo, 1990, p. 4).

Politically, Menem has consolidated executive power vis-à-vis Congress and the Supreme Court (recent reforms have produced a relatively safe majority of judges in support of the president's economic policies), and he has actively courted the armed forces. Military salaries have been increased above public sector guidelines; executive pardons were granted to convicted generals for their violations of human rights during the 1976–83 dictatorship, and also to the 1987 and 1988 mutineers against a constitutional administration. Menem's relations with the church are cordial, in contrast to the opposition mounted by the hierarchy against Alfonsín due to a divorce law passed by Parliament in 1987.

The period of transition to democracy, or to what some authors have called democratic modernization (Nef, 1986), has brought about certain patterns that may well characterize the 1990s short of the eventuality of a military coup in quite extreme circumstances.

The overextension of the economy's financial sector, which Menem has begun to curtail in some areas, needs to be redressed and brought down to scale as a permanent policy. Therefore, industrial investment has to be encouraged and stimulated in selected areas: it should become an integral part of the state's policies for the poststructural adjustment period and the needed industrial reconversion. Also, a serious restructuring of the state is in order. All-out privatizations may not be the only road. Replacing inefficient state monopolies by private multinational penetration in major areas of the economy and public services entails severe risks. One is the age-old question of profit motive versus social needs, and the state's own regulatory powers vis-à-vis major economic groups. Another is that foreign and domestic capital will usually concentrate in upscale markets, more developed regions, and their transportation and communication networks—Buenos Aires, Córdoba and Rosario—relegating the rest of Argentina to second-class status and further contributing to the socioeconomic polarization already indicated.

There were two important electoral events in the 1980s. The 1983 victory of UCR's Alfonsín over the PJ's Italo Luder showed a realignment of forces in Argentine politics; Peronism was defeated in open balloting for the first time. And the 1989 victory of Menem over the UCR's Eduardo Angeloz indicated that alternation between competing political rivals could also occur normally. Both the PJ and UCR—the largest, best-organized parties in the country—possess a certain distinctiveness in comparison to Latin American counterparts. For instance, neither of the two has *permanently* articulated interests from a large proportion of national and foreign entrepreneurs, or the agricultural bourgeoisie (Di Tella, 1987). This situation parallels the striking absence in the political spectrum of a strong, mass-based Conservative Party capable of winning some elections without recourse to fraud (see the 1930–43 period). This factual evidence points, in part, to a better understanding of the frequency of military-civilian conspiracies in Argentina. The dichotomy of popularly based parties (usually seen as populists or reformists, but with crucial differences as the liberal-democratic tradition in the UCR or a major presence of organized labor in the PJ) and socioeconomic groups deeply entrenched in different areas, with the state regularly attempting to perform a mediating role, is another fundamental feature of the political system. It is still too early to assess if Carlos Menem's extraordinary about-face in joining forces with historical adversaries (Bunge and Born, the agropecuarian interests, some neoconservative politicians) becomes the starting point of a new social and political alliance in Argentina that can combine growth (with a diminished kind of redistribution that is the Peronist model), free market policies, and political stability. Many of Menem's recent allies supported repressive military regimes in the not-too-distant past, a relevant instance of continuities between civilian and military administrations in the field of economic programs.

The relative modernization and democratization that transformed the PJ under the leadership of Antonio Cafiero and his *renovadores* (partisans of renewal) has been placed on the back burner during the early part of Menem's term. Menem's own political career mixed a demand for primary elections within the PJ (he won handily over Cafiero in 1988) with a penchant for confidential, back-room strategies of negotiations at the top. This last dimension is the prevailing one in Menem as president: he has managed to keep the party at bay until time comes for his announcing a new policy, which is then submitted to the party's ratification or presented for approval to Peronist parliamentary groups. Power, as indicated previously, is concentrated in the executive—another Argentine political tradition—and negotiations between President Menem and interest groups take precedence over other matters. This is clearly shown in another pattern that may characterize the 1990s. While the president (this was also true about Alfonsín) permanently dispenses the ministrations of *maximum arbiter* for governmental and party affairs, cabinet posts have undergone a deterioration in their original functions. Many times ministers cease to be "secretaries" of the president and carriers of official policies, and function rather as representatives of major corporate players to the executive. Menem's original ministers resembled a "cabinet of corporations," although some of them were later replaced by loyal friends and political cronies.

The panorama for the next decade looks more nebulous in the social and political arenas. The survival of Peronism as a movement and as a political actor, or its eventual dispersion into a Center-Right party, a union-oriented faction that could become a labor party of sorts (this possibility is periodically voiced by analysts and journalists), are key variables for any prospective equation. Certain sectors in Argentine society have begun to react against the structural adjustment's effects, but they still do not make up an organized coalition of interests. Unions in the public sector that face severe unemployment, industrialists producing mainly for the domestic market and with a special client relationship with the state and left-wing parties, and groups in need of overcoming traditional antagonisms with Peronism are crucial examples of this loose opposition to a policy of privatizations, free enterprise, and a nonwelfare state. This reversal of what Peronism—in its historical incarnation—usually meant to faithful partisans and moderate sympathizers is complemented in 1990 by the official rhetoric of important Peronist union leaders such as Saúl Ubaldini: when criticizing Menem's programs, Ubaldini recalls the 1940s past of nationalizations, social welfare, and public services. The lack of alternative, practical programs to oppose the president's goals appears as a major shortcoming to the consolidation of such an alliance at this stage. For the time being, the situation validates the perceptive observation that the country "seems to be living entirely in a present determined by various interpretations of the past, not in a present oriented towards the future" (Calvert 1989, p. 279). Argentine history, too, has included Satanization of the past, or a parallel idealization (in spite of recent anecdotes as the 1989 return of the remains of Juan Manuel de Rosas [1793–1877] from an English cemetery); a morbid preoccupation with the dead, especially in politics where the example of Eva Perón (1919–52) always comes to mind; and a "pathological nationalism" that takes over collectively as an integral part of masses' and elites' beliefs, the 1982 Malvinas/Falklands crisis and war being a striking case in point (Escudé, 1987).

Another aspect in need of reassessment will relate to Argentina's place in the complex world scene of the 1990s, with momentous changes in Eastern Europe and the USSR, but with a less dynamic picture in Latin America. The trend toward insularity and exceptionalism, so embedded in contemporary Argentina, has to be reversed in the country's adaptation to the international economic and commercial system, a position favored both by Alfonsín and Menem.

Consequently, Argentina's foreign relations are directly related to many domestic matters already sketched in this chapter, and at times they even mirror some of these key problems. Pragmatism or continuity in external affairs have not been typical. But there are some stimulating exceptions: a peaceful solution to the border conflict with Chile on the issue of sovereignty in the Beagle Channel, supported by a majority of voters in a 1984 nonbinding referendum called by President Alfonsín; and the reestablishment of diplomatic and economic relations with Great Britain, after an intensive series of negotiations strongly supported by President Menem. Trade and other economic links with the European Economic Community (EEC) were among the motives behind Menem's acceptance of the exclusion of matters about sovereignty from the negotiations, although Argentina remained free to pursue its own claims peacefully at the United Nations and other international arenas. The EEC quietly supported Argentina's and Britain's normalization of relations: it was only after this return to normality that the Europeans signed with the South American nation an agreement of cooperation, as they had previously done with Brazil and Venezuela. Italy and Spain, within the EEC, may well improve their respective relations with Argentina during the 1990s, but they cannot become a new fulcrum for Argentina's traditional export staples as Britain used to be in the past (these and other nations in the EEC had reached a high degree of self-sufficiency in the production of cereals and beef since the 1970s, and consequently introduced protectionist barriers to Argentine imports).

Relationships with the United States, the hegemonic power in Latin America, will be decisive in the new decade vis-à-vis its government, the banks, and productive investors who could be attracted to a stable Argentina with social peace instead of unrest, some degree of continuity and coherence in official policies, and the elimination of an overdeveloped, mainly speculative financial system. Taking all of this into account, Menem's rapprochement with the United States may not be the most rewarding option in the long run. Argentina's own participation in the Non-Aligned Movement may well decrease during the 1990s, paralleling the Third World's evident crises of identity and ideologies. It is hoped that the benign neglect usually manifested by Argentine political leaders about Pacific Rim countries may turn around and transform itself in pragmatic initiatives with some nations in the area, during the coming years. As former Foreign Minister Dante Caputo stated in the United Nations, Argentina is "a Western, non-aligned developing country" (Calvert, 1989, p. 211).

By the mid-1990s, on the other hand, it is expected that a Southern Cone regional common market may be operative among Argentina, Brazil, Chile, and

Uruguay, in conjunction with a Latin American global free trade arrangement. Economic integration may proceed more smoothly in this era of market openings and privatizations than was the case during the 1960s, when ISI and state protectionism made the task a very elusive one. Here, as in many other instances, the U.S. government's apparently favorable position to a huge North American/Latin American free trade area will need to be seriously analyzed from the perspectives of dependency, hegemony, and the Latin American nations' own basic needs and expectations.

A domestic pattern that may become operational in the 1990s is the perceived recourse to compacts that may strengthen liberal democracy and guarantee some long-term consensus among political parties and strong sectoral interests. (This, by the way, is a well-ingrained tradition of Peronism: the 1955 Acuerdo de la Productividad [Productivity Agreement], the 1973 Pacto Social [Social Pact], etc.) To be effective, accords between the government and opposition forces to defend the democratic system against present or future encroachments (e.g., the military), will require a profound change of habits in powerful actors. One scholar has argued, "the question to redefine is not that democracy accepts the corporations, but that [the corporations] accept the democratic rules of the game" (Itzcovich, 1987, p. 239).

Still, another feasible development may prove to be what the Uruguayan writer Eduadro Galeano (1987) has called *democraduras* (a portmanteau Spanish word suggesting a simultaneous presence of democracy and dictatorship), which for Argentina would imply the coexistence of a deeply corporatized society with a weak institutional system, a hybrid marriage that can also be found in other realms than the political. Argentina combines "the worst of economic systems" and it is a hybrid, mixing "socialism without a plan and capitalism without a free market" (Cavallo, 1989).

To sum up, the descending circularity of Argentina's more recent history would need to be substantially altered in the 1990s if the country wishes to arrive at the twenty-first century without the crippling legacy of a not-fully-assimilated nineteenth and mid-twentieth centuries' past.

REFERENCES

Abalo, Carlos (April 23, 1990). "Una apuesta para revivir el pasado." *Nuevo Sur*, economic supplement, p. 4.

Calvert, Susan and Peter (1989). *Argentina: Political Culture and Instability*. Pittsburgh: University of Pittsburgh Press.

Cardoso, Oscar R. et al. (1983). *Malvinas la trama secreta*. Buenos Aires: Sudamericana/Planeta.

Cavallo, Domingo (September 20, 1989). *The Vancouver Sun*, p. A10.

Christian, Shirley (December 26, 1989). "After Six Months, the Troubles Pile Up for Argentine Leader." *New York Times*, p. 8.

Ciria, Alberto (1983). *Politica y cultura popular: La Argentina peronista 1946–1955*. Buenos Aires: Ediciones de la Flor.

————. (1990). *Treinta años de politica y cultura: Recuerdos y ensayos.* Buenos Aires: Ediciones de la Flor.

CONADEP (1984). *Nunca más* [Report of the National Commission on the Disappearance of Persons]. Buenos Aires: Eudeba.

Coron, Edith (January 14, 1990). "Argentine Attempts to Combat Hyperinflation." *Manchester Guardian Weekly,* p. 13.

Corradi, Juan E. (1985). *The Fitful Republic: Economy, Society, and Politics in Argentina.* Boulder, Colo.: Westview Press.

Di Tella, Torcuato S. (1987). *Evolución del sistema de partidos politicos en Argentina, Brasil y Perú (1960–1985).* Buenos Aires: Fundación Simón Rodriguez—Editorial Biblos.

Dorfman, Adolfo (1983). *Cincuenta años de industrialización en la Argentina 1930–1980: Desarrollo y perspectivas.* Buenos Aires: Ediciones Solar.

Escudé, Carlos (1987). *Patologia del nacionalismo: El caso argentino.* Buenos Aires: Editorial Tesis—Instituto Torcuato Di Tella.

Ferrer, Aldo (1989). *El devenir de una ilusión: La industria argentina desde 1930 hasta nuestros días.* Buenos Aires: Sudamericana.

Gabetta, Carlos (May 1989). "Tant d'espoirs deçus en Argentine." *Le Monde Diplomatique,* p. 23.

Galeano, Eduardo (April 1987). "Las democracias no quieren ser democraduras." *El Porteño.*

Gillespie, Richard (1982). *Soldiers of Perón: Argentina's Montoneros.* Oxford: Clarendon Press.

Goluboff, Eva and Benjamin Hopenhayn (April 1989). "Fuga de capitales y deuda externa (Algo para recordar)." *El Bimestre politico y económico* 43.

Ikonicoff, Moisés (1989). *De la cultura de renta a la economia de producción.* Buenos Aires: Lesaga.

Itzcovich, Victoria (1987). "La Cámara Argentina de Comercio y la Asociación de Bancos Argentinos." In José Nun and Juan Carlos Portantiero (eds.), *Ensayos sobre la transición democrática en la Argentina.* Buenos Aires: Pûntosur.

Lewis, Paul H. (1990). *The Crisis of Argentine Capitalism.* Chapel Hill: University of North Carolina Press.

Majul, Luis (1990). *Porgué cayó Alfonsín: El huevo terrorismo económico.* Buenos Aires: Sudamericana.

Nef, Jorge (1986). "Redemocratization in Latin America or the Modernization of the Status Quo?" *Canadian Journal of Latin American and Caribbean Studies,* 11, p. 21.

Nun, José and Juan Carlos Portantiero (1986). "La consolidación de la democracia en la Argentina." Working Paper No. 1. Buenos Aires: CLADE.

————. eds. (1987). *Ensayos sobre la transición democrática en la Argentina.* Buenos Aires: Pûntosur.

Palomino, Héctor (1987). *Cambios ocupacionales y sociales en Argentina, 1947–1985.* Buenos Aires: CISEA.

Vacs, Aldo (1984). *Discreet Partners: Argentina and the USSR Since 1917.* Pittsburgh: University of Pittsburgh Press.

Waisman, Carlos H. (1987). *Reversal of Development in Argentina: Postwar Counterrevolutionary Policies and their Structural Consequences.* Princeton, N.J.: Princeton University.

CHAPTER FIFTEEN

Micro and Macro Logics of Political Conflict: The Informal Sector and Institutional Change in Peru and Mexico

MAXWELL A. CAMERON

The recent growth of the informal sector has been widely observed throughout Latin America (Touraine,1987; Portes et al., 1989; Carbonetto et al., 1988). Less clear are the political implications of the growing number of workers who find income and employment opportunities in informal economic activities. The objective of this chapter is threefold: (1) to argue that the impact of the informal sector depends on the nature and size of the labor surplus and the capacity of economic institutions and the government to provide income and employment over a sustained period; (2) to explain why the growth of the informal sector leads to demands for institutional change; and (3) to compare how the political systems have responded differently to such demands in Peru and Mexico.

The "informal sector" refers to a set of economic activities that are extremely heterogeneous, ranging from street-hawking to industrial homework. However, they are all characterized by the absence of an explicit and written labor contract, state regulation of wages and working conditions, and a clear separation between ownership of labor and capital (Portes et al., 1989, p. 116). For the purpose of this analysis, there are two principal causes of the growth of the informal sector. First, rapid population growth and rural-urban migration have created a surplus work force in many Latin American countries. Second, government restrictions and inefficient economic institutions have reduced the capacity of the private sector to generate adequate employment and income opportunities in the formal sector.

In societies with a growing population and inefficient economic institutions, the pressures for institutional change are likely to be enormous (North, 1989, pp. 1324–1325). For example, in Peru inefficient economic institutions and population growth have created an informal sector that is a major source of political support for parties—both Left and Right—that advocate changes in property relations. This contrasts with Mexico, where the growth of the informal sector has occurred within the context of a relatively stable assignment of property rights. The government has responded to the loss of material and symbolic resources to control and limit the demands of the informal sector by shifting toward a more market-oriented growth strategy designed to attract foreign capital and increase the productivity and efficiency of Mexican business by exploiting the informal sector.

The persistence and recent growth of the informal sector is partly due to the incapacity of formal labor markets to absorb the expanding work force. The incapacity of the formal sector to provide adequate employment is the outcome of many factors. According to the World Bank (1987, pp. 74–75), these include

a chronically overvalued exchange rate, high levels of industrial protection, high taxes (combined with tax reliefs that encourage the use of capital), labor protection laws, powerful labor unions, credit rationing, and the recent recession . . . the informal economy is also a response to the pervasive regulations that have come to affect economic activity.

The avoidance of labor legislation is also a particularly important factor in the growth of the informal sector. Increases in the cost of labor create an incentive to replace labor with capital, thus reducing the demand for labor. Dipak Mazumdar (1976, p. 656) points out that the distinction between formal and informal sectors turns on the idea that workers in the formal sector are protected, so that wages and working conditions are not generally available to all workers unless they cross certain barriers to entry. Informal workers are unprotected by labor laws or minimum wage legislation; without unions they are neither covered by social security nor legally entitled to arbitration or collective bargaining. As Portes and Benton (1984, p. 615) note, "informal activities appear to expand most in those countries where state regulation of the economy is extensive and cost differentials between the two sectors are significant."

Another factor, sometimes slighted by "growth optimists" among the ranks of neoclassical economists, is surplus labor: Latin American industry has often been unable to absorb the urban work force because of rapid population growth or exodus from rural areas (Carbonetto et al., 1988; Chavez, 1987, p. 23; Touraine, 1987, p. 60–64; Safa, 1987, p. 256). The rapid growth of the population is due to changes in health and technology that have reduced the death rate more rapidly than the birth rate. The natural increase in population growth is supplemented by rapid rural-urban migration due to low rural wages and the stagnation of agriculture—the greater part of poverty in Latin America is rural (see Touraine, 1987, pp. 55–56). As peasants are expelled from the land and unable to find work in the cities, they are absorbed into the informal sector. Is the informal sector evidence of overpopulation or a poorly managed economy? There is no reason to accept this false dichotomy. Policymakers "who see that it is politically impossible to free their labor markets at least want to add as few more people as possible" (Keyfitz, 1989, pp. 119–120).

LABOR MARKET INSTITUTIONS

There are at least two plausible ways in which the problem of the informal sector could be addressed: eliminating institutional rigidities, and supporting the informal sector by providing public goods. Institutional rigidities—collective bargaining, job security, and minimum wage laws—create an incentive for employers to replace labor with capital and avoid legal constraints by transferring resources into the informal sector. As Hernando de Soto (1989a, p. 211) has argued, "institutional rigidity and excessive administrative obstacles and confusion prevent the formal private sector or the public sector in the cities from creating jobs as fast as they were needed to absorb the arriving peasants." The belief that "imperfect protection of property and contract rights for informal citizens diminishes their incentives to save and invest" (World Bank, 1987, p. 75) guides the prevailing wisdom in development circles. In this view, "if the incentive system were to become less discriminatory, the evident dynamism of the population currently engaged in informal activities could, once formalized, lead to greater growth in the economy as a whole" (World Bank, 1987, p. 75).

It is widely accepted that the growth of the informal sector is associated with government restrictions and regulation of the economy (Portes and Benton, 1984, p. 615). Such restrictions introduce transaction costs and inevitably create rent-seeking. [1] Lobbying for favors and protection, bribery, corruption, black markets, and capital flight are endemic features of business in Latin America. Such rent-seeking undermines the framework of public legal order, and creates an environment in which long-term calculations are difficult. To the extent that rent-seeking undermines economic efficiency and aggregate output, workers are forced to supplement the limited employment and income opportunities in the formal sector.

The assignment of stable property rights and the development of a legal-rational bureaucracy is a precondition for sustained economic growth. Yet the elimination of government restrictions in the labor market may not guarantee efficiency or employment. In some Latin American countries the differential between wages in the formal and informal sectors is low (Galin et al., 1986, pp. 69–70); moreover, the "monopoly power exercised by trade unions follows and does not precede the present labor market situation" (Tokman, 1978,

p. 1068). Firms in the modern sector often pay a nonmarket clearing wage (Riveros, 1990, p. 48). The established wage is set by the minimum cost per unit of effort supplied, and that cost includes the rate employers are willing to pay to maintain a stable work force (Mazumdar, 1976, p. 656; Tokman, 1978, p. 1068). Finally, urban labor markets in Latin America cannot be cleared as long as there is a surplus work force. As Lyn Squire (1981, p. 141) points out, "minimum wage legislation and other institutional factors have little influence on labor earnings in the informal sector." Removing such institutional rigidities in the context of unlimited supplies of labor would result in creating uniformly low urban wages. Indeed, the recent experience of declining wages and growing unemployment in Latin America suggests that there is not always an inverse relation between salaries and employment.

One possible effect of eliminating restrictions on the labor market would be to further subordinate informal economic activities to the modern sector. The distinction between the formal and informal sectors turns, as we have seen, on the idea that employment in the formal sector is somehow protected. Thus, the cost advantage of informal economic activities lies in escaping institutional factors that protect modern-sector labor. Once these institutions are removed, self-employed workers could be recontracted by formal firms—but under conditions in which the labor contract no longer implies benefits or protection. Or they could continue to work in small shops, but without a cost advantage, such shops would have difficulty competing with the modern sector. The net effect would be to subordinate more informal firms to the modern sector. This process has already begun in countries that have rolled back labor legislation. Portes and Benton (1984, p. 615) claim that where "the state has consistently adopted antilabor and deregulatory policies, the distinction between formal and informal sectors becomes blurred."

The alternative is to directly support productive informal-sector enterprises to help them compete with firms in the modern sector. Studies of the growth of productive businesses in the informal sector emphasize the need for certain public goods such as law enforcement, property titles, public credit, markets, specialized training, lines of credit, information, and improved technologies (Wines, 1985; Berger and Buvinic, 1988; Bromley, 1978). According to Sarah H. Wines (1985, pp. 33–41), IMF austerity measures may facilitate the penetration of new markets by so-called micro entrepreneurs, but such firms can only compete with the modern sector after they have reached a certain stage in their development.

Wines identifies three stages of growth of informal firms: in the first stage family firms sell directly to the poor; once these firms acquire credit and a stable supply of raw materials they use informal workers paid below the minimum wage; in the final stage, the firms acquire licenses, employ a stable work force, and use more advanced technology. These firms may successfully compete with large domestic producers when squeezed by the removal of subsidies on imports, because the informal sector uses domestic inputs. In the cases Wines examined, the government played a crucial role in providing credit with low transaction costs. The findings of Wines are consistent with those of Vega Castro (1989), who analyzed the impact of trade liberalization on the informal sector. He found that informal firms benefited from being able to acquire foreign technology, and they competed better than their counterparts in the modern sector because they used nonprotected labor and local inputs.

Wines' analysis highlights a crucial consideration. Different policies toward the informal sector will have different income effects depending on the type of instrument used. This leads to the question: What kind of coalition support will be found for alternative policies?

THE DEMAND FOR INSTITUTIONAL CHANGE

In the preceding section I implied that the growth of the informal sector leads to "demands" for institutional change. As the World Bank (1987, p. 75) put it, a less discriminatory incentive system could lead to "greater growth in the economy as a whole." Demands for institutional change come from groups who feel that they could capture part of that growth under different institutional arrangements. [2]

Institutions can be defined as "rules, enforcement characteristics of rules, and norms of behaviour that structure repeated human interaction" (North, 1989, p. 1321). According to North, fundamental price changes lead to changes in economic institutions. Population growth is the most important historical cause of price changes. If the parties to an exchange feel they can do better with a new contract, they will use their bargaining power to change the prices and renegotiate the contract. If the renegotiation involves altering a fundamental rule, resources may be devoted to changing the rule. The outcome of such efforts may depend on the balance of power, free rider problems, and the strength of norms (North, 1989, pp. 1324–1325).

The price change created by the growth of the informal sector is obviously the wage bill. The cost advantage of informal economic activities lies in the intensive exploitation of abundant cheap labor and the avoidance of transaction costs associated with legality. For example, there are costs associated with legal registration, state regulation, labor legislation, and social security benefits (Portes et al., 1986, pp. 728–729).

Groups have different motivations for wanting to renegotiate contracts. Much of the private sector would like to share in the benefits of cost reduction by eliminating government restrictions. Some people in the informal sector would like to capture a greater share of the benefits of growth through access to public goods without losing the advantages of being in the informal sector. Other informal entrepreneurs feel that their growth is inhibited by the absence of public goods like secure property rights and liability for damage. Hernando de Soto (1989b, pp. 6–7) has argued that informal firms are unregistered and legally unprotected; they do not operate within a framework of clearly specified property rights and cannot rely on legal enforcement mechanisms. Without secure property or liability, informal units cannot grow and benefit from economies of scale.

Other demands for institutional change come from citizens who want to internalize the negative externalities of informal economic activities. In reducing private costs, informal economic activities introduce public costs (Murillo and Cartier, 1988, p. 12). These may include crowding of streets by hawkers, unsanitary working conditions, extensive use of child labor, the spread of diseases in informal food stands, or unsafe transportation. Internalizing the costs of these activities requires either eliminating or monitoring and organizing them.

The capacity of the informal sector to lobby for institutional change is often inhibited by collective action and free rider problems, as well as legal persecution. The precarious legality of informal economic activities multiplies obstacles to growth and organization inherent in small-scale production. However, informal organizations do merge around the defense of property and collective security.

Chris Birbeck's (1978, p. 1182) study of Cali, Colombia's garbage pickers shows how conflicts emerged in the absence of a framework of property rights that led to a demand for institutional change:

Since the garbage pickers not only work independently but are also paid by the piece it is inevitable that conflicts should arise, particularly over the possession of certain choice materials that come out of the garbage. At best this may be resolved by argument, although in the somewhat impulsive and violent atmosphere of Cali's lower class such conflicts have even led to murder.

Over time, however, informal organizations emerged to restrict entry into the garbage dumps and prevent robbery on the site. Payoffs to the police reduced the threat of repression, and the tractor drivers were paid to drive more slowly so that more could be extracted from the dump. In their search for allies, the informal sector often turns to political parties and other political entrepreneurs. The following section turns to the more political issues.

POLITICAL SYSTEMS AND THE INFORMAL SECTOR

Beyond the most general observations, we know little about the effects of growth of the informal sector on political systems. A review of the literature reveals no single or "modal" impact of the informal sector on politics. One possibility is that they swell the ranks of movements in opposition to austerity, increasing the saliency of class in politics. Thus, in Chile, the informal sector played a key role in opposition to the military regime (Campero, 1987). An obscure clause of the constitution allows workers who have been laid off to form unions; these unions played an active role in the protests against the Pinochet government.

The informal sector has often been seen by policymakers as a "shock absorber," a buffer against the effects of austerity. Yet the growth of open unemployment in the 1980s in Latin America suggests that informal employment "did not function as an effective countercyclical mechanism against the contraction of the modern sector" (Portes et al., 1989). Some analysts have begun to see the informal sector as a potential threat to the capacity of the political system to manage, contain, articulate, and channel the demands of the urban poor (Matos Mar, 1984).

The informal sector can also reinforce more traditional clientelistic political parties, or be easily coopted into state-sponsored structures and associations. Janice E. Perlman's study (1986) of Rio de Janeiro found the shantytown dwellers to be "a group readily available to control and manipulation from above." Manuel Castells (1983) found the Mexican urban poor were controlled and integrated into the political system through a network of caciques (political bosses) linked to the ruling party. According to Amparo Menendez-Carrion (1986), the Ecuadorian informal sector has reinforced clientelistic leaders. Their preferences reflect a pragmatic response to the lack of security and institutional protection in a society where individuals find their role in society precariously structured.

The following analysis examines Peru and Mexico in comparative perspective. The purpose is to illustrate the argument outlined above; I do not attempt a comprehensive treatment of the subject for each case.

PERU AND MEXICO IN COMPARATIVE PERSPECTIVE

The growing disparity between population growth and employment in Peru has created a massive informal sector. Mexico's demographic pressures are less dramatic than those of Peru; rapid economic growth between the 1940s and mid-1970s created substantial employment, and migration to the United States provided another outlet for the labor surplus. Thus, whereas there is a surprising degree of consensus in Peru about the need for profound institutional change, the demand for institutional change in Mexico has been limited by the government, which has sought to remove restrictions on the economy in order to recover growth.

By liberalizing and deregulating the economy, the Mexican elite sought to maintain the framework of political institutions that has guaranteed relative political stability since 1917. The intention of the elite was to stimulate growth through market-oriented measures and negotiate a "debt reduction dividend." President Salinas said "the reduction of the debt and the sale of state companies opens a margin . . . we are going to use to attack social ills." Salinas began a $1.3 billion public works program. In visits to Mexico City shantytowns to introduce new services, he proclaimed that "this is why we renegotiated the foreign debt" (*New York Times,* February 3, 1990). At the same time, President Salinas wanted fewer distributive commitments allocated through corporatist intermediaries like the labor unions. He wished to end the system of corporatist interest representation and replace it with a more direct relation between the PRI (Institutional Revolutionary Party) and individual citizens (Cornelius et al., 1989, p. 29).

In Peru, reformist ideas ranged from the supply-side populism of President García (1985–90), to the working-class radicalism of Lima's mayor Barrantes Lingan (1983–86), and pro-free-enterprise "popular capitalism" espoused by the new president, Fujimori. Political parties across the spectrum supported different kinds of institutional change. Some groups, associated with de Soto, focused on altering the assignment of property rights—through "popular mortgages" or the old populist strategy of granting land titles to the poor. Others, especially the left, actively promoted forms of state intervention, such as loans, health projects, or industrial parks (Annis and Franks, 1989, p. 19). Under President García, Peru experimented with a heterodox approach to economic management. García attempted a demand-led reactivation of the economy by stimulating wage-good consumption by the informal sector. García and his advisors implemented a process intended to "informalize" the economy by "reorienting public investment and expanding credit, training and technical support to small farmers and the informal sector" (Annis and Franks, 1989, p. 14).

Whereas the García government hoped to reactive the Peruvian economy by stimulating the informal sector, recent Mexican administrations have supported the use of cheap labor as a stimulus to foreign investment and a way of rationalizing local firms. The informal sector is a prop for trade liberalization. One of the most significant ways in which the Mexican government has pursued policies of investment liberalization is through the formation of in-bond industries in the border towns and Mexico City. These *maquila* plants are used by transnational firms to assemble products using Mexico's cheap and abundant labor supply. Maquila plants and industrial home work have become common in Mexico, as modern-sector firms attempt to shift production onto low-cost segments of the work force (see Beneria and Roldan, 1987). The Mexican government actively encourages the articulation between formal and informal sectors, arguing that Mexican businesses must use subcontracting mechanisms to become competitive globally. Why have state policies toward the informal sector been so dramatically different in Peru and Mexico?

The growth of the informal sector leads to "demands" for changes in the incentive system by groups who feel they could capture part of the resulting growth under different institutional arrangements. Peruvian economic institutions have failed to generate adequate employment and income opportunities; the relative gains from changing the incentive system—to unleash the dynamism of the informal sector—are great. As a result, intense demands for institutional change have come from a broad range of groups. The rights of the informal sector have been championed by all major political parties in Peru, each outbidding the other with offers of institutional change.

In Mexico, the gains from institutional change have only recently become apparent, and the government is moving quickly toward a more market-oriented strategy of growth, partly to prevent the kind of radical demands for change that have emerged in Peru. The demands for institutional change are still less strident, and have come more from technocrats seeking to increase the overall efficiency of the economy to forestall the collapse of the system. Mexico's demographic pressures are less dramatic than those of Peru. Population growth has sharply declined in recent years. However, the population remains young and is growing: 1 million people enter the work force every year. The percent of the population living in urban areas has also increased. However, the degree of urban concentration actually declined between 1970 and 1980, and people are now leaving Mexico City faster than they are entering.

In the period between the 1940s and the mid-1970s, the Mexican party elite managed an economy that grew at a very rapid and sustained level. The performance of the economy guaranteed the ruling party sufficient "rents" to integrate and control the informal sector through clientelistic mechanisms and cooptation, thereby preserving its dominant position. According to Susan Kaufman Purcell and John F.H. Purcell (1980, p. 200), the Mexican political system "was an alliance among elites for the distribution rather than the redistribution of wealth."

Purcell and Purcell also note that Mexican populism has "always been highly successful at activating particular categories of people." The expansion of the political elite through this process increased the number of people who received "economic payoffs" from the system: "Whether or not such improvement is at the expense of those who already had economic benefits depends on the rate at which the economy is able to grow." Under conditions of growth, the newly incorporated groups were given a share of the rents, and conflict was kept to a minimum. If the economy could not grow fast enough, the new groups received a payoff from the existing surplus.

By contrast, poor overall macroeconomic performance in Peru can be partly attributed to the lack of restraint on rent-seeking by elites. Newly mobilized groups have been included in the political system at the expense of the performance of the economy. Over time, the rate of private saving and investment has declined, while the rate of public investment increased. Much of the public investment was debt-financed and unproductive. This has contributed to an uncertain business environment, capital flight, and speculation.

Peruvian populism in the 1980s was based on building a political relationship with the informal sector through reactivating the economy with demand-stimulus growth. Yet it turned out to be almost impossible to institutionalize a relationship with the informal sector based on the kind of exchange of tangible rewards-for-support characteristic of populist leadership. For example, the APRA party's program of credit did not create the basis for an institutionalized relationship between APRA and the informal sector. Likewise, the public works projects were temporary in nature and did not provide a vehicle for the consolidation of an independent power base for García. They were, however, a burden on the deficit. Once foreign reserves were exhausted, García faced a serious economic crisis without political institutions to support his presidency. The response of the government was to attempt to nationalize the banks. This desperate move paralyzed the economy.

The corporatist structure of the Mexican state cannot effectively organize the growing informal sector indefinitely. Clearly the state has reduced its role as a source of public employment and in distributing wealth. As Wayne Cornelius (1986, p. 1) puts it, by the 1980s Mexico had "entered an era of economic instability, institutional rigidity, uncertainty (for both individual citizens and institutions), erosion of traditional state-society relationships, and the breakdown of the elite consensus that had buttressed the post–1940 development model."

The Mexican strategy of technocrat-led change emphasizes trade and investment liberalization, deregulation, and privatization. Rather than designing institutional change to support the informal sector, the Mexican state has encouraged the formation of in-bond industries in the border regions, which extensively use cheap labor. Industrial home work in Mexico City also appears to be on the rise, and industrial home workers are highly dependent on modern-sector firms. The growth that is expected from further integration into the global economy will be used to support the regime through public works. The informal sector will be increasingly subordinated politically and economically.

CONCLUSION

The growth of the informal sector leads to demands for changes in the incentive system by groups who feel that they could capture part of the resulting economic growth under different institutional arrangements. Peru has a massive labor surplus and economic institutions incapable of generating income and employment over a sustained period. The demands for institutional change in Peru have been dramatic: political parties have responded by attempting to change the structure of incentives that discriminate against the informal sector.

In Mexico, institutional change is confined to eliminating government restrictions on the market and seeking to exploit the informal sector through more extensive use of subcontracting. More dramatic institutional change—a new specification and assignment of property rights and enforcement mechanisms—is unlikely unless the existing institutions are utterly incapable of generating income and employment, either because of the growth of the surplus population, or because of unrestrained rent-seeking by elites.

NOTES

1. The term "rent-seeking" refers to (directly) unproductive economic activities involving an increase in a return to an investment over its next best opportunity cost.

Competition for rents may involve a dead weight loss to the economy. For a discussion see Krueger (1977, p. 291); Bhagwati (1982).

2. I refer to the "demand" for institutional change, using microeconomic language as a metaphor, following Keohane's (1983, p. 142) discussion of the phenomena that affect the desire for regimes in international politics.

REFERENCES

Annis, A. and J. Franks (1989). "The Idea, Ideology, and Economics of the Informal Sector: The Case of Peru." *Grassroots Development,* 13, no. 1.

Benería, L. and M. I. Roldán (1987). *The Crossroads of Class and Gender.* Chicago: University of Chicago Press.

Berger, M. and M. Buvinić (1988). *La mujer en el sector informal.* Quito: Nueva Sociedad.

Bhagwati, J. (1982). "Directly-Unproductive, Profit-Seeking (DUP) Activities." *Journal of Political Economy,* 90.

Birbeck, C. (1978). "Self-Employed Proletarians in an Informal Factory: The Case of Cali's Garbage Dump." *World Development,* 6, no. 9/10.

Bromley, R. (1978). "Organization, Regulation and Exploitation in the So-Called 'Urban Informal Sector:' The Street Traders of Cali, Colombia." *World Development,* 6, no. 9/10.

Campero, G. (1987). *Entre la Sobrevivencia y la Accion Politica.* Santiago: ILET.

Carbonetto, D. et al. (1988). *Lima: Sector Informal,* 2 vols. Lima: CEDEP.

Castells, M. (1983). *The City and the Grassroots.* Berkeley: University of California Press.

Chavez, E. (1987). *El Mercado Laboral en la Ciudad de Arequipa.* Lima: Fundacion M. J. Bustamante de la Fuente.

Cornelius, W. (1986). *The Political Economy of Mexico Under de la Madrid: The Crisis Deepens, 1985–1986.* San Diego: University of California at San Diego.

Cornelius, W. et al. (eds.) (1989). *Mexico's Alternative Political Futures.* San Diego: University of California at San Diego.

De Soto, H. (1989a). *The Other Path.* New York: Harper and Row.

———. (1989b). "Structural Adjustment and the Informal Sector." In J. Levitsky (ed.), *Microenterprises in Developing Countries.* London: Intermediate Technology Publications.

Galin, P. et al. (1986). *Asalariados y Clases Populares en Lima.* Lima: IEP.

Keohane, Robert O. (1983). "The Demand for International Regimes." In S. Krasner (ed.), *International Regimes.* Ithaca, N.Y.: Cornell University Press.

Keyfitz, N. (1989). "The Growing Human Population." *Scientific American,* September.

Krueger, A. O. (1977). "The Political Economy of the Rent-Seeking Society." *American Economic Review,* 64, no. 3.

Matos Mar, J. (1984). *Crisis del Estado y Desborde Popular.* Lima: IEP.

Mazumdar, D. (1976). "The Urban Informal Sector." *World Development,* 4, no. 8.

Menendez-Carrion, A. (1986). *La conquista del voto en el Ecuador.* Quito: Editora Nacional.

Murillo, G. and W. Cartier (1988). "Urbanization, the Informal Sector and Migration: Issues for Research and Cooperation," *Canadian Journal of Development Studies,* 9, no. 1.

North, D. C. (1989). "Institutions and Economic Growth: An Historical Introduction."
    World Development, 17, no. 9.
Perlman, J. (1986). *The Myth of Marginality.* Berkeley: University of California Press.
Portes, A. et al. (1986). "The Urban Informal Sector in Uruguay: Its Internal Struc-
    ture, Characteristics and Effects." *World Development,* 14, no. 6.
Portes, A. et al. (eds.) (1989). *The Informal Economy.* Baltimore: Johns Hopkins Uni-
    versity Press.
Portes, A. and L. Benton (1984). "Industrial Development and Labour Absorption: A
    Reinterpretation." *Population and Development Review,* 10, no. 4:589–611.
Portes, A. and M. Johns (1989). "The Polarization of Class and Space in the Contempo-
    rary Latin American City." In L. Canak (ed.), *Lost Promises.* Boulder, Colo.:
    Westview Press.
Purcell, S. K. and J.F.H. (1980). "State and Society in Mexico: Must a Stable Polity
    Be Institutionalized?" *World Politics,* 32, no. 2.
Riveros, L. (1990). "Recession, Adjustment and the Performance of Urban Labor Mar-
    kets in Latin America." *Canadian Journal of Development Studies,* 11, no. 1.
Safa, H. (1987). "Urbanization, the Informal Economy and State Policy in Latin Amer-
    ica." In M. P. Smith and J. R. Feagin (eds.), *The Capitalist City.* London: Basic
    Blackwell.
Squire, L. (1981). *Employment Policy in Developing Countries.* New York: Oxford Uni-
    versity Press.
Tokman, V. E. (1978). "An Exploration into the Nature of Informal-Formal Sector Re-
    lationships." *World Development,* 6, no. 9/10.
Touraine, A. (1987). *Actores Sociales y Sistemas Politicos en America Latina.* Santiago:
    PREALC.
Vega Castro, J. (1989). *El Sector Industrial Informal y Las Politicas de Liberalizacion
    del Comercio Exterior en el Peru.* Lima: Instituto de Investigacion y Docencia.
Wines, S. W. (1985). "Stages of Micro Enterprise Growth in the Dominican Informal
    Sector." *Grassroots Development,* 9, no. 2.
World Bank (1987). *World Development Report 1987.* New York: Oxford University
    Press.

CHAPTER SIXTEEN

The State and Economic Crisis in Mexico: Restructuring the Parastate Sector

JUDITH TEICHMAN

Since 1982, following the decline in world oil prices, Mexico has faced an ongoing economic crisis—a crisis characterized by strict adjustment policies, a dramatic drop in living standards for most Mexicans, and sporadic threats of a debt moratorium. Coincident with and related to this economic crisis has been a deepening political crisis. Opposition to the government's handling of the economic crisis, combined with a return to the traditional political tactics of electoral fraud, precipitated the emergence of an opposition political front—the Democratic National Front (FDN). By the 1988 federal elections, FDN, led by Cuauhtémoc Cárdenas, posed an unprecedented political challenge to the Institutional Revolutionary Party (PRI), which had ruled Mexico unchallenged for the last 50 years. Even in the face of what is widely believed to have been extensive electoral fraud, the PRI presidential candidate, Carlos Salinas de Gortari, received the lowest proportion of the popular vote ever received by a PRI presidential candidate (50.7 percent). Opposition to the government's handling of the crisis has continued unabated since 1988 in the form of labor strikes, marches, demonstrations, and opposition electoral victories.

In response to Mexico's economic crisis, President de la Madrid (1982–88) initiated a program of economic restructuring, a strategy geared toward making Mexico's exports competitive in manufactured goods. A fundamentally important component of this new program, which has been pursued even more vigorously by current President Salinas de Gortari, is the restructuring of Mexico's enormous parastate (companies owned wholly or partially by the state) sector. This chapter examines the changes that have occurred in Mexico's parastate sector since 1982 and argues that they have important implications for Mexico's traditionally stable authoritarian regime. These changes have been instrumental in undermining the traditional alliance between organized labor and the state and in inciting a serious challenge to the regime's revolutionary and nationalist credentials. Moreover, opinion on the issue of parastate restructuring is deeply divided, with powerful business interests as strong proponents of an intensification of the program, pitted against opposition leftist parties and trade unions. The following paragraphs suggest some of the most important ways in which Mexico's parastates have, in the past, helped to sustain a stable political order.

MEXICO'S POLITICAL STABILITY AND THE PARASTATE SECTOR

Most observers have explained the "success" of the Mexican political system in terms of a judicious combination of revolutionary mythology, preemptive reform, co-optation through patronage, with the addition of selective doses of repression if all else fails (Stevens, 1974; Hellman, 1983). The parastate sector not only occupies an important place in Mexican revolutionary mythology, but it has also been an important instrument of both reform and patronage.

While the Mexican constitution of 1917 establishes the Mexican state as responsible for both the social welfare of the population and for economic growth, it was not until the administration of President Lázaro Cárdenas (1934–40) that a number of bold social and nationalist measures firmly linked the PRI with Mexico's revolutionary heritage and to the interests of peasants and workers. In particular, the immensely popular nationalization of the foreign-owned petroleum industry in 1938 and the later establishment of what would become Mexico's most important state-owned industry, Petróleos Mexicanos (PEMEX), affirmed the nationalist credentials of the official party. In addition, state led economic growth until the mid-1960s made possible preemptive reform (Coleman and Davis, 1983)—piecemeal concessions in the areas of wages and social benefits made to selective groups—which served to stave off unrest, particularly from the most highly organized sectors of the labor movement and to shore up the regime's legitimacy.

The role of the parastate sector in postwar economic growth has its legal basis in Mexico's constitution, which establishes the state as the "rector of national development" and directs that the state is to have responsibility over "strategic areas" and "priority areas."[1] Following the establishment of the Bank of Mexico in 1925, state development banks were set up and state enterprises were created in the petroleum and electricity sectors and in infrastructure, such as railways. A number of important parastates were established as a consequence of the state's reformist social welfare role; for example, the

Mexican Institute of Social Security (IMSS) was founded in 1944 to provide health and social security services to workers, and the National Company of Popular Goods (CONASUPO, state-run food stores providing basic foods and staples at subsidized prices) had its origins in the 1950s. In addition to the parastates set up for social welfare and economic development, a third type of parastate began to appear more frequently from the mid-1960s as the economy began to stagnate. These were years of growing political unrest during which the government felt compelled to take over private-sector enterprises in order to maintain employment and ensure social peace, as occurred, for example, with government acquisitions in the sugar industry in 1968 (on this see Purcell, 1981).

Whereas in 1940 there were 57 parastates, by 1983 the number reached 1,155 (see Table 16.1). By 1977, spending in the parastate sector reached a high of 55 percent of total public-sector federal outlays (Teichman, 1988, p. 158) and the parastates accounted for 78 percent of the federal government's long-term external debt. [2] In 1982, 28 enterprises were wholly owned by the government; it owned a majority of shares in over 500 and held minority ownership in the remaining. The rapid economic growth of the postwar period, propelled by Mexico's state-led industrialization policies, produced a rapid rise in the growth of state expenditure (Griffiths, 1972, p. 48; Gribomont and Rimez, 1976, p. 785). The discovery and development of petroleum after 1972 further accelerated the expansion of the parastate sector particularly PEMEX (Teichman, 1988, p. 158).

The proliferation of parastates provided employment for workers, while their increasingly powerful unions were able to exact social benefits unavailable to most other sectors of the working class. For Mexico's middle class, the state became an important source for economic and career opportunities (Smith, 1979), as members of the middle class entered the public bureaucracy in increasing numbers. Economic growth, in expanding the revenues available to the party state apparatus, ensured the lubrication of patronage networks that involved government officials, businessmen, and top labor leaders, known

Table 16.1
Disincorporation and Creation of Parastate Entities, 1983–90 (numbers at the beginning of each year)

1983	1984	1985	1986	1987	1988	1989	1990*
1,115	996	964	870	696	n.a.	463	324

*As of March 1990.

Sources: 1983–87: Andrade (1987, p. 135); 1989: Latin American Weekly Report, June 8, 1988, p. 8; 1990: Proceso, March 12, 1990, p. 18.

as *camarillas* (Camp, 1984; Grindle, 1977)—a vital source of political incorporation. Labor union leaders, such as petroleum leader Joaquín Hernández
Galacia ("La Quina"), were able to amass enormous wealth as did private-
sector businessmen who benefited handsomely from government contracts and
cheap inputs. [3]

Mexico's economic crisis has resulted in a dramatic reversal of parastate expansion. The decline of petroleum prices beginning in 1981, combined with the
government's decision to continue the pace of government borrowing and
spending and increasing interest rates, pushed the Mexican economy to the
verge of collapse by 1982. Although President de la Madrid called immediately
for reform of the parastate sector, his administration proceeded cautiously.
Commitment to the implementation of such a program increased over time in
response to worsening economic circumstances. During the de la Madrid
years, the parastate restructuring program may be divided into two phases:
(1) 1983–85, a period that witnessed a brief attempt at economic reactivation,
during which both trade liberalization and parastate restructuring are initiated
and pursued cautiously; (2) mid-1985–88, which marks a phase characterized
by a return to austerity policies, invigorated commitment to trade liberalization, and further policies to deepen the restructuring of the parastate sector.
The first two years of the Salinas administration (1989–90) represent a third
phase. While the general thrust of the de la Madrid economic program is continued, we witness an even stronger commitment to the fundamental changes
within the parastate sector.

PARASTATE REFORM DURING THE DE LA MADRID YEARS (1983–88)

The 1983 National Development Plan called for parastate restructuring as
integral to economic restructuring: It was believed that rationalization of the
transportation system and increased production and productivity of parastates
would facilitate export competitiveness. While during the first three years of
the de la Madrid administration measures were taken to stimulate "in bond"
industries, import controls remained in effect. Similarly, policy reform in the
parastate sector did not reflect a firm commitment to abandon past practices:
there was a sharp reduction in total government outlays, and in the absolute
level of expenditure in the parastate sector (particularly in the petroleum industry), but the parastate sector increased its proportion of total federal government expenditure (see Table 16.2). Moreover, the government resisted
IMF pressures that subsidies be reduced or eliminated. This is seen in 1984
when the proportion of monies transferred by the federal government to the
top three social parastates—IMSS, the Institute of Security and Social Services for Workers of the State (ISSSTE), and CONASUPO—as a proportion
of total transfer payments made by the federal government to the parastate
sector, reached 40 percent (see Table 16.3), with 33 percent going to CONAS-

UPO. Over 97 percent of the monies transferred to CONASUPO in 1983 and 1984 were for price subsidies. [4]

In the face of opposition Popular Action Party (PAN) victories in the 1983 municipal elections and impending elections in 1985, strike activity, and land invasions, the government felt compelled to let up on its stiff austerity program by early 1985 (*Quarterly Economic Review of Mexico*, No. 1, 1985, p. 116). Investment picked up, the decline in minimum wages abated, and positive economic growth was achieved in 1984 and 1985 (see Table 16.4).

However, this brief foray into economic reactivation was short-lived. Increases in the cost of production and U.S. import barriers were discouraging Mexican manufacturing exports to the United States, while deterioration in petroleum prices beginning in 1985, combined with rising interest rates, further eroded foreign exchange earnings. A sharp deterioration occurred in Mexico's balance of payments and GDP fell to –3.8 percent in 1986 (see Table 16.4). As the public deficit as a percent of GDP approached 10 percent, the IMF suspended loan disbursements to Mexico. In the face of a growing outcry against further austerity, the finance minister was dismissed and the government began to take an increasingly radical stand in its negotiations with the IMF. Although the resulting IMF agreement marked an important departure from traditional IMF policy, [5] it accelerated the process of economic restructuring. As part of the agreement, the World Bank pledged $1,900 million to help finance structural changes of the Mexican economy (Banamex, August 1986, p. 345).

Table 16.2
Parastate Finances, 1982–86 (parastates under budget control)

	1982	1983	1984	1985	1986
% Total Federal Expenditures[1]	40.7	44.5	47.5	43.1	35.9
% Long Term External Public Debt[2]	73.5	66.6	63.4	63.8	57.9
% of Total Federal Investment[3]	27.6	19.7	19.5	17.6	17.6
Transfers to Para states as % total federal expend.	10.7	13.2	13.1	12.0	7.9
PEMEX Expenditure as % Parastate[4]	25.2	20.4	19.0	19.5	19.9

Sources: [1] Calculated from Banamex, July 1987, pp. 252-253, 256; September 1988, p. 502. [2] Calculated from de la Madrid (1987, pp. 212-213). [3] and [4] Ibid., pp. 103-105.

Table 16.3
Distribution of Federal Government Transfers to the Parastate Sector,
1982–86 (% total transfers)

	1982	1983	1984	1985	1986
IMSS	8.4	5.4	7.0	7.1	8.3
ISSSTE	7.7	2.9	–	–	–
CONASUPO	23.3	17.8	33.0	29.0	28.1
CFE*	37.3	43.1	34.5	35.1	29.7
Railways	9.8	10.9	6.4	6.9	8.9

*Federal Electricity Commission

Source: Calculated from de la Madrid (1987, pp. 1115-1117).

Table 16.4
Selected Basic Economic Indicators, 1982–89

	1982	1983	1984	1985	1986	1987	1988	1989*
Real GDP % Change[1]	.5	-5.3	3.7	2.8	-3.8	1.5	1.1	3.0
Real Wages[2]	100	77	72	71	65	61	53	n.a.
Investment % Growth[3]	-15.9	-27.9	5.5	6.4	-0.7	-0.7	n.a.	n.a.

*preliminary
Sources: [1] 1982-86: Trebat (1988, p. 76); 1987-89: Mexico and Central
America Report, Latin American Newsletter, January 1990: 6. [2] Dornbusch
(1990, p. 169). [3] Bendensky and Godínez (1986, p. 66).

The reemergence of the economic crisis had reinforced the belief among Mexico's rulers that greater efforts were necessary to stimulate manufacturing exports. Hence trade liberalization efforts were stepped up: exporters were given special privileges in the importation of inputs and tax exemptions, import permits were replaced by tariffs, tariffs were reduced, and in 1986 Mexico joined GATT—a decision that required, among other things, reduction in the size of the public enterprise sector to produce an internationally competitive industrial sector. And as Mexico's economic difficulties continued through 1987 and 1988 (new loans were delayed because Mexico was unable to obtain its critical mass necessary from the private banking sector and petroleum prices dropped again in 1988), the need to further reduce government expenditure gave additional impetus to the parastate restructuring program. By late 1987, concerned with the rising level of inflation (it had reached 150 percent), the administration responded with its Pact of Solidarity, signed by representatives of the government, workers, and peasants. Although containing certain heterodox features—exchange controls, price and wage controls—the Pact represented an invigorated commitment to economic liberalization and to parastate restructuring.

The regime's policy of restructuring the parastate sector responded more to outside events than to a preconceived plan. Although over 200 state enterprises had been disincorporated (liquidated, sold, or fused) during 1983 and 1984, it was not until 1985 that a procedure and criteria for disincorporation were established with the Federal Law of Parastate Entities. While enterprises continued to be disincorporated in clearly nonstrategic/nonpriority areas (such as in the media, soft drinks, and tourist industries), the program now began to affect enterprises that were politically symbolic, if not strategically important. The government began a concerted effort to divest the state of its holdings in air transportation: in the face of labor opposition to the reduction of routes serviced by the airline, Aeroméxico was liquidated and its union thereby disbanded and the other state-owned airline, Mexicana de Avación, was put up for sale. The state began to withdraw from its activities in two sectors having political and economic significance: petroleum and mining. Some 64 petrochemical products were reclassified from primary to secondary in order to open up their production to private capital and La Compañía Minera de Cananea, the government-owned copper company, where a strike against foreign owners in 1906 is widely seen as a prelude to the Mexican Revolution (*Proceso*, August 23, 1989, pp. 146 ff.), was slated for privatization.

At the same time, the government moved to ensure policy and budget control of the parastates remaining under its jurisdiction. Legislation passed in 1985 established new administrative bodies, composed of representatives from the ministries of Finance and Budget and Planning, to oversee the activities of the strategic parastates. In addition, Agreements for Financial Rehabilitation and Structural Change, signed between the federal government and individual parastates, committed the parastates to production, investment, and export goals; to the elimination of transfers, particularly subsidies; and to price increases (Secretaría de Controlaría, 1988, pp. 62–63). Another type of agreement ensured against budget overruns in the parastates under federal government budget control. A special effort was made to institute tighter control over PEMEX. Following the appointment of a tough financial manager, Ramón Beteta, as director general, payments by contractors of commissions to the Petroleum Union for its Social Fund were outlawed and the Union's right to let out a proportion of all PEMEX contracts was abolished. The top levels of PEMEX were replaced with teams deemed to be more sympathetic to the shift in government policy and the Foreign Oil Trade Company (COCEP), composed of representatives from the most important economic ministries, was set up to establish policies on foreign sales.

The results of these control mechanisms went a considerable way in achieving state objectives. In 1986 the parastate sector's proportion of total government expenditure dropped to 35.9 percent (see Table 16.2). Between 1983 and 1988, the parastate sector's proportion of the total public deficit went from 31.9 to 15.3 percent (Secretaría de Controlaría, 1988, p. 62). But the government had, by now, been forced to move more concertedly against transfer payments to the parastate sector. Federal government transfer payments to the parastate sector as a portion of federal government outlays declined in 1986 (Table 16.2). Expenditures on capital projects (investment) in the parastate sector, which had dropped markedly in 1982, continued to fall off (Table 16.2). By 1988, the government claimed to have withdrawn totally from the production of consumer durables and from five branches related to the production of intermediate goods (Secretaría de Controloría, 1988, p. 31).

PARASTATE RESTRUCTURING UNDER PRESIDENT SALINAS (1989–90)

In general terms, President Salinas' economic program represented a continuation of policies pursued during the de la Madrid years. The Pact for Stability and Economic Growth (PECE), which replaced de la Madrid's Solidarity Pact, continued price controls on basic products, exchange rate controls, and called for further restraint on public expenditure. And like the de la Madrid administration, President Salinas faced an ongoing struggle with foreign creditors. But in the face of strong electoral opposition during the 1988 federal elections, Salinas had been forced to take a much stronger position on the hemorrhage of capital imposed by payments on the debt. Threatening moratorium on a number of occasions during 1988 and 1990, Mexico's negotiators demanded reductions in the payments of interest and principal (*Latin American Weekly Reports*, May 25, 1989, p. 7; March 15, 1990, p. 12). [6]

The Salinas administration also proceeded more forcefully in the area of parastate restructuring with the stated objective of further increasing the efficiency and export competitiveness of parastates. While carrying out the privatizations announced in the last years of the de la Madrid administration, a number of new policies were announced in 1989 and 1990. Moreover, these new initiatives were combined with tough measures against union resistance and a concerted onslaught against collective labor agreements in the parastate sector. Union power diminished as leadership was changed at will and labor agreements set aside.

In 1989 the sale of the government's shares of the telephone company, Teléfonos Mexicanos, was announced and the government's withdrawal from iron and steel proclaimed in early 1990—both state-owned companies in this sector, Siderúrgica Lázaro Cárdenas-Las Truchas (SICARTSA) and Altos Hornos, were to be put up for sale and the banks, nationalized by the López Portillo administration in 1982, were to be reprivatized. The announced privatization of SICARTSA followed the dismissal of all workers when the union resisted the government's modernization program, which included the dismissal of some 1,000 workers. Less than a year earlier, the Union of Altos Hornos had accepted a reduction of over 500 jobs and the elimination of 18 clauses from its labor contract (*Proceso*, May 1, 1989, p. 10). Along similar lines, the Salinas administration declared the bankruptcy of Cananea and ended relations with its union when workers went on strike to protest the government's 1988 announcement that the company would be privatized. Only in those sectors with acquiescent union leadership (such as electricity and telephones) was the administration able to move forward with modernization plans without major resistance. Even CONASUPO, considered sacred as a support for the most marginal members of society, was no longer immune: nine of its industrial plants and over 600 commercial outlets were to be privatized.

Severe expenditure and investment cutbacks continued in PEMEX (Banamex, April 1990, p. 195) and 30,000 temporary workers were laid off in 1989 (*Proceso*, May 22, 1989, p. 31). Petroleum labor leader La Quina and other top petroleum union leaders were arrested on corruption charges, and the government imposed a leadership more amenable to its modernization plans. Those plans included a sharp curtailment of state benefits to petroleum workers and their union and minimal wage increases (*Proceso*, July 31, 1989, p. 31). Fifteen petrochemical sectors previously restricted to the state were reclassified and thereby opened up to private investment. Foreign capital was encouraged to participate in the exploration of oil and gas, and private firms, both domestic and private, now replaced PEMEX's exclusive role in the job of marketing Mexican petroleum abroad.

Official statements of parastate policy continued to follow specific decisions in the parastate sector. It was not until March 1990 that the government enunciated its National Plan for Modernization of Public Enterprise (PRONAMEP). It was now officially admitted that, with regard to parastate restructuring, "the concept of 'priority' must be periodically subject to revision" (*Proceso*, March 19, 1990, p. 19). [7]

THE POLITICAL IMPLICATIONS OF PARASTATE RESTRUCTURING

Throughout the period 1982–85, policymakers demonstrated a commitment not to diminish state participation in activities where state action, for historical reasons, was considered not only legitimate but also important: communications, petroleum, mining, and social welfare. However, as Mexico faced renewed economic difficulties after 1985, this commitment was abandoned and parastate restructuring was pursued more forcefully.

The most immediate and strongest opposition came from the parastate workers' unions. This was especially true of PEMEX, where de la Madrid's program of restructuring severely undermined the traditional alliance between top petroleum labor leaders and the government (Teichman, 1988, pp. 70ff.). The abolition of commissions from petroleum contractors and the inability of PEMEX to let contracts withdrew an important source of economic resources from the petroleum union leadership.

Top petroleum labor leaders became outspoken critics of the president and government policy. The conflict between the administration and La Quina ultimately resulted in Beteta's resignation (on this see *Proceso,* February 23, 1987, p. 10). Attempts to gain financial control of the petroleum sector were to prove very costly politically, however. La Quina and other top petroleum leaders gave only grudging and formal support to the presidency of PRI candidate Carlos Salinas (as secretary of budget and planning he had been the man behind the attempt to gain financial control over PEMEX), while rank and file petroleum workers are believed to have given support to Cuauhtémoc-Cárdenas. [8] Salinas' removal of the Petroleum Union's leadership was likely motivated as much by the desire for political reprisal as it was by the requisites of economic modernization.

Labor unrest was rife in the parastate sector in general between 1982 and 1988 and intensified in 1989 and 1990. Parastate wage demands in 1987 were firmly resisted by the de la Madrid administration and, as we saw, the Salinas administration reacted harshly to any union resistance toward government plans for modernization and privatization. Indeed, insofar as modernization invariably meant reduced jobs and benefits to workers, reduction in the power of labor unions was a prerequisite of parastate restructuring.

Since one of the most important sources of political incorporation in Mexico has been the judicious and selective use of patronage to ensure labor quiescence, the sharp reduction in government expenditure and investment in the parastate sector has reduced the government's ability to co-opt the country's most powerful labor unions. Political support cannot be assumed if material rewards are no longer forthcoming. This scenario is seen most clearly in the case of PEMEX. The imposition of labor leaders more amenable to parastate restructuring may be successful in the short term, but inevitably will run into increasing difficulties. Labor leaders must either be able to meet the most pressing demands of their rank and file, or they must be able to selectively co-opt troublesome subelites within their ranks. Mexico's economic difficulties and the government's economic program now render even the latter difficult. Moreover, opposition political parties have in the past taken up the causes of disaffected labor groups. There will be more opportunities to do so in the future.

The political fallout of restructuring the parastate sector has implications beyond the growing disaffection between organized labor and current state managers. The dismantling of the parastate sector is an extremely sensitive political issue in a country where regime legitimacy has, in the past, rested upon the historic economic and social vocation of the state. The statist position taken by the FDN in the 1988 federal election campaign represented a clear repudiation of de la Madrid's plan to restructure the parastate sector (*Latin American Weekly Report,* June 16, 1988, p. 10).

Parastate restructuring, however, was pursued even more relentlessly after 1988. Not surprisingly, the banner of nationalism has continued to be taken up by Cuauhtémoc Cárdenas and the various left-wing opposition parties, although the original opposition electoral front has fallen into disarray. This opposition has continued to characterize the parastate restructuring program as antinational, and as representing a threat to national sovereignty (*Proceso*, November 6, 1989, pp. 10–11). Both the official workers' movement and the Left parties have remained critical of the government's treatment of union demands and of uncooperative labor leaders—including the arrest of the top petroleum union leaders. The Confederation of Mexican Workers (CTM), the official labor organization, has become increasingly critical of the government's economic policy in general and of its parastate program in particular. Privatization of parts of CONASUPO was criticized as contributing to further reduction in living standards of workers.

The vigorous pursuit of parastate restructuring, on the other hand, brought increased business confidence and business support for the regime, particularly for the presidency of Carlos Salinas. Indeed, the fact that, during the de la Madrid years, the business community pressured heavily for privatization of PEMEX, CONASUPO, and the reprivatization of the banks has led the Left to charge that the enthusiasm of the government for privatization stemmed from its desire to please the private sector (*Proceso*, August 21, 1989, p. 37). The most powerful business interests—called the Monterrey Group, which controls the peak organization known as the Coordinating Entrepreneurial Council (CCE)—while lauding the government's trade liberalization measures, have repeatedly called for a reduction in the level of state intervention in the economy. The CCE, a vociferous supporter of privatization, which sees the parastate sector as a highly inefficient contributor to the public deficit, has pressured the government to accelerate its program of privatization (*Proceso*, November 6, 1987, p. 24). On the other hand, the small and medium business sector, represented by the National Confederation of Transformation Industries (CANACINTRA), has criticized both the government's austerity measures and its parastate restructuring program. Reflective of its dependence on government largess, CANACINTRA has complained about the high prices of parastate products and services and irregular payments to supplier firms (*Proceso*, January 26, 1987, pp. 28–30).

Given the depth of the economic crisis and the severe cutbacks in the state sector, government benefits to the private sector are now considerably more selective than in the past. A small group of large companies (those represented by the CCE), which have been receiving most of the export incentives, produced one-half of nonpetroleum exports (Banamex, August, 1986, p. 370). Moreover, the government in effect came to the financial rescue of a number of the largest and most externally indebted firms when it established a financial agency to cover the exchange risk for private companies rescheduling their debts. In short, under present circumstances, there are far fewer national businessmen bound to the state with the promise of lucrative contracts and other financial rewards than in the past. The reduction in the size and the role of the parastate sector has contributed to this change.

CONCLUSIONS

While the drastic reduction in government spending alone would have reduced the role of parastates, restructuring of the parastate sector ensures that elimination or reduction of the old co-optative role of that sector will acquire a degree of permanence. Institutional changes have ensured that control over government expenditures is now more centralized—the ability of those in charge of parastates to maintain the loyalties of camarilla members (parastate management, union leaders, and client business owners and management) through the distribution of patronage has become problematic. In addition to this diminution of the state's ability to co-opt potentially politically threatening elements through a flexible patronage system, the state's strategic role in the economy and its ability to administrate a variety of selective social programs is now under threat.

This analysis of the Mexican case suggests an incompatibility between the requisites of economic modernization—the neoclassicial formula entailing the withdrawal of the state from the economy—and policies necessary to create a modicum of political stability. While few would call Mexico a democracy, its form of authoritarianism has been more benign than has occurred elsewhere in Latin America. Legitimacy shored up by an activist state has been instrumental in making state repression a relatively rare occurrence in Mexico. While government rhetoric has linked economic modernization with political modernization—that is, with a greater respect for electoral results, and an end to corruption within the government and unions—recent political trends in Mexico have been disturbing: despite the concession of an opposition gubernatorial victory in Baja California, electoral fraud appears to have continued, the government has continued to manipulate corrupt union leadership, and political assassinations of opposition party activists have been on the rise. The economic program in place since 1983 has produced political polarization in Mexico: between big business interests, which are enthusiastic proponents of trade liberalization and state withdrawal from the economy, and leftist opposition parties and trade unions, which have remained highly critical of the government's economic program. This polarization of positions is especially notable with regard to the restructuring of the parastate sector. Mexico's ongoing economic difficulties have given rise to policies that have resulted in an intensification of political conflict—conflict that may well make the ultimate resolution of those difficulties more difficult.

NOTES

1. These areas include the printing of money, mail, telegraph, railways, radio and communications via satellite, the emission of money by a Central Bank, petroleum and other hydrocarbons, basic petrochemicals, radioactive minerals, and the generation of nuclear energy and electricity.

2. Calculated from Banamex, July 1987 and September 1988; and from de la Madrid (1987).

3. According to Roger Hansen (1980, p. 87), "no other Latin American political system has provided more rewards for its new industrial and commercial agricultural elites."

4. Calculated from de la Madrid (1987).

5. According to the new agreement, government expenditure would be allowed to reach 10 percent of GDP, a growth rate of 3–4 percent would be allowed for 1987, and additional funds would be made available should the price of petroleum fall below $9.00 per barrel.

6. Negotiations with Mexico's private creditors dragged on until early 1990, when the banks finally responded to Mexico's menu of three options: reducing interest payments, reducing principal payments, or providing new loans.

7. Spoken by the secretary of budget and planning, Ernesto Zedillo, at his presentation of the new program.

8. *Proceso* provides a breakdown of electoral results for almost all of the petroleum zones and alleges that La Quina secretly helped the Cárdenas electoral campaign (*Proceso*, July 25, 1988, p. 27).

REFERENCES

Andrade, Guido Párraga (1987). "Anexo Estadístico." *Empresa Pública, Problemas y Desarrollo.* 1, no. 4 (January–June 1987).

Banamex. *Examen de la situación económica de México.* Various months.

Bendendsky, Léon and V. Godínez (1986). "The Mexican Foreign Debt: A Case of Conflictual Co-operation." In Riordan Roett (ed.), *Mexico and the United States.* Boulder, Colo.: Westview Press.

Camp, R. A. (1984). *The Making of a Government.* Tuscon: The University of Arizona Press.

Coleman, K. M. and C. L. Davis (1983). "Preemptive Reform and the Mexican Working Class." *Latin American Research Review,* 8, no. 1.

de la Madrid, M. (1987). *Quinto informe de gobierno, 1987, Estadístico.*

Dornbusch, R. (1990). "Mexican Debt." In Dwight S. Brothers and Adele E. Wick (eds.), *Mexico's Search for a New Development Strategy.* Boulder, Colo.: Westview Press.

Gribomont, C. and M. Rimez (1976). "La política económica de gobierno de Luis Echeverría (1971–1976), un primer ensayo de interpretación." *El Trimestre Económico,* XLIV, no. 176.

Griffiths, Brian (1972). *Mexican Monetary Policy and Economic Development.* New York: Praeger.

Grindle, Merilee (1977). *Bureacrats, Polticians and Peasants in Mexico.* Berkeley: University of California Press.

Hansen, Roger (1980). *The Politics of Mexican Development.* Baltimore: Johns Hopkins University Press.

Hellman, Judith Adler (1983). *Mexico in Crisis,* 2nd ed. New York: Holmes and Meier.

Purcell, S. K. (1981). "Business Government Relations in Mexico: The Case of Sugar." *Comparative Politics,* 13, no. 2.

Secretaría de Controloría de la Federacíon (1988). *Restructuración del sector parasta-tal.* Mexico City.
Smith, Peter (1979). *Labyrinths of Power.* Princeton, N.J.: Princeton University Press.
Stevens, E. (1974). *Protest and Response in Mexico.* Cambridge, Mass.: MIT Press.
Teichman, Judith A. (1988). *Policymaking in Mexico.* Boston: Allen and Unwin.
Trebat, Thomas J. (1988). "Mexican Foreign Debt, Old Lesson, New Possibilities." In Riordan Roett (ed.), *Mexico and the United States.* Boulder, Colo.: Westview Press.

CHAPTER SEVENTEEN

Prospects for Economic and Political Change in Cuba in the 1990s

ARCHIBALD R.M. RITTER

As Cuba enters the 1990s, it confronts extreme uncertainty and the likelihood of major economic and political change after having been cast adrift by the Soviet Union and Eastern Europe and after a long period of internal systemic blockage and paralysis.

Cuba's world has fallen apart. The international system in which it functioned for 30 years has changed at high velocity. Its strategic place in the bipolar Cold War system is gone. Its special trade and aid relationship with the Soviet Union is being phased out. The countries after which it modeled its economic and political institutions have judged those institutions to be inadequate and are in the process of replacing or drastically modifying them. Moreover, Cuba's own economic and political systems possess flaws that make them unsustainable, despite the significant social advances that have been achieved since 1959.

Any discussion of Cuba's prospects is extremely difficult for a number of reasons. First, the experience of Central Europe in 1989–90 suggests that the nature and pace of change, after long periods of blockage, can be exceedingly rapid and are certainly unpredictable. Second, we are almost totally lacking in any solid systematic and quantifiable information concerning the climate of public opinion on political matters within Cuba. There appear to be no scientific political opinion surveys that have been made public, and indeed if there were, could we ascertain the extent to which the responses to state-sponsored surveys reflected genuine opinion rather than protective verbal camouflage?

Third, personality factors, and of course the role of President Castro, are difficult to predict. Fourth, there are continuing imponderables in the international strategic crucible in which Cuba has been located, and in particular in prospective relations with the United States. Fifth, the future role and actions of the Cuban community outside Cuba are also difficult to estimate.

Despite these formidable difficulties, the central objective of this chapter is to explore some of the factors that will help to determine the course of events in Cuba during the 1990s and to sketch some of the possible scenarios for future change. These explorations of prospective economic and political change should be considered as tentative and suggestive rather than prognosticative, as there are clearly many foreseeable and unforeseeable ways in which future events could unfold. There also are many possible future economic and political structures that are conceivable for Cuba.

The chapter begins with a brief discussion of the changes that have occurred and are likely to continue occuring in the international economic and political systems in which Cuba must operate, and that will compel major changes in Cuba. Cuba's domestic economic and political systems are discussed briefly. Despite a strong social development record in the past, neither the political nor the economic systems will be sustainable for long as a result of fundamental weaknesses in their functioning and due to changes in the international environment. Prospective changes in the 1990s for Cuba's economic and political system are explored in the form of a number of scenarios. Finally a short summary is presented.

THE INTERNATIONAL GEOPOLITICAL AND ECONOMIC ENVIRONMENT

The international environment within which Cuba must exist was dramatically transformed from 1988 to 1990. By the end of 1990, changes that earlier seemed inconceivable were in place and were proceeding further. Among the most significant of these on-going political changes for Cuba were the following:

- the *internal political problems of the Soviet Union,* including the drive for a more authentic participatory system and the pressures for decentralization and indeed the dissolution of the Union, together with the formal centralization of emergency powers of President Gorbachev
- the *phase-down of the Cold War,* and the new spirit of cooperation between the USSR on the one hand and NATO and the United States on the other, illustrated by their partial agreement on managing the Gulf Crisis of 1990–91, and the provision of emergency assistance by NATO countries to the USSR
- the growing *convergence of the political systems* of the countries of Central or Eastern Europe (and perhaps the Soviet Union) to West European-style pluralistic multiparty electoral systems

- the continued global *shift away from one-party authoritarianism* toward multiparty systems—almost complete in Latin America, in process in Asia and Eastern Europe, and commencing in Africa

The changes in the international economic environment with relevance for Cuba have been just as dramatic and include:

- the virtual *collapse of the "socialist international system"* including COMECON
- the *phase-out of Cuba's privileged status* in trade and aid relationships with the Soviet Union and East European countries
- the restructuring and replacement of the old systems of *central planning* with more decentralized and more marketized systems in Eastern Europe and the USSR
- the on-going trends toward *global economic integration* and simultaneously toward the formation of *regional trading groupings*

These changes have important implications for Cuba. The phase-down of the Cold War means that Cuba's strategic value to the Soviet Union has been reduced and may disappear entirely. The rapid though unsteady and uncertain moves toward marketization of the economy and toward more authentic popular participation and multiparty pluralistic political systems in Central Europe and the Soviet Union imply that Cuba no longer serves as a demonstration model for Soviet orthodoxy in the Third World. Indeed, Cuba's adherence to a political model that has been rejected in Eastern Europe and the Soviet Union appears to have generated hostility between Cuba and the governments of some of the latter countries, most notably of Czechoslovakia. The movement toward multiparty pluralistic democracy in most of the world—including virtually all of South America, the English-speaking Caribbean and Haiti, Mexico, growing numbers of Asian countries, as well as Eastern Europe—and the growing rejection of one-party political systems in Africa mean that Cuba is increasingly seen as an international political pariah rather than the "wave of the future" in its unswerving dedication to a one-party monopoly.

The movement toward marketization of the Soviet economy together with the difficulties it has been undergoing in its transitional processes since about 1988 have made it increasingly unable economically as well as unwilling politically to continue its heavy subsidization of the Cuban economy. The phase-out of implicit subsidies to Cuba will have major impacts on the Cuban economy beginning on January 1, 1991.

The level of subsidization of the Cuban economy by the Soviet Union has been most generous. Soviet subsidization has enabled Cuba to live beyond its means, to be insulated from the instabilities of the world economy, to enjoy an illusion of rapid growth and of economic prosperity, and to run an activist foreign policy of a type usually associated with major powers. In order to gauge the impact of the phase-out of Soviet assistance on Cuba, a brief summary of the character and possible magnitudes of Soviet assistance is presented in the following paragraphs.

Soviet subsidization is controversial in concept and difficult to measure. One method that permits some estimation of magnitudes is to define as assistance or "implicit subsidization" the value of the various elements of the relationships with the Soviet Union in comparison with the value of these elements if Cuba had participated in the same manner and degree in the world economy and at world prices. However, measurement of such subsidization is complicated by the absence of realistic exchange rates for the peso and the ruble and by lack of knowledge concerning the quality of Soviet exports to Cuba.

As is well-known, the main components of Soviet subsidization of Cuba were hidden in the above-market prices for Cuban sugar and nickel exports to the USSR and the below-market price (prior to 1986) for petroleum exports from the USSR to Cuba. Cubans have rejected the idea that such pricing involves subsidization. In the words of President Castro: "No one gives us things. We buy them and we pay for them. If our sugar receives a higher price than the world dumping price, it is still a fair price, because it put an end to the phenomenon of unequal terms of trade" (cited in *Journal of Commerce*, March 9, 1990, p. 1). In 1987 the sugar subsidy amounted to $2.6 billion, at official exchange rates for the peso, ruble, and dollar, or about 21 percent of Ingreso Nacional Creado (INC, a close approximation of GDP) (Ritter, 1990, p. 126). In the same year the petroleum subsidy had turned negative, as Cuba paid an above-world price for its imports from the Soviet Union, again at official exchange rates equivalent to approximately 5.4 percent of INC.

A second component of Soviet assistance was the reexportation of sugar and petroleum. In the 1980s, Cuba was permitted to buy sugar on the international market at the "free market" price for resale to the USSR in fulfillment of long-term sugar export commitments. This permitted a profit to be received, the magnitude of which depended on the price differential and the exchange rate at which the dollar "free market" price was converted to Cuban pesos. Similarly, the USSR permitted Cuba to reexport Soviet petroleum on the basis of an agreement that provided that if petroleum consumption and importation levels declined vis-à-vis previously planned levels due to energy conservation, the petroleum that was "saved" could be reexported at world prices and in convertible currency. This transaction was a paper transaction only, with the petroleum traveling physically from the USSR to Eastern and perhaps Western Europe. Net profits from these transactions amounted to about 3.9 percent of INC at official exchange rates (Ritter, 1990).

Since 1960, Cuba has continuously run a bilateral trade deficit with the USSR, reaching as high as 1.5 billion pesos annually in 1986–87. These annual deficits are the main source of the debt to the USSR which has been placed at 16 billion rubles, or $23.5 billion at official exchange rates (*Izvestia*, March 3, 1990). It is not clear whether this debt will ever be repaid, although R. Gonzalez Vergara, a Cuban vice-secretary in the Council for Mutual Economic Assistance (CMEA) prior to his defection in June 1990, stated that the USSR expected Cuba to begin repayment in 1995 in dollars at an exchange rate to be determined in 1991 (*Ottawa Citizen,* 1990). Interest payments on the Soviet debt have also been continuously forgiven or postponed. Finally, the Soviet Union has provided military assistance to Cuba of unknown economic or commercial value. As noted earlier, the real value of Soviet assistance is not known because of our lack of knowledge of realistic exchange rates for the peso and ruble and of the genuine quality of Soviet exports to Cuba. If one allows for overpricing and low quality of such Soviet exports in the captive Cuban market, the value of Soviet assistance declines significantly. Taking all this into consideration, net Soviet implicit subsidization of the Cuban economy can be estimated at 15 to 40 percent of INC in the 1980s, depending on the year and the exchange rate assumptions utilized (Ritter, 1990). The "quid pro quo" for this assistance was Cuban support for the Soviet Union in the Cold War, and the demonstration of the success of the Soviet model in the Third World.

Soviet subsidization began to be phased out in 1991. Movement toward a market-determined exchange rate (i.e., ruble devaluation) and world prices for traded commodities would eliminate the margins that made implicit subsidization possible. The general orientation of Soviet policy under Gorbachev— namely, the preoccupation with marketization and structural transformation, economic stabilization, and avoidance of economic breakdown—means that the Soviet Union has lost the capability to foster or prop up Cuba as well as interest in doing so. Indeed, if any of a variety of possible economic and political "breakdown" scenarios were to occur in the Soviet Union, one probable consequence would be an immediate termination of such subsidization.

Just as Cuba is being cast adrift by the Soviet Union and from the dissolving socialist bloc, the rest of the world is being propelled simultaneously toward intensified global economic integration and the formation of regional trading spheres or blocs. Cuba therefore confronts major challenges in reinserting itself in the international system.

Global economic integration will be furthered by a number of forces, even in the absence of strong positive results from the 1990 GATT negotiations. Among the forces promoting global economic integration are:

- the intensification of the interaction of the countries of Eastern Europe with the rest of the world

- the installation of a genuine common market in the European Community by January 1993 and the link-up of the European Free Trade Association (EFTA) with the EEC

- the unsustainability of import substitution and the shift in practice and in conventional wisdom toward export-oriented development strategies in the Third World

- the imperatives created to earn foreign exchange to service large external debts on the part of many highly indebted developing countries

At the same time, a number of forces are pushing toward the formation of regional trading spheres, including:

- the establishment or reinvigoration of regional integration schemes among developing countries
- the EFTA, EEC, East European linkage intensification noted above
- North American and Western Hemispheric movements toward the establishment of free trade areas (of a still undetermined character and depth)

The risk for Cuba in this dual movement toward global integration and regionalization is that it will be left "out in the cold." As a small country with a limited resource base, Cuba must specialize and utilize its comparative advantage, diversify and increase its exports, and participate fully in the international division of labor if its economic potential is to be realized and if material levels of living are to be improved sustainably. To expand its exports and foreign exchange earnings, Cuba needs to be able to obtain better access to markets, particularly in the Western Hemisphere and the United States, its natural geoeconomic sphere. It also must undertake those internal economic reforms that will enhance productivity gains and improve its competitiveness in the international system.

THE UNSUSTAINABILITY OF CUBA'S ECONOMIC AND POLITICAL SYSTEMS

Cuba's development record since the victory of the revolution in 1958 is well known. Through a set of deep-cutting changes in the political system, in social and economic organization and in resource allocation generally, Cuba made rapid and large gains in terms of social or human development, including education, health, the reduction of open unemployment, the reduction of poverty, and improvement in the equity of income distribution. These achievements are of obvious importance and have done much to improve the quality of life for a broad strata of the population and also to improve the quality of human resources. A substantial proportion of the improvements in all these areas were made in the 1960s, however—though education and medicine have been improving steadily since.

The economic record is mixed, but also seriously flawed. After a bad decade in the 1960s, economic growth was quite strong and consistent from about 1970 to 1985 (with a few bad years). This positive experience was due both to internal factors (policy pragmatism and stability, a major investment effort, the mechanization of the sugar harvest, and the release of labor for employment elsewhere) and external factors (Soviet assistance and the expansion of hard-currency foreign loans.) However, after 1985 economic growth rates declined and became negative (see Table 17.1). This was due to a decline in the real value of implicit subsidization after 1985, the halting of new convertible currency loans owing to the moratorium declared on debt repayment in 1985, and internal problems of inefficiency and low productivity.

Table 17.1
Cuba: Major Macroeconomic Indicators, 1978–89

	1978	1979	1980	1981	1982	1983	1984	1985	1986	1987	1988	1989
National Value Added[1] (Real)												
Growth Rate[3] (%)	7.0	0.6	-5.3[3]	20.8[3]	5.1	5.4	7.5	4.6	1.4	-3.3	+0.1	+0.9
Growth Rate per capita (%)	5.9	-0.2	-5.3	+20.8	4.2	4.5	6.4	3.5	0.3	-4.3	-1.2	-0.2
Investment (Real)												
Growth Rate (%)	-5.5	-0.6	5.3	20.0	-11.5	+13.8	+17.0	+7.5	-21.0	-20.0	+8.5	-2.0[4]
Productivity Change[2,3] (%)												
Output per Worker (%)	8.2	1.7	-6.2	19.5[3]	3.6	1.9	3.9	3.5	-1.5	-3.6	+4.3	-3.9[4]
Merchandise Trade												
Socialist: Exports CuP.m.	2,916	2,884	2,786	3,179	4,172	4,765	4,909	5,323	4,699	4,797	4,766	
Economies: Imports CuP.m.	2,849	3,053	3,613	4,114	4,908	5,414	6,072	6,718	6,412	6,692	6,626	
Balance CuP.m.	67	-169	-827	-935	-736	-649	-1,163	-1,395	-1,713	-1,895	-1,860	
Market: Exports CuP.m.	524	615	1,181	1,045	761	770	568	660	626	604	753	
Economies: Imports CuP.m.	724	635	1,014	1,000	623	808	1,155	1,265	1,156	919	954	
Balance CuP.m.	-200	-20	-167	+45	+138	-38	-587	-605	-530	-315	-201	
Convertible Currency: Balance CuP.m.	-136	+99	+367	+284	+606	+441	+73	+67	-164	+34.2	+78.1	
Exchange Rates												
Official Rate CuP./$US[1]	.75	.73	.71	.78	.85	.87	.90	.92	.83	1.00	1.00	1.00
Terms of Trade (1981 = 100)	108	100	111	100	79	92	89	87	82			
Latin America: Growth Rate Per Capita Gross Domestic Product (%) (excluding Cuba)			2.8	-1.9	-3.5	-5.0	1.2	1.3	1.3	0.7	-1.5	-1.0

Sources: CEE (1985), pp. 100, 161, 193, 381; BNC-CEE (1987), p. 11; BNC (May 1987; May 1989); UNCTAD (1988), p. 533; CEPAL (1989); CEE (1990); Rodríguez (1990).

Notes:
1. "Productive" sectors only; excluding education, health, social security, finance, and administration.
2. Changes in value added per worker, constant 1981 prices.
3. Dramatic changes in growth rates and productivity arise largely from changes in the sugar harvest.
4. First six months of 1989.

Cuba's economic prospects for the 1990s are not bright from the perspective of late 1990. The ending of the special relationship with the Soviet Union already has created problems concerning petroleum imports. The movement in Eastern Europe and the Soviet Union toward market-based behavior and hard-currency preference by enterprises also was affecting the availability of imports to Cuba. There was an expectation within Cuba of severe economic deterioration, to the point of even discussing the substitution of oxen and bicycles for petroleum-consuming tractors and buses. A termination of the Soviet financing of continuing trade deficits will hurt Cuba as well. Since Cuba's moratorium on servicing its hard currency debt in 1985, Cuba also had to conduct trade with the hard-currency countries on a "cash-only" basis, with little recourse to borrowing from either private banks, bilateral lending agencies, or international financial institutions.

Finally, while Cuba has emphasized export diversification by commodity and destination, and while it has had some limited success, its dependence on traditional exports continues to be very high, with sugar still accounting for 74.6 percent of its total gross exports in 1988 (not allowing for high soft-currency sugar prices, or for the reexportation of imported petroleum and sugar [CEE, 1989, p. 426]). Export diversification and expansion has been hurt badly by the trade embargo of the United States. However, the rigidities of Cuba's central planning system, the lack of incentive and freedom for enterprises to cultivate foreign markets directly, the lack of market-oriented realism in the general price structure, the absence of a private medium-scale enterprise sector, and the deepening cultural and behavioral impacts of a bureaucratized society have all damaged Cuba's ability to compete in the international economy. In other words, for Cuba to pay its own way internationally by expanding and diversifying its exports will ultimately require basic change in the economy and perhaps Cuban society more broadly.

There are a number of interlocking sources of the systemic problems of the economy, including the near absence of a middle-range private sector; hypercentralization of decision-making, and the absence of markets and an economically rational price mechanism.

There is a small private sector in Cuba, which includes officially recognized microenterprises that employed some 28,600 persons in 1988 or about 1.1 percent of total employment (CEE, 1989, p. 192). There is additional unrecorded full-time and part-time employment in various officially unrecognized activities, such as garment-making, shoe repair, electronic repair, house renovation/repair and construction, secretarial services, transportation, tradesmen's services—these constituting a significant "informal sector." There is also an ubiquitous "black market" where goods and services of all sorts are exchanged illegally, and with almost the entire population participating in one capacity or another. However, middle-sized private enterprises were abolished with the Revolutionary Offensive of 1968 and are effectively nonexistent at present.

Despite the vibrance of at least parts of the micro enterprise or informal sector and the pervasiveness of the black market, the abolition of most small- and medium-sized private businesses has hurt Cuba badly. By abolishing such enterprises, a large amount of "human capital" was eliminated, including varying combinations of entrepreneurship, managerial skill, technical knowledge, and marketing know-how. The effects of this approach over time have been serious: some 25 to 30 years of pragmatic learning and innovation by small business entrepreneurs have been lost. The bureaucratized and centralized planning system in the public sector has not been able to replace the decentralized initiative and self-activation of hundreds of thousands of small business owner-operators. The result is that Cuba appears visually as a material desolation without the myriad of small businesses that make modern life convenient and agreeable. There are other harmful consequences of this situation. First, the range and quality of goods and services available to citizens is far below what would be possible with a different approach. Second, the economy has been sluggish and slow to respond to new opportunities created by technical changes and changing consumer demand, in comparison with other countries at roughly similar levels of development. Third, the ability of the economy to diversify and expand exports in a range of new nontraditional areas has been impeded. Fourth, the division of labor within the economy and the creation of numerous new specialist enterprises (as firms "spin off" particular functions to new enterprises) has also been blocked, with consequent productivity losses that increase over time.

Hypercentralization of economic decision-making was a well-publicized problem in the 1960s, with the failures of the 10-million-ton sugar harvest and the Havana "Green-belt" program. In both these cases, the hierarchial command structure of economic management permitted decisions reached at the level of President Castro to reorient the energies of much of the population in massive programs that turned out to be ill-conceived, economically foolish, and exceedingly costly to the Cuban people. These programs were subsequently reversed, and it appeared in the 1970s and early 1980s that Castro and Cuba had become more pragmatic and deliberative in economic matters. Unfortunately recent examples of this pattern of decision-making, including the shutdown of the farmers' markets in 1985, continuing massive investment in the trans-Cuba *autopista*, and in high-technology medicine, suggest that the roots of this hypercentralization are systemic in nature. President Castro wields so much power and influence—through the party, the Council of Ministers and National Assembly, and his domination of the media and national life generally—that his decisions are quickly adopted and implemented without serious criticism or evaluation anywhere in the political system or the system of economic management. This degree of centralized decision-making creates a certain "macroflexibility" in Cuba's economy and society: decisions can be reached and implemented rapidly so that natural, human, and capital resources can be mobilized and deployed quickly. The weakness of hypercentralization is that the mistakes that inevitably emerge are massive in scale.

The demarketization of the Cuban economy has resulted in an intensifying bureaucratization of the system. This phenomenon has been severe because bureaucracies are supposed to perform all of the control, coordination, allocation, and activation functions performed by the market mechanism. Bureaucratism manifests itself in a variety of ways: expansion of numbers of personnel throughout the system; conversion of managers from entrepreneurs to "order-takers"; extreme subdivision of functional tasks among bureaucrats, with a lack of flexibility among persons and an absence of general managerial savoir faire; promotion on the basis of political criteria rather than on aptitude (Cruz, 1990); loss of sight of the real purpose of enterprises (to serve Cuban citizens); and preoccupation with procedures and immediate private rewards. The result of this is further pressures toward economic paralysis and rigidity, waste, and inefficiency.

Demarketization also means that the structure of prices bears little relationship to genuine economic scarcities. Without an economically rational structure of prices, there is no way in which enterprises can accurately ascertain whether they are utilizing inputs of all sorts efficiently in producing those outputs that are of greatest relative value to the Cuban people. For example, the absence of a meaningful and unified exchange rate—that is, a relative price for all foreign vis-à-vis domestic goods and services—means that no enterprise can know if it is using foreign and domestic inputs in optimal combination. There appears at this time to be no workable alternative to the price mechanism, imperfect though it may be, for allocating resources efficiently in a complex economic system. No country can afford to waste or in effect to destroy its scarce natural, capital, and human resources, decade after decade, by abstaining from using the price mechanism.

Cuba's political system is also unsustainable. One-party authoritarianism has been and is being rejected elsewhere. A monopoly over the polity and society generally by the Cuban Communist Party, which in turn is dominated by President Castro, is inherently incompatible with authentic participatory democracy. It is a matter of time before the system is changed.

Cuba's political system, outlined in the constitution adopted by the Communist Party in December 1975, involves a three-tier governmental structure, with Municipal and Provincial Assemblies and a National Assembly (see Alvarez, 1985 for a detailed outline and discussion of this system). Citizens elect directly a representative from their electoral district for the Municipal Assembly. The Municipal Assemblies then select the delegates for the 14 Provincial Assemblies and also for the National Assembly, which is constitutionally the supreme organ of the political system. The executive of the National Assembly is the Council of State, whose president (Castro) appoints a Council of Ministers, which runs the public administration.

In theory this system might appear to be reasonably democratic: with multi-candidate elections for representatives to the Municipal Assemblies; with requirements that deputies at all levels report back to the electors at the district level; and with deputies being subject to recall by their electors. However, if one defines democracy simply as the ability of citizens to influence and control the selection of those in leadership positions and to shape the policies, procedures, and objectives adopted in the relevant assemblies, then one would conclude that at the municipal level the system is somewhat democratic, but at the provincial and especially the national level, it is less democratic.

The National Assembly in practice has been dominated by the Communist Party which, with its youth affiliate, accounted for 96.7 percent of the elected deputies in 1976 (Ritter, 1983, p. 199). Moreover, in 1976, 30 of the 31 members of the Council of State were also members of the Central Committee of the Communist Party. In 1987 Central Committee members continued to predominate in the Council of State (Azicri, 1988, pp. 90–93). In sum, it appears that the National Assembly is somewhat of a shell within which the Communist Party conducts its business. Why do party members dominate the National Assembly and its Council of State so completely? This arises because in the Municipal Assemblies, the delegates appear to select their party superiors or leading personalities for the National Assembly. It then appears that President Castro, not unnaturally, selects mainly Communist Party Central Committee members to the Council of State.

There is some questioning and debate within the National Assembly. However, in some of its meetings, President Castro dominates the discussion totally, taking and fielding questions, directing questions or criticisms to certain ministers, and pronouncing, analyzing, criticizing, and summarizing on most issues, although he has not been the president of the National Assembly itself. (This was especially the case for the first day of the July 11–12, 1990 meetings of the Assembly [see *Granma*, July 12, 1990, pp. 1–4].)

The National Assembly also appears to be designed by the constitution to be amateurish and inconsequential. It meets only twice annually, for two to three and one-half days each meeting, and with very heavy workloads in terms of legislation to pass, budgets and socioeconomic plans to approve, reports to consider, and so on. It is not possible for the Assembly to play a significant role within such a brief period of time. Furthermore, the deputies work on a part-time basis in the National Assembly, maintaining their regular employment and remuneration, and lacking any type of support staff or financial resources to assist in their legislative duties. On the other hand, the 20 "working commissions" that have been established on a variety of areas have played an active role in analyzing issues and preparing draft legislation. They also command some resources for their functioning.

While the National Assembly has been disappointing so far in fulfilling its constitutional mandate as "the supreme power of the state" representing and expressing "the sovereign will of the people" (Article 67, Alvarez, 1985, p. 257) it could evolve into such a body if it were to become more professional and if the single-party monopoly were replaced with a multiparty or multifaction arrangement.

The party monopoly extends beyond the Organos del Poder Popular to all of the civil organs of society (unions, women's organizations, small farmers' associations, etc.), over the media, and over the formulation and dissemination of ideology. In these circumstances, opposing views or officially unacceptable criticisms can not be effectively voiced. Organization for unsanctioned political objectives is also impossible or difficult—witness the difficulties faced by the various human rights groups in Cuba.

FACTORS SHAPING CUBA'S PROSPECTS

Cuba confronts major economic and political challenges in the near future. Politically it must move toward more authentic democratization, which most likely requires the establishment of a multiparty pluralistic political system and an end to the current Communist Party monopoly control over the media and the civil organs of society. Economically, Cuba must begin to "pay its way" in the international system, mainly though not solely in view of the on-going phase-down of Soviet subsidization. It must increase its foreign exchange earnings by expanding and diversifying its exports of goods and services. This in turn requires deep-cutting internal changes in economic organization, including an expanded role for private middle-sized enterprises, a reduced role for centralized planning in the system, and an increased role for the market mechanism. (This is argued at length in Ritter, 1991.)

In moving toward liberalized economic and political systems, Cuba will be preoccupied with a number of major concerns. First, it undoubtedly will try to maintain the social programs, especially in education and public health, that have operated so successfully to promote human development. Second, there will inevitably be significant transitional costs as Cuba moves toward a partially marketized mixed-ownership economy. (It is unlikely that any Cuban government in the foreseeable future would move toward the privatization of the sugar sector, natural utilities, or other very large state enterprises.) These transitional costs will include the transformation of current underemployment into open unemployment and the various other problems associated with deep structural change in the economy. Institutional innovations such as unemployment insurance will be necessary to reduce and contain such costs. Third, there can be little doubt that a movement into a mixed market economy will increase income disparities, especially as those entrepreneurs who are early arrivals in new activities earn high profits prior to the intensification of competition and consequent profit reduction. These phenomena will require important institutional innovations, especially the introduction of the progressive income tax.

In any exploration of Cuba's prospects for the future, the *role of President Castro* is obviously of central importance. Since the success of the rebellion in 1959 and even before, Castro has dominated the political scene. Not only did he lead the guerrilla forces in the 1950s but he has been the paramount decision-maker ever since. His persona is of "historic dimension" and "larger than life." He has been successful in defending his vision of revolutionary social change, in maintaining what may be a "revolutionary consensus," and in spear-heading the high egalitarianism of Cuban society. He has also done much to keep the revolution more or less "on track" in contrast to other similarly placed authoritarian leaders whose egomania and xenophobia have generated extreme social disfunctionality (such as Ceaucescu in Romania, Kim Il Sung in North Korea, and Enver Hoxha in Albania). On the other hand, Castro's over-powering central role has resulted in massive and costly mistakes, as noted earlier. As of late 1990, it appeared that Castro's role had become intensely conservative. He appears to be intent in preventing change of almost any sort and in preserving the political and economic status quo. He appears not only to impose a paralysis upon Cuba, but also proposes extreme economic austerity and what is, in effect, a "retreat to the mountains" for the Cuban people as a means of dealing with the looming foreign exchange crisis while maintaining the political system and economic institutions intact.

The absence of reliable public opinion surveys and the internal political cli-mate (which likely induces many people to wear "political masks" to camou-flage their real views and feelings for purposes of self-defense in a monolithic system) means that we have little idea as to what the Cuban people actually think of their president. It is likely, but unprovable, that Castro enjoyed consid-erable popular support in the past. Has this support been maintained in the 1990s as the socialist regimes of Eastern Europe collapsed and as economic conditions within Cuba worsened? Once again this is impossible to ascertain. Some evidence in this regard comes from a survey conducted unofficially by four brash journalists from *El Norte* (Monterrey, Mexico) in Havana in March 1990 with a methodology that was unavoidably impressionistic and unscientific (interviews with 400 Cuban adults in Havana, on the basis of a questionnaire). In response to the question, "Do you believe that Fidel Castro is a hero?" 26 percent responded "yes," 31 percent said "no," and 43 percent replied "now no, but before yes he was." To the question, "What do Cubans think of Fidel Castro?" 40 percent stated that he was "the most important television artist," 35 percent said "he was good, but not the people around him," 21 percent stated that he was a dictator, and 4 percent gave a negative but unprintable reply. These results are interesting and perhaps suggestive, but unfortunately they are also inconclusive and provide no insight into changes in public opinion over time. In any case, support for Castro appeared to be "soft" in March 1990. It was likely somewhat weaker in 1991 and is probably volatile.

Will Castro continue to oppose meaningful movement toward political plural-ism and economic liberalization? As of the end of 1990 this appeared to be prob-able. If this continued to be the case, then Castro would have to be ousted as "Lider Maximo," "Ceaucescu-style," before such change could occur. On the other hand, it is not impossible that Castro himself may reach the conclusion that political pluralization and economic liberalization were desirable and inevitable, so that conceivably he might attempt to ride the tigers "Gorbachev-style" and orchestrate such reforms himself. Is this improbable? Perhaps. Still, when the Albanian Communist Party (after Hoxha) supports the legalization of opposition parties, the establishment of a multiparty system, and multiparty elections (in February 10, 1991), the replacement of central planning with "the mechanisms of a market economy," and with mixed public and private investment, then analogous shifts within Cuba and under Castro are not inconceivable (*Ottawa Citizen*, January 5, 1991, p. A7).

The role of the United States is clearly of major significance in influencing the course of events within Cuba. Since the break of diplomatic relations, the imposition of the trade embargo, and the Bay of Pigs, U.S. policy toward Cuba seems to have been totally counterproductive and so wrong-headed that virtually no other country in the world considers it appropriate or useful to follow a similar policy. U.S. policy has undoubtedly damaged the Cuban economy and hurt the living standards of the Cuban people. On the other hand, it has also likely contributed to the radicalization of the regime, thereby consolidating popular support for Castro as the champion of Cuban nationalism and independence. A less hostile U.S. approach to Cuba, including termination of the embargo (generally an approach similar to that vis-à-vis the countries of Eastern Europe) would very likely have stimulated more pragmatic economic policy and a more liberal political system right from the start.

Political and economic normalization of relations at this time would eliminate the anti-U.S. underpinnings of Castro's leadership, and would destroy the excuse that the need for war-preparedness required a militarized political system. Economic normalization would stimulate Cuban exports, U.S. tourism, direct foreign investment from the United States, transfer of technology from the United States, and a significant role for entrepreneurs in the Cuban community outside Cuba in Cuba's import and export trade and in a variety of business ventures. All of these would be of benefit to the Cuban economy and the material well-being of the Cuban people. Very likely, the process of marketization and economic liberalization would be strengthened and accelerated by the imperatives, opportunities, and challenges of renewed economic interaction with the United States.

Economic normalization would be of significant benefit to the United States—though relative to the size of the U.S. economy the material benefits would be small. As the natural geoeconomic partner for Cuba, and with the Cuban community in the United States available to help reforge economic relations, the United States would gain major export markets, new sources of imports, and an outlet for foreign investment. Undoubtedly the Cuban community itself, and in particular the city of Miami and state of Florida, would gain most from economic normalization because that location is poised to play an important springboard and intermediary function in the development of renewed economic linkages. The United States will face significant competition from Japan as a trade partner with Cuba, as Japan is cultivating the Cuban market for capital goods very effectively. From this standpoint, the sooner the United States normalizes its relations with Cuba, the better for its own economic interests.

If there are significant economic benefits from normalization for the United States and especially for Florida's Cuban community, and if political liberalization were more likely to take place in an environment of normal relations with the United States, why has that country not moved decisively toward normalization of relations already? This is indeed a mystery that baffles observers outside the United States and presumably many within.

POSSIBLE SCENARIOS FOR CHANGE

Having discussed briefly some of the factors that will shape Cuba's prospects, a number of possible scenarios for change are presented below.

Scenario 1: Normalization-Induced Liberalization

One interesting scenario—probably the result of wishful thinking—would envisage the United States normalizing relations with Cuba (without detailed preconditions) followed by gradual economic liberalization as Cuba pragmatically responds to its external and internal economic challenges and by gradual political liberalization as well.

Will the United States normalize relations with Cuba soon? This is dubious; there appears to be a feeling that after sustained U.S. pressures, Castro is finally "on the run" and hence now would not be the time to relax the pressure. On the other hand, normalization would both give Castro an excuse and generate the compulsion from public opinion to liberalize the economy and pluralize the polity.

Scenario 2: Liberalization Orchestrated by Castro

A second scenario would involve economic and political liberalization initiated and orchestrated by President Castro, Gorbachev-style, even in the absence of U.S.-initiated normalization of relations. As noted, however, this is improbable though not inconceivable. Its probability will increase if a number of the countries of Central Europe meet economic success and pluralistic political stability relatively soon.

The risk of this option for Castro is that if the floodgates for reform are opened, it may become difficult for him to stage-manage or control the processes of change that would likely acquire a momentum and logic of their own.

Already a process of partial change has been initiated. Some 50 percent of the membership of the Central Committee of the Communist Party was dropped in late 1990. The next five-year Party Congress, scheduled to meet in the first half of 1991, is supposed to emphasize openness and criticism. Such an emphasis may actually occur in view of Cuba's worsening pariah status as the socialist world changes and if the domestic economy deteriorates sharply in the face of the phaseout of Soviet subsidization and the reduction of trade with Central Europe. However, the chances of the party, under Castro's influence, reforming itself fundamentally, or promoting a more deep-cutting political pluralism and economic liberalization, seems remote at this time.

Scenario 3: Romanian-Style Collapse

Another possibility is for a spontaneous mass uprising, unforeseen and unforeseeable, provoked by some minor issue, which leads to a rapid "meltdown" of the old system, in the style of the popular revolutionary overthrow of President Ceaucescu of Romania at Christmas 1989. Again this is not inconceivable, but neither is it probable at this time. President Castro appears to enjoy substantial personal public support. Moreover, most of the population has benefited from the social programs, income redistributive reforms, and reduction of open unemployment. A reasonable proportion of the population (that 25.3 percent over 45 years of age) has personal recollections of the situation prior to the revolution, and a much larger proportion undoubtedly has indirect memories of this. It would seem that much of the population perceives the regime as legitimate, although hard evidence on this is absent.

On the other hand, one could imagine circumstances in which this scenario might occur. For example, if in the face of U.S.-initiated reconcilication and normalization President Castro continued to prevent economic and political liberalization and continued the heavy prohibition of opposition and suppression of opposing views, a pent-up and furious popular explosion conceivably could occur. To repeat, such an eventuality is most improbable at present, although some factors could change the probabilities in future.

Scenario 4: Castro-Enforced Status Quo

Perhaps the most probable short-term scenario is for no meaningful change, with Castro effectively maintaining the status quo. It is improbable that Castro now will abandon or modify significantly his vision of the revolution and of the direction in which Cuba should go. The status quo may be sustainable for some years, especially if the transitional costs to economic liberalization in Central Europe are high and prolonged, and despite worsening domestic economic performance. Indeed, if the reform movement in the Soviet Union were to be reversed, a situation that appeared increasingly likely in January 1991, the status quo in Cuba may be maintainable for longer.

Ultimately, however, the status quo is unsustainable in Cuba economically and politically, as argued in the previous sections of this chapter. Castro cannot hold the entire system together forever. Presumably when he retires, dies of old age, or is otherwise removed as president of Cuba and head of the Communist Party, change will occur, perhaps very rapidly. One could envisage a period of military rule, Polish-style, while opposition groups organized themselves and built legitimacy and support. Or one could imagine the Communist Party itself adopting reformist measures in an effort to reduce the appeal of the opposition (Soviet- or Albanian-style). Or one could imagine more explosive popular movements against an unpopular Raul Castro who is slated to become president after his brother Fidel.

In summary, Cuba's future is obscure and may unfold in a variety of different ways. In time, however, political pluralism and economic liberalization will come regardless of President Castro's current views on the matter.

CONCLUSION

This chapter has attempted to explore Cuba's economic and political prospects, clearly an ambitious and risky task. It was argued that the phase-out of generous Soviet subsidization of the Cuban economy and the demise of special trade relations with the countries of Eastern Europe together with the simultaneous movement toward global economic integration and regionalization had created a need for Cuba to intensify its efforts to compete effectively in the international system and to "pay its way." Improved export performance ultimately will require reduced reliance on central planning, greater emphasis on the market mechanism, and an expanded role for middle-sized private enterprise. Current domestic economic problems also required these institutional reorientations and policy reforms. It was also argued that the current system of centrally managed and restricted democracy is essentially undemocratic and therefore unsustainable.

The prospects for change in Cuba depend significantly on two factors—namely, the future role of President Castro and that of the United States. Neither of these is predictable, unfortunately. A variety of possible scenarios for change were briefly described and assessed. Two of these—political and economic liberalization after a U.S.-initiated normalization of relations, and a Castro-initiated liberalization (in the absence of normalization with the United States—are likely to be of low probability at this time. A third scenario, a Romanian-style popular insurgence overthrowing Castro and the Communist Party, also was not judged to be probable at this time, mainly because in contrast to the Romanian case, the Cuban regime appears to enjoy significant support and a high degree of legitimacy, although this cannot be substantiated with confidence. A fourth scenario—that the current status quo would be maintained ultimately by President Castro—was considered to be the most probable scenario in the short term. In the longer term, however, the status quo is unsustainable; postponement of reform is only likely to make it more rapid and riskier when it does come.

REFERENCES

Alvarez Tabio, F. (1985). *Comentarios a la Constitucion Socialista.* Havana: Editorial de Ciencias Sociales.

Azicri, M. (1988). *Cuba: Politics, Economics and Society.* London: Pinter Publishers.

Banco Nacional de Cuba-Comité Estatál de Estadísticas (BNC-CEE) (September 1987).

CEPAL (December 1989). *Preliminary Overview of the Economy of Latin America and the Caribbean, 1989.* Santiago, Chile: CEPAL.

———. (December 1990). *Preliminary Overview of the Latin American Economy, 1988.* Santiago, Chile: CEPAL.

Comité Estatál de Estadísticas (CEE), Republic of Cuba (1985; 1989). *Anuario Estadístico de Cuba.* Havana: CEE.

———. (1990). *La Economía Cubana en 1989.* Havana: CEE.

Cruz, Soledad (July 8, 1990). "Eliminar las causas de los azares." *Juventud Rebelde,* p. 2.

El Norte (March 20, 1990). Monterrey, Mexico. "Empeora Cuba con Castro," pp. 1, 7–10.

Granma (July 12, 1990). "Inicío sus sesiones la Asamblea Nacional del Poder Popular," pp. 1–4.

Ottawa Citizen (September 13, 1990). "Cuba Faces Hard Times," p. 8.

Ottawa Citizen (January 5, 1991). "Albanian Rulers Vow Reforms," p. 7.

Ritter, A.R.M. (1983). "The Authenticity of Participatory Democracy in Cuba." In A.R.M. Ritter and D. H. Pollock (eds.), *Latin American Prospects for the 1980s: Equity, Democratization and Development.* New York: Praeger.

———. (1990). "The Cuban Economy in the 1990s: External Challenges and Policy Imperatives." *Journal of Interamerican and World Affairs,* Autumn.

———. (1991). "Cuba in the 1990s: Economic Reorientation and International Reintegration." In J. Kirk and S. Halebsky (eds.). *Cuba's Struggle for Development: Dilemmas and Strategies.* Boulder, Colo.: Westview Press, forthcoming.

Rodriguez, J. L. (1990). "El Proceso de Rectificación y la Economía Cubana en 1990." Unpublished manuscript. Havana: Centro de Investigaciones de la Economía Mundial.

UNCTAD (1988). *Handbook of International Trade and Development Statistics, 1987 Supplement.* New York: United Nations.

General Bibliography

Altimir, O. "Income Distribution Statistics in Latin America and their Reliability." *Review of Income and Wealth*, Series 33, no. 2 (June 1987).

Berry, A., "Predicting Income Distribution in Latin America during the 1980s." In A.R.M. Ritter and D. H. Pollock (eds.), *Latin American Prospects for the 1980s: Equity, Democratization and Development*. New York: Praeger, 1983.

Bruno, M. et al. (eds.). *Inflation Stabilization: The Experience of Israel, Argentina, Brazil, Bolivia, and Mexico*. Cambridge, Mass.: MIT Press, 1988.

CEPAL. *Magnitud de la Pobreza en America Latina en los Años Ochenta*. Santiago, Chile: CEPAL, 1990.

Cornia, G. A., Jolly, R. and Stewart, F. (eds.). *Adjustment with a Human Face*, Vols. I and II. Oxford: Clarendon Press, 1988.

Cortazar, R. (ed.). *Políticas Macroeconómicas: Una Perspectiva Latinoamericana*. Santiago, Chile: CIEPLAN, 1988.

DeSoto, H. *The Other Path*. New York: Harper and Row, 1989.

Economic Commission for Latin America and the Caribbean. *Preliminary Overview of the Latin American Economy, 1990*. Santiago, Chile: ECLAC, 1990.

Galleguillos, N. and Nef, J. "The Trend Towards Democratization and Redemocratization in Latin America: Shadow and Substance." *Latin American Research Review*, 23, no. 3 (Fall 1988), pp. 131–153.

Hartlyn, J. *The Politics of Coalition Rule in Colombia*. New York: Cambridge University Press, 1988.

Hecht, S. and Cockburn, A. *The Fate of the Forest: Developers, Destroyers and Defenders of the Amazon*. London: Verso, 1989.

Kirk, J. and Halebsky, S. *Cuba's Struggle for Development: Dilemmas and Strategies.* Boulder, Colo.: Westview Press, 1991.

Mahar, D. J. *Government Policies and Deforestation in Brazil's Amazon Region.* Washington, D.C.: World Bank, 1989.

Malloy, J. (ed.) *Authoritarianism and Corporatism in Latin America.* Pittsburgh: University of Pittsburgh Press, 1987.

O'Donnell, G., Schmitter, C. and Whitehead, L. (eds.). *Transitions from Authoritarian Rule: Prospects for Democracy.* Baltimore: Johns Hopkins University Press, 1986.

Picado Sotela, S. *La Mujer y los Derechos Humanos, Decenio de Naciones Unidas: Igualdad, Desarollo y Paz.* Costa Rica: Instituto Interamericano de Derechos Humanos, 1986.

Ritter, A.R.M. and Pollock, D. H. *Latin American Prospects for the 1980s: Equity, Democratization and Development.* New York: Praeger, 1983.

Roniger, L. "Caciquismo and Coronelismo: Contextual Dimensions of Patron Brokerage in Mexico and Brazil." *Latin American Research Review,* 20, no. 2, pp.71–99.

Sachs, Jeffrey D. (ed.). *Developing Country Debt and the World Economy.* Chicago: University of Chicago Press, 1989.

Stepan, A. *Rethinking Military Politics: Brazil and the Southern Cone.* Princeton, N.J.: Princeton University Press, 1982.

Teichman, J. A. *Policymaking in Mexico.* Boston: Allen and Unwin, 1988.

Touraine, A. *La parole et le sang: Politique et société en Amérique latine.* Paris: Odile Jacob, 1988.

UNICEF. *The State of the World's Children, 1990.* Oxford: Oxford University Press, 1990.

Index

About the Editors and Contributors

MAXWELL A. CAMERON is Assistant Professor in the School of International Affairs at Carleton University, Ottawa.

DAVID H. POLLOCK is an Adjunct Professor in the School of International Affairs at Carleton University, Ottawa.

ARCHIBALD R.M. RITTER is an Associate Professor of Economics and International Affairs at Carleton University, Ottawa.

REMONDA BENSABAT is in the Department of Political Science, University of Toronto, Canada.

ALBERT BERRY is a Professor of Economics at the University of Toronto.

JULIAN CASTRO REA is completing a Ph.D. in the Department of Political Science, Université de Montréal, Canada.

ALBERTO CIRIA is a Professor of Political Science at Simon Fraser University, Vancouver, Canada.

GRACIELA DUCATENZEILER is a Professor in the Department of Political Science, Université de Montréal.

PHILIPPE FAUCHER is Professor in the Department of Political Science, Université de Montréal.

MYRON J. FRANKMAN is a Professor in the Economics Department of McGill University, Montréal.

NIBALDO GALLEGUILLOS, originally of Chile, is a Professor in the Department of Political Science, University of Toronto.

DAVID GLOVER is an Associate Director of Economic Policy, Social Sciences Division, International Development Research Centre, Ottawa.

ENRIQUE V. IGLESIAS is President of the Interamerican Development Bank.

GARY McMAHON is a Program Officer for the International Development Research Centre in Ottawa.

JORGE NEF, originally from Chile, is a Professor of Political Science at the University of Guelph in Canada.

YVONNE RIAÑO is a Ph.D. candidate in the Department of Geography, University of Ottawa, Canada, and also works in the International Development Research Centre, Ottawa.

LUIS RONIGER is a Professor of Sociology at Hebrew University, Jerusalem.

GERT ROSENTHAL, a citizen of Guatemala, is the Executive Secretary of the UN Economic Commission for Latin America and the Caribbean, in Santiago, Chile.

MICHAEL SMALL is working with the Canadian International Development Agency, Ottawa.

ELIZABETH SPEHAR is the Program Director for Latin America in the International Centre for Human Rights and Democratic Development in Montréal.

JUDITH TEICHMAN is a Professor in the Department of Political Science at the University of Toronto.

ROLF WESCHE is a Professor in the Department of Geography at the University of Ottawa.